INSIGHT GUIDES

Created and Directed by Hans Höfer

alaska

Project Editors: Janie Freeburg and Diana Ackland
Update Editor: Giselle Smith
Managing Editor: Andrew Eames

Editorial Director: Brian Bell

APA PUBLICATIONS

This book is a brand new edition of *Insight Guide: Alaska*, and is an essential tool for anyone who wants to make the most of a challenging land. It is one title in the award-winning series created in 1970 by Hans Hofer, now chairman of Apa Publications. Each of the 190 titles, which cover all major travel destinations, encourages readers to celebrate the essence of a place rather than try and tailor it to their expectations, and is edited according to Höfer's conviction that, without insight, travel can narrow the mind rather than broaden it.

One key to the books' quality is the input of experienced project editors. In the case of this book, that input was twofold: **Janie Freeburg** graduated from the University of California, Irving, with a degree in Comparative Cultures, followed by studies in commercial art and graphic design, and has since edited a number of publications.

Freeburg

Ackland

Diana Ackland was an editor on *Good Housekeeping* magazine who went on to serve as vice-president of Sequoia Communications, the Santa Barbara company she runs with her husband. Together, they set about assembling an expert team of writers and photographers.

Field editor **Roy Bailet** wrote several of the chapters and compiled the mass of information on all parts of Alaska for the Travel Tips section. Bailet hails from Craig, Alaska, and brought first-hand experience to his piece on Alaska's bush pilots.

Contributing the chapter on Katmai National Park is **Kathy Hunter** of Palmer, Alaska. Hunter is a graduate of University of Alaska, Fairbanks School of Journalism. Freelance writer and editor **Kyle Lochalsh** contributed the informative piece on remote Cape Krusenstern National Monument.

Mike Miller, a member of the State House of Representatives, and partner in the firm Alaska Books, wrote the pieces on Juneau, the Inland Passage communities, as well as the Misty Fjords National Monument article.

Jeff Brady, editor/publisher of the *Skagway News*, wrote the chapter "Skagway, the Fun City." Brady started the paper after leaving the University of North Carolina.

Miller

Jeff Brady

Writer **Mark Skok** was born in Anchorage, grew up in Washington state, and returned to continue his interest in Alaska's back country. His article on beautiful Prince William Sound is in this book. **Chris Blackburn**, writer of the Kodiak Island chapter, has contributed to a number of diverse US publications. **Chris Carson**, who wrote the chapter on the Kenai Peninsula, has worked on newspapers from Lewiston, Idaho, to Kenai, Alaska.

Katy Korbel, author of the Anchorage chapter, has lived in the Great Land since childhood. Born in Panama, she moved to Alaska as a young girl. Writer and photographer **Gloria J. Maschmeyer** co-authored the chapter on Anchorage.

The substantial chapter on Fairbanks and the Interior of Alaska was penned by **Bill Bjork** and **Debby Drong-**

Bill Bjork

Barber

Bjork, both native Minnesotans and teachers. A 1977 canoe trip in the far north led to teaching positions in a remote Athabascan village.

Park ranger/naturalist **Rick McIntyre** contributed the chapter on Denali National Park as well as the feature on Alaska's wild flowers and wildlife, not to mention several photographs. For the past decade he has worked at Denali in the summers.

Leslie Barber, a member of the Citizen's Advisory Commission on Public Lands, wrote the piece on Gates of the Arctic National Park.

Diane Brady

Diane Brady contributed the piece on Glacier Bay National Park, an area she has toured many times as a commercial pilot for an air taxi service out of Skagway.

One of the most unusual pieces of writing in this book is the combined work of **Julie** and **Miki Collins**. Twin sisters who make their living hunting and trapping in the remote Alaska bush, they have built their own cabins, grown and preserved their own food, and raised a pack of sled dogs.

Outstanding photojournalism goes hand-to-hand with text in Insight Guides. Photographers whose images grace the pages of this book include **Mireille Vautier** and her **Photothèque Vautier-de Nanxe** in Paris, and **Jeff Shultz, Harry Walker, Allan Seiden** and **James McCann, Tony Stone Worldwide, Mark Skok, Lee Foster, Maxine Cass, Kim Heacox, Angela White, Julie & Miki Collins** and **Carol Kaynor**. Historic pictures are from the collection of **Bruce Bernstein** and from **Topham Picturepoint**.

Debby Drong-Bjork

Thanks especially go to **Thomas F. Honan**, director of marketing, Holland America Westours, and in his capacity of chairman of the Alaska Visitors Association Marketing Council (AVAMCO), and to **Dave Giersdorf**, owner/director of Exploration Holidays and Cruises, for his support.

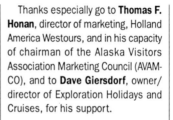

Smith

This new edition was revised by **Giselle Smith**, editor of *Seattle* magazine, and an enthusiastic traveler to Alaska. Smith has contributed to Insight Guides on Seattle and the Pacific Northwest.

She recruited new contributors **Bill Sherwonit**, who writes about Winter in Alaska and the Wrangell-St Elias National Park, **Byron Ricks**, who writes about the appeal of ecotourism, **Kris Capps**, who describes visiting Alaska's Natives, and **Rebecca Gleason**, who revised and rewrote the historical section of the book.

Sherwonit and Capps are both residents of Alaska; Sherwonit started his working life as a geologist but after a spell as a journalist in the Lower 48 (contiguous United States) is now a freelance author.

New pictures for this edition came from **Harry Walker**, with additional contributions from **Bill Sherwonit** and **Brian** and **Cherry Alexander**. The overall co-ordination for this project was undertaken by **Roger Williams** and **Andrew Eames** in Apa's London office, with proof-reading and indexing by **Mary Morton**.

CONTENTS

Maps

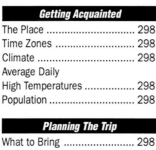

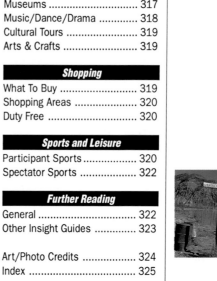

THE LAST FRONTIER

Alaska: the Great Land, the Last Frontier – more than 580,000 sq. miles (1½ million sq. km) that taunted early explorers and still defies modern-day researchers. The hint of urban sophistication in Anchorage rapidly gives way to the frontier, where whale-hunting expertise may be far more useful than a college education.

Alaska has both lush rain-drenched forests and barren wind-swept tundras. It boasts lofty mountains and endless swamps, along with a handful of high-rise buildings and uncountable numbers of one-room log cabins. Within hours of dining sumptuously in a first-class restaurant it is possible to tread on ground that has never known a human footprint: ground belonging to the grizzly bear and wolf and only shared reluctantly.

This varied land is best viewed from a light plane or surveyed from a canoe; it cannot be seen properly from a car, and would take forever to cover on foot. Alaska is an outdoor world, a wilderness, a land of many faces, few of which can be explored by moving from hotel to hotel.

The Alaskan experience includes the sheer wonder of finding what hides beyond the horizon or over the next ridge. No one person has ever seen it all; no one person ever will. Therein lies the essence of Alaska. Something new, something different and something unique always waits around the next bend in the river or twist in the trail. Only those who have looked upon Alaska, however briefly, can appreciate its fierce and unforgiving majesty.

Preceding pages: totem face; totemic hydrant; blanket-tossed native. Double-page spreads: Mount Brooks; a living glacier at Tracy Arm; Prince of Wales Island; hiker in the Arctic National Wildlife Refuge. Left, sleeping-car attendant.

NDARY LINE ON CHILKOOT PASS

Despite its rugged appearance, Alaska is actually quite young, geologically speaking. Composed of fragments of the earth's crust that rafted from the Pacific area on the backs of crustal plates and then "docked" together, the entire region is still in the process of coming together.

Its youth and placement on the globe are also responsible for much of Alaska's diversity. America's largest state boasts arctic tundra, 5,000 glaciers, ice fields, four mountain ranges (including the highest mountain in North America, 20,320-foot/6,195-meter Mount. McKinley otherwise called Denali), broad valleys, immense forests, active volcanoes, 12 major river systems, three million lakes and islands beyond counting.

Alaska is more than twice as large as its closest competition, Texas, and it has 33,900 miles (54,500 km) of seacoast – 50 percent more than the contiguous United States.

With all this land mass, it's not surprising that Alaska has six distinct geographic areas.

Arctic Alaska stretches north from the southern edge of the Brooks Range to the Arctic Ocean. This region – harsh but not barren – contains huge stretches of tundra that flower spectacularly in the nightless summer. The average midsummer temperature is 40°F (4°C), while temperatures in midwinter reach -17°F (-26°C). The area's minimal precipitation – about 5 inches (13 cm) a year – qualifies it as a desert.

Southeast Alaska (also known as the Panhandle) is a narrow, 400-mile (640 km) strip of land sandwiched between the Pacific Ocean and Canada, and cut off from the rest of Alaska by the towering Saint Elias range. Southeast is covered by huge forests nurtured by the region's mild climate: readings of 60 or 70°F (15 or 20°C) are not uncommon in the summer, and in the winter the mercury does not often dip below -10°F (-12°C).

Southcentral Alaska lies along the Gulf of Alaska. A region of mountains, fjords and lakes, it boasts Prince William Sound, the Kenai Peninsula, Cook Inlet and Kodiak Island, as well as the fertile Matanuska Valley. Temperatures vary from a -20°F (-29°C) in winter to 60°F (15°C) in the summer.

Southwestern Alaska is the home of the Aleutian islands, which stretch 200 miles (320 km) west into the Bering Sea. A warm current from Japan meets the icy northern air over the Aleutians, creating the rain and fog that enshroud the islands. Temperatures on the islands range from 0°F (-17°C) in winter to 50–60°F (10–15°C) in summer.

Alaska's Interior is a broad lowland cradled between the Brooks and Alaska mountain ranges. Within the Interior are the mighty Yukon, Tanana and Kuskokwim rivers. In some areas, birch and spruce thrive; others support only vast reaches of tundra. Temperatures here can drop to below -50°F (-45°C) in the winter and climb into the 70–80°F (20–25°C) range in the summer.

Western Alaska and the Bering Sea coast stretch from the Arctic Circle down to Bristol Bay. Much of the land is treeless tundra underlain with permafrost; the Yukon and Kuskokwim rivers flow through this harsh land on the final leg of their journey to the sea. Temperatures in this region range from 0°F (-17°C) in the winter (with frigid wind-chill factors) to 60°F (15°C) in the summer.

The Alaska Natives: Who were the people who first thrived in such an unforgiving – environment? Anthropologists believe the ancestors of the Alaska Natives – who were also the ancestors of the Natives found today in North and South America – migrated in three waves over a land bridge which joined Siberia and Alaska thousands of years ago.

When Europeans first encountered Alaska Natives in the early 18th century, there were dozens of tribes and language groups throughout the region, from the Inupiat Eskimos in the arctic region to the Tlingits in the relative lotus land of southeast Alaska. Today, these first Alaskans are divided into several main groups: the southeastern Coastal Indians (the Tlingits and Haidas), the Aleuts, the Athabascans, and the Eskimos.

The Coastal Indians: These were probably in the first wave of immigrants to cross the land bridge; they initially settled in Canada, and had only been living in Alaska for hundreds, rather than thousands, of years before

Preceding pages: customs post between Alaska and Canada in 1898. **Left**, from true Native stock.

European contact. Of this group the Tlingits were the most numerous; they claimed most of the coastal Panhandle, leaving a small southern portion to the less populous Haidas. (In the late 1800s these two subgroups were joined by the Tsimshian, Coastal Indians who emigrated from Canada to Annette Island off the southeastern coast.)

The mild climate and plentiful resources of the Panhandle allowed the Coastal Indians to develop a rich culture. They had leisure time to devote to social pastimes, travel and trade. They enjoyed ceremony and drama, and the traditional recitation of family histories and bloodlines kept an accurate account of generations.

The Coastal Indians had great respect for the natural world, which provided them with all they needed. They believed that fish and animals gave themselves willingly to humans, and strove to acknowledge and honor that sacrifice. A bear killed for meat might be brought to the house, greeted with a welcome speech and placed in a seat of honor for a day or two. The bones of a consumed salmon were always returned to the river where it had been caught to allow reincarnation. Great care was taken to return all the bones; otherwise the fish would return deformed.

The Coastal Indians lived in a capitalist society that allowed private ownership. Each household owned economic goods while the

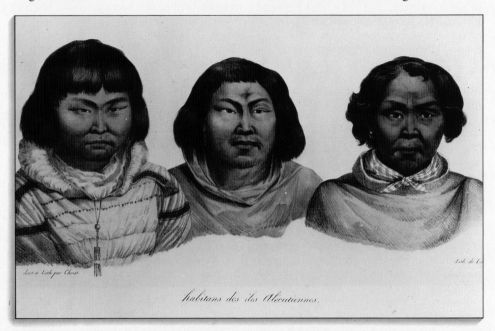

habitans des îles Aléoutiennes.

The remarkable painted designs developed by the Coastal tribes feature abstracted fish and animals, often in bold patterns of black and red. They lavishly decorated the goods they crafted: utensils, clothing, masks, canoes, trade goods, ritual objects and the characteristic totems (or totem poles) that marked family residences.

The Tlingits were excellent navigators, and were known to travel more than 1,000 miles (1,600 km) south to trade with Native peoples in the Pacific Northwest. The standard of currency was "blanket value," based on blankets made of cedar bark, dog and goat hair.

clan owned religious titles and objects. For example, the whole group or sections within the group might own the right to perform a certain dance or practice a profession such as seal hunting. But individuals within the group usually owned weapons and clothing, and anything they had made themselves.

In the social organization of the Tlingits and Haidas, status was determined by wealth. Ownership of goods, privileges such as the right to light ceremonial fires or dance a certain dance, and prestigious family background were all important in achieving status as a noble. In order to maintain position, a person of power demonstrated wealth by giving a ceremonial "potlatch" during which he would give away, destroy or invite his guests to consume all his possessions and food. Those who received goods at one potlatch were expected to reciprocate and "better" their host in future. Another important feature of the potlatch was the traditional recitation of family histories and bloodlines.

The Athabascans: The Athabascan Indians of Alaska's harsh Interior were hunters and inland fishermen. Most lived in small nomadic bands along the region's rivers. Theirs was a difficult life: They travelled for days without food and existed in temperatures of -50°F (-45°C) or colder without shelter or fire. Endurance and physical strength were

Some Athabascan groups inhabited permanent winter villages and summer fishing camps. Most Athabascan bands consisted of a few nuclear families, and had limited internal organization. Leadership was acquired by great warriors or hunters.

Athabascans also gave potlatches for a variety of reasons: to mark a death, to celebrate a child's first successful hunt, as a prelude to marriage. Those who aspired to leadership were expected to host especially memorable potlatches. At such a potlatch the would-be leader would give away all his possessions – and then prove his prowess by providing for himself and his family for an entire year without accepting outside help.

prized; game was often run down on foot over difficult terrain.

Athabascans hunted salmon, rabbits, caribou and bear with the help of snares, clubs, and bows and arrows. But despite their inventive hunting methods – deadfall traps for moose, driving large game into water – periods of famine were not uncommon. Because they were semi-nomadic and hunted on foot, the Athabascans designed extremely efficient snowshoes – one type for hunting, another for walking – made of birch.

Left, Yukon River Natives. **Above**, young unmarrieds in their best furs.

The Athabascans used birch from the vast Interior forests to make canoes, containers, sleds and even cradles. Clothing was of animal hides, decorated with porcupine quills colored with plant dyes.

The Aleuts: This Native group settled the windswept islands of the Aleutian Chain approximately 10,000 years ago. The name "Alaska" comes from their word "Alaxsxag," which means "the object toward which the action of the sea is directed." This name demonstrates the Aleuts' strong attachment to the sea, which provided them with all of life's necessities. Although their location on the island chain allowed them to harvest the sea's bounty, they also had to contend with unpredictable weather – high winds, fog and blinding rain – as well as earthquakes.

Aleut fishing technology included fish spears, weirs, nets, hooks and lines. Various darts and nets were used to obtain sea lions and sea otters. Whales were killed with a poisoned, stone-bladed lance. Upon being thrust into a whale, the lance head detached. When the poisoned tip worked its way to a vital spot the whale would die, usually within three days, and the carcass would drift to shore where the Aleuts awaited it. Women and children also gathered shellfish along the beaches at low tide.

Aleut society was divided into three cate-

Aleuts wore little clothing indoors and during the summer. When weather made it necessary, they donned hoodless, knee-length parkas; in cold weather they added knee-length skin boots. Waterproof overgarments made from the intestines of sea lions were also worn, and this waterproof material was also fitted over the tops of their skin boats to keep hunters dry.

Because of a ready supply of grass in the summer, Aleut women became skilfull at basketry – their baskets were so closely woven that they could even hold water. Mats and some clothing were also made this way.

The Eskimos: The Native group most familiar to non-Alaskans, Eskimos were di-

gories: honorables (usually respected whalers), common people and slaves. At death the body of an honorable was mummified, and sometimes slaves were killed in honor of the deceased. The one- and two-man skin boats used by the Aleuts were called "bidarkas" by the Russians. Because of their dependence on the sea, Aleuts seldom went over a mile inland, but they did develop a clever method of transportation over snow. Aleut skis were made by drying hair-seal skins over wooden frames. When the traveller went uphill the hair would dig into the snow and act as a brake; on the downhill journey the hair would lie flat to provide speed.

vided into two distinct subgroups in Alaska. The Inupiat Eskimos settled in Alaska's arctic region, while the Yup'ik lived in the west.

For the Inupiat especially, life was a constant struggle against hunger and the cold. Seasonal food was stored against future shortage and for the long dark winter; and even though his own family might be wanting, a hunter always divided a fresh kill evenly throughout the community. Because food was a primary concern, status within a village was determined by hunting ability.

A recent find at Barrow has given archeologists insight into the world of the arctic Eskimos before European contact. Excavation has uncovered five members of an Eskimo family in their wood and sod house. The family was apparently crushed to death hundreds of years ago by an enormous piece of ice that must have rafted in from a stormy sea. Autopsies performed on the bodies revealed the effects of seasonal starvation and accumulated soot inside the group's dwelling. One of the five, a 42-year-old woman, had survived bacterial pneumonia, an infection of the heart valves, arthritis, trichinosis and blood poisoning. She had also recently given birth.

Eskimo village sites were chosen according to availability of food sources. The arctic coast people depended on seal, walrus and

the summer dogs were used as pack animals.

Women were skilled in basketry and sewing. They stitched and fitted waterproof garments made of animal intestine and fish skins. The Eskimos' everyday clothing of trousers, boots and coats were sewn from skins and fur, sometimes in complex geometric designs. The coats, called parkas, featured an attached hood and ruff.

Eskimos are renowned for their fine carving, especially their small ivory pieces. In early times household utensils and weapons were beautifully ornamented. Using wood, bone, baleen (bony plates that line the mouths of baleen whales), walrus ivory and fossil mammoth tusks, Eskimos crafted dishes and

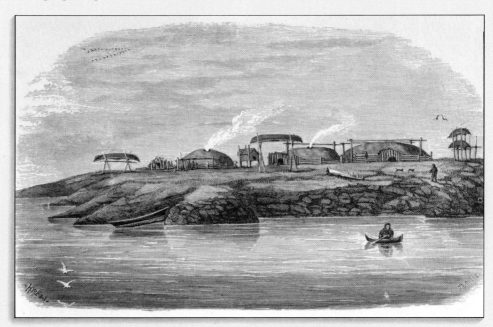

whale, while the inland Eskimo lived on caribou, birds and other small game animals. Eggs were gathered by all, and berries, roots and wild greens were eaten fresh or preserved in skin containers or baskets.

The Eskimos used boats called *umiaks* to hunt larger sea animals. They also used smaller, one-man craft, called *kayaks,* from which comes the modern boats of the same name. Both were made of a frame of wood covered with skins or hides. Sleds and dog teams were used for winter travel, and during

Left, traditional waterproof canoe made from animal hide. **Above**, Native village.

knives, oil lamps, small sculptures and game pieces, and goggles to protect their eyes from the glare off of snow and ice. The *ulu,* or woman's knife, can be found in tourist shops today and is appreciated by contemporary cooks for both its beauty and its utility.

European Contact: By the time the first Europeans arrived in the 18th century, these Alaska Native groups had inhabited their respective homelands for hundreds of generations. Their lives were often difficult, but they had refined methods for hunting, for clothing and for making peace with the animals and environment that supported them.

Then came the Russians.

THE RUSSIAN INVASION

The story of Russia's invasion of the land long inhabited by Alaska Natives actually begins with a Dane, Vitus Bering. In 1741, Bering, on a mission of exploration for Peter the Great, set sail from Russia with two tiny vessels, the *Saint Peter* and the *Saint Paul*.

The ships, both two-masted crafts only 80 feet (24 meters) long, left the Siberian port of Petropavlovsk on June 4, 1741. Six days later, Bering, in command of the *St Peter*, and Alexei Chirikof, the captain of the *St Paul*, lost sight of each other in a thick fog. Both commanders continued to sail east.

On July 15, Chirikof sighted land – probably, historians say, the west side of Prince of Wales Island in southeast Alaska. He sent a group of men ashore in a long boat. When the first group failed to return, he sent a second. Eerily, that group also vanished. Chirikof pulled anchor and moved on.

In the meantime, on July 16 Bering and the crew of the *St Peter* sighted a towering peak on the Alaska mainland – Mount St Elias, which at 18,000 feet (5,500 meters) is second only to Mount McKinley in height. Turning westward, Bering anchored his vessel off Kayak Island while crew members went ashore to explore and find water. Georg Wilhelm Steller, ship's naturalist, hiked briskly along the island, taking notes on plants and wildlife. Here he first recorded for science the striking blue-and-black jay which bears his name. Bering was anxious to return to Russia before bad weather came, and so turned westward, leaving the magnificent country behind him unexplored.

Chirikof and the *St Paul* returned to Siberia on October 9 with news of the new land they had found. But Bering's concern over bad weather had proved prophetic: his ship was battered by relentless storms, and in November he and his crew were forced to land on one of Russia's uninhabited Commander Islands. Bering, ill with scurvy, died on the island, and soon thereafter high winds dashed the *St Peter* to pieces. The stranded crew wintered on the island; when the weather

improved the 46 survivors managed to build a crude 40-foot (12-meter) boat from the wreckage of the *St Peter*. They set sail for Petropavlovsk on August 12, 1742, and arrived safely on August 27.

Bering's crew returned to Russia with sea otter pelts – soon judged to be the finest fur in the world. Spurred by the riches represented by the furbearing marine life and mammals Bering's crew had discovered, Russia threw itself wholeheartedly into setting up hunting and trading outposts.

Native contact: For the Native populations of Alaska, the coming of the Russians was an unprecedented disaster. The Russians quickly expanded throughout the Aleutian Islands, furiously hunting the marine life that had supported the Aleuts for so many generations. Even worse, the Russians brought with them European diseases to which the Aleuts had no defenses. As word spread of the riches in furs to be had, competition among Russian companies increased and treatment of the Aleuts deteriorated.

Catherine the Great, who became Czarina in 1763, proclaimed goodwill toward the Aleuts and urged her subjects to treat the

<u>Left</u>, Grigor Ivanovich Shelikof, who founded the first Russian settlement in Alaska. <u>Right</u>, the Natives were not always welcoming.

Natives fairly. But Catherine was thousands of miles away, and the hunters' all-consuming quest for furs caused them to overlook Aleut welfare. Hostages were taken, families split up, individuals forced to leave their villages and settle elsewhere. The Aleuts revolted that year, and won some victories. but the Russians retaliated, killing many and destroying their boats and hunting gear, leaving them with no means of survival.

Eighty percent of the Aleut population was decimated by violence and disease during the first two generations of Russian contact. The survivors became little better than slaves.

Other Europeans: About this same time, the British were continuing their search for the Northwest Passage, the fabled water route between the Atlantic and the Pacific. And so Captain James Cook sailed to the Aleutians in 1778. The Russians tried to impress him with the extent of their control over the region, but Cook saw how tenuous was the position of this ragtag group of hunters 3,000 miles from their homeland.

Although Cook died in Hawaii after visiting Alaska, his crew continued on to Canton, China, where they sold sea otter pelts obtained in Alaska for outlandishly high prices. Britain was interested. Cook's expedition spurred the English to increase their sailings along the northwest coast – and the Spanish, who were well established on the coast of California, followed suit.

Gaining a foothold: The Russians were determined to dig in and keep Alaska's fur wealth for themselves. One particularly determined Russian, Grigor Ivanovich Shelikof, arrived in Three Saints Bay on Kodiak Island in 1784 with two ships, the *Three Saints* and the *Saint Simon*. A third had been lost on the long journey from Russia.

The indigenous Koniag, wary of the foreigners, harassed the Russian party. Shelikof, who intended to use the Koniags to hunt sea otters and needed their obedience, responded with appalling violence.

As reported by Ivan Peel, acting governor general of Irkutsak and Kolyvan, "They said Shelikohov (sic) loaded two bidarkas with his people...and with the armed band murdered about 500 of these speechless people; if we also count those who ran in fear to their bidarkas and, trying to escape, stampeded and drowned each other, the number will exceed 500. Many men and women were taken as prisoners of war. By order of Mr. Shelekohov (sic), the men were led to the tundra and speared, the remaining women and children, about 600 altogether, he took with him to the harbor and kept them for three weeks. The husbands who succeeded in escaping the murder began to come. Shelekohov returned their wives to them, but he retained one child from each family as hostage."

Having established his authority on Kodiak Island, Shelikof founded the first permanent Russian settlement in Alaska on the island's Three Saints Bay, built a school to teach the Natives to read and write Russian, and introduced the Russian Orthodox religion.

In 1790 Shelikof, now back in Mother Russia, hired Alexander Baranof to manage his Alaskan fur enterprise. Baranof moved the colony to the northeast end of Kodiak island, where timber was available. The site chosen by Baranof is now the city of Kodiak.

Russian members of the colony took Koniag wives and started families whose names continue today: Panamaroff, Petrikoff, Kvasnikoff, Chichenoff. Baranof himself proved brilliant at managing the rough Russians who were the permanent hunting contingent on Kodiak Island. He also set up comparatively humane ground rules for interaction with the Koniag Natives.

In 1795 Baranof, concerned by the sight of non-Russian Europeans trading with Natives in southeast Alaska, established Mikhailovsk six miles north of present-day Sitka. He bought the land on which Mikhailovsk was built from the Tlingits; but in 1802, while Baranof was away, the neighboring Tlingits, perhaps rueing their decision to allow the strangers onto their territory, attacked and destroyed Mikhailovsk. Baranof returned with a Russian warship and razed the Tlingit village. He then built the settlement of New Archangel, which became the capital of Russian America, nearby.

Meanwhile, as Baranof secured the Russians' physical presence in Alaska, the trade activities in the Americas. But despite the best efforts of Baranof and others, the Russians never fully colonized Alaska; for the most part they clung to the coast, shunning the rugged inland. And by the 1830s, the Russian monopoly on trade in the region was weakening. The Hudson's Bay Company, formed by the British in 1821, set up a post on the southern edge of Russian America in 1833. The English company was more organized and better run than the Russian-American Company, and soon began siphoning off trade.

Colonial powers: The Americans were also becoming a force. Baranof began to depend heavily on American supply ships, since

Shelikof family continued to work back in Russia to win a monopoly on Alaska's fur trade. In 1799, Shelikof's son-in-law, Nikolay Petrovich Rezanov, had acquired the charter of monopoly for the American fur trade from Russian Czar Paul I. Rezanov then formed the Russian-American Company. As part of the deal, the Czar expected the company to establish new settlements in Alaska and carry out an expanded colonization program.

By 1804 Alexander Baranof, now manager of the Russian-American Company, had consolidated the company's hold on fur

Left, Captain Cook. **Above**, New Archangel.

they came much more frequently than Russian ships. In addition, Americans could sell furs in the Canton, China market, which was closed to the Russians.

The downside of the American presence was that American hunters and trappers encroached on territory the Russians considered theirs. In 1812, a settlement was reached. The Russians had exclusive rights to the fur trade above 55°N latitude, the Americans below 55°N latitude. The agreement soon went by the wayside, however, and with Baranof's retirement in 1818 the Russian hold on Alaska was further weakened.

When the Russian-American Company's

charter was renewed in 1821, it stipulated that the chief managers from then on be naval officers. Unfortunately, most naval officers did not have any experience in the fur trading business, so the company suffered under a string of sometimes well-meaning but incompetent "governors."

The second charter also tried to cut off all contact with foreigners, especially the competitive Americans. But this strategy backfired, since the Russian colony had become used to relying on American supply ships, and America had become a fur customer. Eventually the Russian-American Company entered into an agreement with the Hudson's Bay Company, even giving the British rights to sail through Russian territory.

Although the mid-1800s were not a good time for the Russians in Alaska, for those coastal Alaska Natives who had survived contact – primarily the Aleuts, Koniags and Tlingits – conditions improved.

The Tlingits were never conquered and continued to wage guerrilla warfare on the Russians into the 1850s. The Aleuts, many of whom had been removed from their home islands and sent as far south as California to hunt sea otter for the Russians, continued to decline in population through 1840. For them, the officers of the Russian-American Company were a blessing: these managers established schools and hospitals for the Aleuts, and gave them jobs. Russian Orthodox clergy moved into the Aleutian Islands; Father Ivan Veniaminof, famous throughout Russian America, lived among them and developed an Aleut dictionary and grammar. Slowly the Aleut population began to grow.

But by the 1860s the Russians were seriously considering ridding themselves of Russian America. Zealous overhunting had decimated the furbearing animals, and competition from the British and Americans exacerbated the situation. This, combined with the difficulties of supplying and protecting such a distant colony, brought about a waning of interest. A Russian emissary approached US Secretary of State William Henry Seward about a possible sale, and in 1867 the US Congress, at Seward's urging, agreed to buy Russian America for $7.2 million, just under 2 cents an acre.

Left, Seward (sitting) urges the Russian minister (standing) to sign the sale document for Alaska.

The truth of the matter was, America wasn't sure what, exactly, it had just bought. Vast regions of Alaska remained unexplored. The interior had remained little touched by Russians, who had stayed in the coastal areas. In 1865, Robert Kennicott, part of a Western Telegraph surveying effort, had led his surveying crew to Nulato on the banks of the Yukon. Western Union had decided to lay a telegraph line across Alaska to Bering Strait where it would connect with an Asian line. Kennicott died the following year at Nulato. Among Kennicott's contingent were several scientists and, upon Kennicott's death, William H. Dall took charge of scientific affairs. The Western Union expedition conducted the first scientific studies of the region and produced the first map of the entire Yukon River. That same year (1866), workers finally succeeded in laying an Atlantic undersea telegraph cable, and the Alaskan overland project was abandoned. Dall returned to Alaska many times, recording and naming many geographical features. Dall sheep and Dall porpoise bear his name.

The Alaska Commercial Company also contributed to the growing exploration of Alaska. In the last decades of the 1800s the company began building trading posts along the interior's many rivers. One by one, small parties of trappers and traders entered the Interior. And, though the federal government provided little money to officially explore the region, every now and then an Army officer would broadly interpret his orders and do a little reconnaissance on his own.

In a four-month journey, Lt. Frederick Schwatka and his party rafted the Yukon from Lake Lindeman in Canada to Saint Michael near the river's mouth on the Bering Sea. Lt. Henry T. Allen made an even more remarkable journey. In 1885 Allen and four others left the Gulf of Alaska, followed the Copper River, crossed a mountain range and traveled down the Tanana River to the Yukon, portaged to the Kanuti and then the Koyukuk rivers. Allen went up the Koyukuk, then back down to the Yukon, crossed over to

Left: Francis Seward, architect of the American purchase of Alaska. **Right**, early supply tent.

Unalakleet on the coast, and then made his way to Saint Michael. Allen explored about 1,500 miles (2,400 km) of Interior Alaska.

But whether the United States knew what it had or not, the territory still needed to be governed. Unfortunately, back in Washington, D.C., legislators had their hands full with post-Civil War reconstruction issues, and little time to dedicate to Alaska. As a result, a US Army officer, General Jefferson C. Davis, was put in charge.

Gold: It was the discovery of gold in the

Yukon in 1896 that finally made the United States (and the rest of the world) sit up and take notice of America's northern possession. A wave of fortune hunters clamored for passage to the Klondike strike. The Klondike was in Yukon Territory, Canada, not Alaska (as many would-be miners believed). But the easiest route to the Canadian territory was by ship to Skagway, in Southeast Alaska. Once in Skagway, miners had their choice of two brutal passes across the mountains to the Yukon gold fields: White Pass, also called Dead Horse Trail, because it was littered with the corpses of pack animals, or the Chilkoot Trail, an old Native route.

However, many who didn't make their fortunes in the Klondike strike brought their search for gold back to Alaska.

Alaska, in fact, had plenty of gold of its own. An earlier strike in Juneau had established that city in Southeast Alaska. Gold was found in Nome in 1899. And a serendipitous combination of fortune and misfortune led to both a gold strike and the birth of Fairbanks, Alaska, in the early 1900s. For several years Felix Pedro had been prospecting in the Tanana Hills of the interior, searching for a gold-rich creek he had stumbled upon years earlier but had been forced to abandon. As the summer of 1901 drew to a close, the luckless Pedro was about

farther if he could work the *Lavelle Young* through the shallow river channel, but if he couldn't, Barnette agreed to be put ashore wherever upstream progress was halted.

Barnette didn't anticipate disembarking in the middle of nowhere on a slough off the main Tanana River, but that's where Felix Pedro found him. It was a match made in heaven: Pedro and his partner were delighted to be saved the long walk to Circle City, and Barnette was equally delighted to see his first customers walking out of the wilderness.

As an appropriate end to the fairy tale, in July 1902 Pedro struck gold, and the would-be goldminers who flooded the area transformed Barnette's wilderness outpost into a

to set out with his partner on a 165-mile (265-km) walk to Circle City for another grubstake. It was then that Pedro spotted smoke coming from the banks of the Chena Slough.

The smoke was the final chapter in the failed effort of E.T. Barnette to get thousands of dollars worth of supplies up the Tanana River to Tanana Crossing, a point on the proposed Valdez-to-Eagle trade route. Barnette had convinced the captain of the steamer *Lavelle Young* to take himself, his wife, his partner and supplies up the Tanana against the captain's better judgment. The latter agreed to go to where the Chena River entered the Tanana. He would take Barnette

booming town. Named Fairbanks in honor of a US senator, the burg grew as more miners and new businesses came to the Chena. Public services, libraries and hospitals all eased the early days in Fairbanks. True, the town had shanties along its fringes, but the city center offered many of the conveniences of Lower 48 communities. Traffic came and went on the river, and an overland route to Valdez cut days off a trip to the Lower 48.

Eventually the Tanana Mining District out of Fairbanks became a huge gold producer. There were strikes in other places, as well, such as Fortymile. The gold acted as a powerful magnet for Americans and Europeans.

Of course, not everyone in Alaska was a goldminer. Many found ways to profit from the gold rushes without actually panning for the metal themselves. At Ruby Creek, for example, a strike in 1907, and a more substantial one in 1910, brought the predictable rush of miners to the area and the town of Ruby was born. Newcomers arrived from up and down the river, some by small riverboats, others on large paddlewheelers, The steamers required several cords (a cord is approximately 130 cubic feet) of wood daily to keep them moving, and residents along the river supplemented their trapping and fishing by maintaining wood lots.

Ruby grew from a tent city in 1911 to a

Wrangell-St. Elias Mountains. The mine extracted more than 591,535 tons of copper ore from the earth, and in its heyday employed more than 800 workers.

The more traditional ways of life – fishing, in particular – also provided a livelihood for many Alaskans, particularly after canning was introduced. In 1878 businessmen built the first two canneries at Klawock and Sitka. In 1883 the Arctic Pack Company established a cannery at Nushagak Bay, where they were able to exploit the immense runs of salmon. Two years later the Alaska Packing Company opened a cannery across the bay. And by 1908, ten canneries ringed Nushagak Bay. Kodiak's first canneries were built in

bustling river port. With running water in summer months, a theater, several shops and cafes, Ruby sought to provide all the amenities of its upstream rival, Fairbanks. By 1917, at the height of the rush, creeks south of Ruby had yielded $875,000 worth of gold.

Other ways of life: There were other precious and semi-precious metals to be mined in Alaska as well, particularly copper. In 1910, the richest copper mine in the world started operation at Kennecott in the

Left, trudging up treacherous Chilkoot Pass en route to the Klondike. **Above**, mail sleigh, complete with reindeer and a gold dredge behind.

the late 1800s, when word of phenomenal fish runs became widespread. Rumors of being able to cross streams on the backs of salmon drew fishermen from far and wide.

By the turn of the century, commercial fishing was gaining a foothold in the Aleutian islands. Packing houses salted cod and herring. Salmon canneries were opened.

Another traditional occupation, whaling, continued with, unfortunately, a modern disregard for overhunting. Bowhead whales, the awesome behemoths of northern seas, led a parade of whale hunters to the high Arctic. Following routes they had used since the end of the Pleistocene age, the bowheads migrated twice yearly through Bering Strait on their run from the southwestern Bering Sea to summer feeding areas in the Beaufort Sea. Weighing a ton per foot and reaching lengths of 60 feet (20 meters), bowheads filter their food through large plates of baleen and carry huge quantities of oil in their tissue. Sadly whalers seeking the oil pursued the bowhead to the edge of extinction.

Indeed, the American fishing, canning and whaling operations – as well as walrus hunting – were as unchecked as the Russians' hunting had been. In the Aleutians, a deputy marshal was appointed in 1884 to maintain order under the laws of Oregon. The Aleuts were suffering without the fur seals and sea

otters they needed to survive. Not only did the Aleuts need the animals for food; they used their skins for the coverings of their boats. Without boats, Aleuts couldn't hunt.

Even worse, Americans had expanded into Interior and Arctic Alaska, aggressively exploiting the furbearers, fish and other game that Natives in those regions depended on.

World War II: After Pearl Harbor some farsighted military officers feared for the safety of the Aleutians. These fears were proved legitimate on June 3, 1942, when the Japanese launched an air attack on Dutch Harbor, a US naval base on Unalaska. The US forces at Dutch Harbor managed to hold

off the planes, and the base survived the attack, and a second, with minor damage. But on June 7, the Japanese landed on the islands of Kiska and Attu, where they overwhelmed Attu villagers and a white schoolteacher. The villagers were taken to Japan and interned for the remainder of the war. Aleuts from the Pribilofs and Aleutian villages were evacuated by the United States to southeastern Alaska.

In fall 1942, the US Navy began constructing a base on Adak from which to strike the Japanese invaders, who were digging in on their two captured islands. On May 11, 1943, American troops landed on Attu, determined to take the island back from the Japanese. The bloody battle wore on for more than two weeks. The Japanese, who had no hope of rescue because their fleet of transport submarines had been turned back by American destroyers, fought to the last man. The end finally came on May 29 when the Americans repelled a banzai charge. Some Japanese remained in hiding on the small island (only 35 miles long and 15 miles wide/56 km by 24 km) for up to three months after their defeat. When discovered, they killed themselves rather than surrender.

The taking of Attu was the second bloodiest battle of the Pacific theater; only Iwo Jima was more costly in terms of human lives.

The US then turned its attention to the other occupied island, Kiska. From June through August, tons of bombs were dropped on the tiny island. But the Japanese, under cover of thick Aleutian fog, escaped via transport ships, on July 28 and 29. After the war, the Native Attuans who had survived internment in Japan were resettled to Atka by the federal government, which considered their home villages too remote to defend.

World War II affected Alaska in unexpected ways. The US had finished the Alaska-Canada Military Highway (Alcan) during the war. Running from Great Falls, Montana, to Fairbanks, the road was the first stable link between Alaska and the Lower 48.

By the end of the war, Alaskan cities had swelled. Anchorage, for example, had grown from 4,200 people in 1940 to 8,000 in 1945. Two other great catalysts of change were just around the corner: statehood and oil.

Left, prospectors. **Right**, bearded sourdough and his bugle remember an era of work and wealth.

After its purchase by the US in 1867 Alaska was governed at different times by the US Army, the US Treasury Department and the US Navy. Finally, in 1884, the federal government declared the territory the District of Alaska, and a civil government was appointed by President Chester Arthur.

By the turn of the century, a movement pushing for Alaska statehood had begun. But in the Lower 48, legislators worried that Alaska's population was too sparse, its location too distant and its economy too unstable

Egan was sworn in as the first state governor.

Disaster: It was not long before the young state underwent its first trial by fire. On March 27, 1964, the Good Friday Earthquake struck southcentral Alaska, churning the earth for a heart-stopping four minutes. At an estimated 8.7 on the Richter scale, the Good Friday quake is one of the most powerful ever recorded. One hundred and three Alaskans were killed – most of them drowned, being unable to outrun the quake-triggered *tsunamis* (tidal waves) that tore apart the

for the territory to be a worthwhile addition to the US.

World War II and the Japanese invasion of Attu and Kiska highlighted Alaska's strategic importance, and some began to take the issue of statehood more seriously in the Lower 48. But it was the discovery of oil at Swanson River on the Kenai Peninsula in 1957 that truly helped to dispel the image of Alaska as a weak, dependent state. Oil, when added to the resources already known to exist in the territory, tipped the balance, and on January 3, 1959, Alaska became a state. Juneau, which had been the territorial capital, continued as the state capital. William A.

unfortunate towns of Valdez and Chenega.

Throughout the Prince William Sound region towns and ports were destroyed, land uplifted or shoved downwards, islands tilted. The uplift destroyed salmon streams – the fish could no longer negotiate waterfalls and other barriers to reach their spawning grounds. Ports at Valdez and Cordova were beyond repair – what land and mud slides hadn't claimed, fire did.

At Valdez, an Alaska Steamship Company ship was lifted by a huge wave over the docks and out to sea. Amazingly, most hands survived. Witnesses on shore swore that at one point they could see daylight all the way under the ship. There were few witnesses, however: many of those who had been waiting on the dock to greet the ship were swept to their deaths.

At Turnagain Arm off the Kenai Peninsula, the incoming salt water killed trees and caused cabins to sink into the mud. In Anchorage, huge chunks of road asphalt piled on top of each other like shingles. At Seldovia, near the junction of Kachemak Bay and Cook Inlet, well-developed fish processing facilities and an active fishing fleet were laid

to come into their own, participating in state and local government and flexing their voting muscle. More than 200 years after the arrival of Vitus Bering, Natives of all ethnic groups united to claim title to the lands wrested from them by Europeans. With no imperatives, the government responded slowly. Then, in 1968, the Atlantic-Richfield Company discovered oil at Prudhoe Bay, catapulting the issue of land ownership into the headlines.

Prudhoe Bay is on Alaska's Arctic coast.

waste, along with Seldovia's harbor.

On Kodiak, a *tsunami* wiped out the villages of Afognak, Old Harbor and Kaguyak, and damaged other communities. Seward, a thriving port town at the southern terminus of the Alaska Central Railroad, also lost its harbor.

Oil and land: Despite the catastrophe, Alaskans managed to rebuild many of the devastated communities. And four years later, Alaska experienced an upheaval of another sort. In the mid-1960s, Alaska Natives began

Left, Native Alaskan bark house and barkers. **Above**, the 1964 earthquake in Anchorage.

Drilling at such a remote location would be difficult enough – but transporting the resulting crude to refineries in the Lower 48 seemed almost impossible. The best solution seemed to be to build a pipeline to carry the oil across Alaska to the port of Valdez (rebuilt a few miles from the ruins of the old Valdez). At Valdez the oil would be loaded onto tanker ships and sent by water to the Lower 48. The plan was approved – but a permit to construct the pipeline, which would cross lands involved in the Native land claims dispute, could not be granted until the Native claims were settled.

With major petro dollars on the line, there

was new urgency for an agreement with the Natives, and in 1971 the Alaska Native Claims Settlement Act was signed. In it, the Natives relinquished aboriginal claims to their lands; in return they received title to 44 million acres of land and were paid $962.5 million. The land and money were divided among 13 regional, four urban and more than 200 village Native corporations established for the purpose. Some have handled their funds wisely; others have not, leaving some Natives land-rich and cash-poor.

The settlement compensated Natives for the invasion of their lands. It also opened the way for all Alaskans to profit from the state's tremendous natural resource, oil.

terrain. And to help the pipeline survive an earthquake, it was laid out in a zigzag pattern, so it would roll with the earth instead of breaking up.

The first oil took 38 days, 12 hours and 54 minutes to travel through the pipeline, arriving at Valdez on July 28, 1977. The total cost of the pipeline and related projects, including the tanker terminal at Valdez, 12 pumping stations, and the Yukon River Bridge, was $8 billion.

The Alaska Permanent Fund: As the potential oil bonanza took shape, Alaska governor Jay Hammond and other state leaders were determined that *this* Alaskan boom would not end like the fur and gold booms – in an

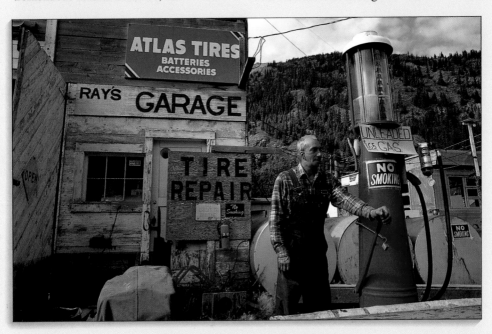

The pipeline: After the Alaska Native Claims Settlement Act, it still remained to actually build a pipeline stretching from Arctic Alaska to Valdez. Between the two points were three mountain ranges, active fault lines, miles and miles of unstable muskeg (boggy ground underlain with permafrost) and the migration paths of caribou and moose. The pipeline was designed with all these factors in mind. To counteract the unstable ground and allow animal crossings, half of the 800-mile pipeline is elevated on supports. The supports also hold the pipe – and its cargo of hot oil – high enough to keep it from melting the permafrost and destroying the natural

economic bust as soon as the resource had disappeared. This time Alaskans would think of the future as well as the present.

To this end, legislators created the Alaska Permanent Fund, which was voted into law in 1976. Twenty-five percent of all mineral lease proceeds are deposited into the fund. Income from the fund is then put to three uses: annual dividends paid to every resident who applies and qualifies; funds added to the principal account to hedge against inflation; and funds appropriated by the state legislature for various uses.

The fund is now one of the largest pools of public money in the United States, and a top lender to the US government. By the year 2000, it is predicted that the fund will produce more revenues for the state than the Prudhoe Bay oil fields.

Moving the state capital: Oil was not the only subject of discussion in Alaska in the 1970s. There was also great debate over whether Juneau, located in the geographically isolated southeast, was the best site for Alaska's capital. There were many who thought that the capital should be more centrally located.

In 1974 Alaskans voted to move their state capital – with the proviso that the new capital could not be located in either Fairbanks or Anchorage. (The two cities had each lobbied

ing, the capital move issue has never completely died; it appeared on ballots again – unsuccessfully – in the 1980s.

Tourism and the environment: In the years following its admission to the US, Alaska discovered another important and growing source of revenue.

Tourism got its start after World War II when men who had been stationed in the region returned home praising the area's natural splendor. And the Alcan highway, as well as the Alaska Marine Highway System (completed in 1963) made the state more accessible than ever before.

Tourism is now big business in Alaska: currently nearly 900,000 people visit the

hard to make sure the other would not receive the benefits of becoming the state capital.) This left few options in sparsely developed Alaska. If not Fairbanks or Anchorage, where? The state governor came up with three options: Willow, Larson Lake and Mount Yenlo. Each potential capital came with a whopping price tag: $2.46 billion, $2.56 billion, and $2.7 billion, respectively. In November 1978 voters rejected a bond issue – in excess of $900 million – intended to finance the move. Although denied fund-

Left, a Chitina garage complete with gravity-fed pump. **Above**, the latest in pipeline technology.

state every year. Once there, they flock to Alaska's top attractions, namely Portage Glacier, the Inside Passage, Glacier Bay, the Ketchikan totems, Mount McKinley (Denali), Skagway's historic district, the Anchorage Museum of History and Art, the University of Alaska Museum and the Kenai River. Grizzly- and wildlife-watching is a main attraction, although only a small proportion of visitors march off into the wilderness, however.

With tourism more and more vital to the state's economy, environmentalism has also risen in importance. Alaskans are working to balance the needs of their remarkable land with the needs of its residents. Much is already well protected – the Alaska National Interest Lands Conservation Act (ANILCA) of 1980 added 53.7 million acres to the national wildlife refuge system, parts of 25 rivers to the national wild and scenic rivers system, 3.3 million acres to national forest lands, and 43.6 million acres to national park land. As a result of the lands act, two-thirds of all American national parklands are now in Alaska.

But tension remains between those who live off the land – such as loggers – and those who wish to preserve it.

The oil spill: No event better illustrates Alaska's struggle to both protect the envi-

ronment and benefit from the state's natural resources than the *Exxon Valdez* disaster. The *Valdez* ran aground on March 24, 1989 in Prince William Sound, releasing 10.8 million gallons (41,000 kl) of crude oil into the water. The oil eventually spread along 1,100 miles (1,760 km) of formerly pristine shoreline.

It was an ecological disaster of unprecedented proportions: According to the US Fish and Wildlife Service, 90,000 to 270,000 sea birds, 2,000 otters and countless other marine animals died as a result of the spill. Exxon spent $2 billion on clean-up in the first year alone.

During the summer of 1989, 12,000 workers descended on the soiled shores of the sound. They bulldozed blackened beaches, sucked up petroleum blobs with vacuum devices, blasted sand with hot water, polished rocks by hand, raked up oily seaweed, and sprayed fertilizer to aid the growth of oil-eating microbes. They worked quickly, to accomplish as much as possible before the onset of winter

For Alaska's tourism industry, the spill (the worst in American history) strained what already had been an uneasy relationship with the state's petroleum interests. Not only did it generate horrendous international publicity at a time when many would-be visitors were making their summer vacation plans, but the influx of clean-up workers filled to capacity virtually every hotel, motel, campsite and restaurant in the Valdez area.

Exxon, working with state and federal agencies, continued its clean-up efforts into the early 1990s. By 1991 there were signs that Prince William Sound was recovering, with Exxon claiming that the Sound was effectively clean. That year salmon returned in force, and millions of pounds had to be thrown away. In some areas, such as Smith Island in the center of the sound, an oil-soaked wasteland directly after the spill, winter storms did more to wash the shore clean than any human efforts.

But there has been concern, particularly among Natives who rely on the sound's rich marine life, that shellfish and other creatures might still be unhealthy to eat. Scientific tests have yielded mixed results, but butter clams, which were feared contaminated with aromatic hydrocarbons, appeared healthy when examined in a lab. It has been difficult to assess competely the damage to wildlife, because the animal populations had not been thoroughly surveyed or understood before the spill, and counting methods after the spill were not foolproof.

Still, the oil spill was a disaster of mammoth – one might say Alaskan – proportions. Prince William Sound seems to be bouncing back, but Alaskans are working hard to make sure their state – beautiful, rugged, delicately balanced – is not put to the test again.

Left, cleaning up on La Touche Island after the *Exxon Valdez*. **Right**, tanker maneuvers in Prince William Sound.

VISITING ALASKA'S NATIVES

A Native tour guide leading a group of professional women on a wilderness river trip out of Arctic Village, in the foothills of the Brooks Range, expertly spotted a moose as the group floated down the east fork of the Chandalar River. If he were alone, he told them, he would shoot the moose for food, since hunting season was open. The women – who came from places such as Pennsylvania and New York – encouraged him to do just that. So he shot the moose and butchered it on the spot.

It wasn't a planned item on the women's travel itinerary – and such an experience isn't likely to happen to most visitors on trips to remote Alaska villages – but the travellers went home with a greater understanding of the state's Native peoples than they possibly could have learned visiting city museums.

Past and present merge: Many Native Alaskans still live a subsistence lifestyle that depends upon collecting meat and fish during the abundant summer months and preparing it for storage to sustain them over the long winter. In the southern part of the state, Natives depend upon deer, salmon and other food from the sea. In the Interior, the Athabascans fish on the rivers and hunt caribou and waterfowl. Further north, Eskimos hunt whale and seals. Most villages are located in remote areas without roads to connect them with cities and luxuries such as grocery stores. Until recently, about the only outsiders who spent any time in villages were friends, relatives, health care workers or teachers. Now the list is growing.

Villages welcome visitors: An international fascination with indigenous people has spread to Alaska, and village residents from Saxman Native Village in Southeast Alaska to Gambell on St. Lawrence Island in the Bering Strait are cautiously opening their doors to visitors. Visiting an Alaska Native village can be a unique adventure for people who are both flexible and open-minded. Organized tours are now offered in at least 10 villages throughout Alaska and by the year 2000, as many as 30 villages may offer tours.

Preceding pages: off-piste again; Yu'pik Natives ice-fishing. **Left,** Nulato boy in his parka.

In these encounters, both the visitors and the visited learn from each other. Visitors learn how Natives live in various parts of the state and along the way discard stereotypes about igloos, wardrobes of animal skins and rubbing noses. "Visitors come with an expectation that they're going to go back in time," says the Alaska Native Tourism Council, an organization formed in 1992 to promote rural tourism and help Native groups who operate tours. "They find out it's going to be very visually familiar in terms of clothing – people wearing Nike tennis shoes – but the culture and life of the people hasn't changed a lot. Value systems are still deeply rooted in the past and in their culture. [The visitors] learn that while it doesn't *look* like what they expected, it *feels* like what they expected."

And Natives learn to share their love for the land and a desire to preserve their way of life and the teachings of their ancestors. In recent years, as more and more young people leave villages for life in the cities, Natives have worked to keep their culture and their language alive. Tourism now provides an impetus for them to do that. Young Natives learn the dances and stories of old, passing them on to their own children and to the rest of the world.

Changes afoot: The 20th century has brought numerous changes to Alaska's Native communities. Thirteen regional and 200 Native village corporations were formed to manage money and land received from the government as a result of the 1971 Alaska Native Claims Settlement Act. The measure approved the transfer of 44 million acres and $963 million to corporations in exchange for giving up their aboriginal rights to the land.

Some of these corporations have been phenomenally successful, parlaying the oil, mineral and other natural resource wealth of their lands into large annual dividends for members. Others have not done as well. Some made bad investments and others were tainted by corruption.

Although snowmachines are largely replacing dog sleds as a means of winter travel and boats with motors replace the skin boats that their ancestors used for fishing and hunting, Natives still follow traditional ways. Now, however, they must have money to buy gasoline for their snowmachines and bullets for their guns. Their subsistence way of life requires modern tools and they meld the old and the new.

It's a delicate balance. Natives struggle to keep their own culture intact as they embrace the conveniences of modern society. Essentially they have a foot in both worlds.

The modern world, which lures away younger Natives, has also brought its share of ills to Native communities and many struggle to overcome high rates of alcoholism and suicide. A number of villages have voted to stay "dry" with no alcohol allowed.

of Huslia. For years, the federal Bureau of Land Management hired young villagers to fight summer forest fires. But a series of rainy seasons put a damper on that. To employ the young people, the village decided to try tourism. It wasn't an easy decision for Huslia. The 250 residents took seven years to achieve unanimous agreement. The first season, only a dozen people visited. The second season, more than 20 arrived, and organizers expect the numbers to grow every year.

Tips for travelers: One of the biggest hurdles for some villagers has been the fear of losing their privacy. Indeed, outsiders who show up unescorted in some villages still receive a chilly reception. Allowing a stranger

Yet modern conveniences have also made life a little easier. Under her fur parka, that Eskimo woman may be wearing a dress bought through a mail-order catalog. Her whaler husband and friends track movements of their prey with a short wave radio, and when the meat is consumed raw, as in the old days, they wash it down with canned pop.

Needs must: For many remote communities, welcoming tourists is a step prompted by an increasingly gloomy economic outlook. "While there is a growing demand for a cash economy in the village, paying jobs are on the decline," says Lary Schafer, who helped begin a tourist program in the Interior village

into their village is like a white man inviting someone into his home.

Some residents worry about tourists unwittingly walking into houses unannounced, as if they were strolling into a Disneyland attraction, or indiscriminately snapping photographs nonstop.

It is common courtesy to ask Natives before photographing them. Some villages, such as Gambell, prefer that you ask before taking *any* pictures in the village. And the travel brochure publicizing Arctic Village specifically prohibits video cameras.

Whether you are visiting as part of an organized tour or on your own, remember that what happens in Native villages is real life, not a tourist attraction. Even on tours, day-to-day community life sometimes takes precedence over visitors' needs.

Read up on the people and their culture before you show up at the airstrip. Visitors on organized tours to Huslia receive two books about Athabascan culture, *Athabascan People of the North* and *Make Prayers to the Raven*. Many other books are available about other Native groups in Alaska and can be found at most libraries.

In some villages, interaction between visitors and residents is controlled and limited, with visitors escorted. Many isolated communities want to break into the tourism busi-

take people to fish camp, we explain that there is a dog team tied up around camp to warn of bears or moose coming in. We tell them not to feed the dogs, they're work dogs," says Audrey Ranstead, who takes tour groups to a Native fish camp on the Yukon River. "We tell them the villagers who work there live in wall tents and that's their private area, not to just walk in there. We ask them to respect their privacy. We set ground rules before we get there and people respect that."

Contact the village council before you show up to make sure residents are open to visitors, or find a tour operator that includes Native villages on its itineraries. The Alaska

ness slowly and tailored tours accommodate that need.

Pack clothing for a variety of conditions. As in all Alaska communities, weather often determines activities. Find out what the average weather conditions are for the area you want to visit and plan accordingly. Keep an open mind. Some visitors get a taste – literally – of the Native lifestyle. Food served in Athabascan villages includes traditional fare, from caribou and moose to bear and beaver.

Learn as much as you can about Native values before you reach a village. "When we

Left, Aniak children. **Above**, Yu'pik dancers.

Native Tourism Council (1577 C St., #304, Anchorage, AK 99510) has a list of villages that welcome visitors.

You can show your respect for Native culture by how you behave. Slow down and don't pepper villagers with personal questions. Observe for a while first, then ask a question respectfully. You will probably get an answer. Be prepared to fend for yourself. Accommodations and amenities are limited and sometimes conditions can be primitive. Don't expect room service and don't count on sticking to a strict time schedule.

Your reward will be an insight into the world of the Alaska Natives.

Two Sisters in the Alaskan Bush

Julie Collins describes how she and her twin sister Miki learned to make their living by hunting and trapping in the remote bush

"All right, boys." The soft command is all I need. As I, Julie, pull the snow hook – the sled anchor – 12 rangy huskies bound forward in unison, slamming into their harnesses to send the loaded dogsled and me flying down the steep hill below our isolated cabin.

"Gee, Loki!" At my order the lead dog swings hard right without breaking his stride, leading the loping dogs out the snowy trail going to our trapline and, 18 miles distant, our nearest line cabin.

The heavily loaded sled skids sharply around corner, requiring all my weight to keep it from flipping as the dogs reach a top speed of 15 miles per hour. Already I've begun to perspire from the heavy work, and by the time the dogs settle into a 10-mile-an-hour trot I've shed my parka despite the 10-below weather.

A good beginning: It's been a typical start except for the remarkable lack of trouble. The sled did *not* clump a sapling in its careening descent; I did *not* have a dog fight, runaway dogs, a last-minute repair job, or a sloppily-loaded sled threatening to buck burlap sacks of frozen fish from the canvas tarp. The towline did *not* disconnect from the sled, sending the dogs flying in formation away down that hill without me. I did *not* run into a one-ton bull moose challenging my right to use the trail.

Still, as the dogs glide effortlessly through two inches of fresh snow on the trail, I must remain constantly alert for unseen dangers: thin ice, deadly water hidden under deep snow, irritable moose, open creeks, or a fresh tree blown down across the trail.

These hazards usually crop up suddenly and without warning. Once I walked up to entangle the 60-foot towline and stepped backwards perhaps six inches off the trail only to have the ice collapse under me. A section of the slough caved in and I plunged into waist-deep water along with three of my dogs. Since I never let go of the towline, which had about 800 pounds of dogs attached

to it, I had plenty of leverage for climbing out, but at 15 degrees below zero (F) the last 10 miles of that trip wasn't too pleasant.

While watching ahead I also have to control the sled with its load of dog food, my own food, emergency gear, trapping gear, rifle and snowshoes – keeping the graceful wooden sled from skidding off the narrow trail into the deep snow. At the same time I must maintain a steady and constant control over the team of sled dogs, braking the sled as it plunges down banks, and running up hills to lighten the load. The dogs are guided

verbally, with commands to tell a leader which trail to take, to order slack dogs to speed up, or to encourage the team as a whole when they begin to tire.

By watching form, ears, eye contacts and attitudes, I can determine whether the dogs scent a moose or an animal in a trap ahead, if they want to fight or balk, if they're happy, discouraged, tired or angry. Sensitive observation and interpretation of this subtle language enables me to keep the dogs at peak performance and alerts me to hazards I may not see myself.

After 10 years of driving dogs under conditions from 50 above to 50 below zero, I now possess a constant alertness for dangers, which hit often and unexpectedly in the depths of the Alaskan bush where I live. Last fall my twin sister Miki and I returned from meeting the twice-weekly mail plane and found grizzly tracks on the beach in front of our house, tracks which had not been there in the morning. During the pitch black night the giant bear returned, plodding through knee-deep water up the bay past our house.

We were alerted by the 14-chained huskies as they roared with wild excitement. Miki, also my constant companion and trapping partner, challenged me to come with her into the darkness to protect our drying fish and hanging moose meat from the great bear.

Outside, we crept softly toward the grizzly, listening to it splash by the water. The bear passed uncomfortably close to us as we stood on the beach.

Miki fired a shot over the bear's head with our .308 rifle while I held a .264 ready in case he answered our challenge. Rather than speed-

ing his departure, the explosion caused the grizzly to stop in mid-stride and raise his head to stare. A second shot had no effect at all, but at the third warning shot the bear moved off – not quickly, but fast enough.

An encounter like that tends to raise one's level of alertness far above normal. But then, so does stalking a bull moose or encountering a vicious, powerful wolverine caught in a feeble trap meant for a much smaller animal.

A hard rewarding life: Life in the Alaskan bush is exhilarating but it is very hard and often tedious. Since very few jobs are available, many people like Miki and myself are self-employed, working as trappers, fishing or making handcrafts. Trapping is one of the hardest, least profitable professions I know, and the rewards are emotional and physical more than monetary. Still, we earn enough to support our dog team, and supplement this with small incomes from selling handcrafts and freelance writing.

Gliding down the trail, the padding of paws and squeaking of sled runners muted by fresh snow, I feel tired but content. Yesterday I may have mushed the dogs 30 miles, tomorrow I may ski 15, but for now my goal is that tiny trapping cabin 18 (30 km) miles

Preceding pages: Gold-miner's cabin in the Wrangells. **Left**, Miki and dog team in a snowstorm. **Above**, bounty from Julie's summer garden. **Above right**, Miki sawing wood.

from home where my sister awaits with a warm fire in the wood stove and a hot meal.

If she were not there, if she were at home or farther out the line, I'd be looking forward to arriving long after the early darkness at a cabin as cold inside as the air outside. I'd have to unharness the dogs alone, light a fire, and chop a water hole through two or three feet of river ice, all in the darkness. After lighting a gas lantern I'd pack 40 gallons of water up the steep bank in five-gallon buckets, cook dog food, start my own meal, feed the dogs, and skin any fur I may have caught along the trail that day.

But today Miki will be there waiting for me, and this thought gladdens me, not only

whole team past, scolding the young dogs who have not yet learned to leave sets alone.

I find a marten in the trap, the first we have caught in 10 days. Although this rich, valuable fur animal is our prime catch, we trap them in cycles, sometimes doing well, and often doing very poorly.

After stopping at the set my dogs are eager to run and they lope on down the trail despite the fresh snow and heavy load. I have been pedaling with one foot on the runners behind the sled for an hour and won't stop until we reach the cabin. Pedaling is part of the routine, whether I am traveling five miles or 50. The work grows tedious and then tiring but I can't quit. With 50 to 80 miles of trapline to

for the work she'll be helping me with, but for her companionship, for I have spent many days alone and know the true meaning of loneliness.

The dogs break into a run and I glance ahead to see their ears pricked tautly, every tugline tight as they strain forward. I see nothing here to spur them on but a set lies ahead, a trap laid in a small cubby baited with rotten moose hide.

"Straight on, Loki! Get up, straight on! Amber -Chevy!" My commands bark out in rapid staccato, first ordering the leader to force the excited dogs past whatever animal may be in the trap, and then guiding the

cover each week by dog team the huskies need that extra boost. Although the team is capable of doing 60 miles a day on a good trail, almost every week we have several inches of fresh snow or wind-blown snow covering the trails.

Miki and I are constantly on the move trying to keep the lines open. Our pace is much slower, especially since we have to clean and bait traps after every snow.

Although we travel exclusively by dog team, most trappers use snow machines on their traplines, and during the summer we all

Above, ready to embark on a canoe trip.

travel by river boat or three-wheeler. Since few roads exist in the bush, any trip to the city is by airplane. Mistakes can be deadly when flying the Alaskan bush but I've been fortunate enough to survive the situations I've gotten myself into as a pilot, although not always without damage. A plane crash some years ago left me with a stiff foot and a couple of scars, and just last winter a broken valve in one cylinder crippled the engine of our Super Cub airplane. Although we finished the flight, we were forced to make an 80-mile detour around mountains because the engine couldn't develop enough power to gain altitude.

Our days are always full and productive. During the summer we grow a large garden to produce most of our vegetables for the year and spend long hours picking berries for fresh fruit and jam. The fish nets must be run daily and the dogs fed with cooked whitefish and rice. Any extra fish are cut and dried for next winter.

In the slow summer months we build dog houses and dogsleds, sew sled bags, dog booties and harnesses. We also tan and sew furs from the winter's catch, making luxurious hats and mitts to sell for spare cash. This small business gives us a much-needed chance to sit quietly sewing for hours at a time – a relaxing break from our over-active lives. And once Miki and I brought a rich red-fox hat into a sporting goods store and traded it for a pair of snowshoes, two sleeping bags, a fishing pole, some pots, gloves and several pair of heavy winter socks.

During the fall we pick 15 or 20 gallons of cranberries. We usually manage to shoot a moose, pack out the meat and hang it for the winter's food. Potatoes and root vegetables are harvested and stored and later in the fall, during the annual fish run, we net 500 to 1,000 whitefish, freezing them whole on a shelf outside in the brisk fall air for the winter's dog food.

As autumn spirals into winter, with graying skies, black ice and white snow, a sense of urgency catches us. We *have* to catch a few more fish before the nets freeze in. We *must* finish that dogsled we've been working on. We have to repair our winter gear, a job we put off during the summer because the garden needed weeding or a fish net needed hanging.

Then the trapping season begins and we hit the trail with bouncing dogs and happy

hearts, for the long, cold, dark season is our favorite. Now our union with our dogs is stronger, more intense, as we spend six to 12 hours nearly every day on the trail with them, scolding or praising them, loving and hating them, guiding, training and *living* dogs.

With winter comes the truly hard work: snowshoeing many miles through deep snow; skiing more miles to set trail; driving dogs 80 to 150 miles each week just to maintain the lines; clearing miles of new trails or brushing out overgrown old trails; and cutting cord after cord of firewood.

By late winter we are tired of the constant work in bitter weather. It's time for a vacation, the only vacation of the year. By early March the bitterest cold has drained away and we take our vacation: a cross-country dog team trip, a grueling journey which may take us 600 miles or more. We travel hard but without a care, the two of us alone with our dogs, following trails or breaking our own through the deep, powdery snow, stopping in villages to make friends but always eager to be off again.

So it goes. The yearly cycle, of putting food up in the summer and fall, of trapping and woodcutting in the winter and spring. The weekly cycle, measured by the mail plane and the trapline rounds, and the daily cycle of mushing dogs and feeding fires.

Home at last: Now the dogs break into a lope again. We are near the cabin; dusk has fallen and we are tired but eager to be home. I smell the rich wood smoke of Miki's fire, see the cheery lantern light beaming through the window.

The dogs crowd by the door as she comes out and together Miki and I unhook each dog and tie them up, unload the sled, and duck inside the warm, tiny cabin. A hot meal follows, of rich chili from ground moose and beans, or tender pot roast with potatoes and garden vegetables, or thick moose steaks with rice and steaming cornbread or raisin bread on the table.

I feed the dogs their meal too, fish and rice with a small piece of liver for each dog, with tallow, dried fish and commercial dog food to fill out their meal. Then, back inside, I pull off my fur mukluks and lie back on the bed, face flushed from the cold wind, muscles a little sore, a bruise on one knee from slamming into the sled when it hit a tree.

But most of all tired – tired but content.

BUSH PILOTS: A SPECIAL BREED

In the 1920s Alaska and the airplane became partners in a relationship best described as complicated bliss. Despite an obvious need, early 20th century Alaska wasn't equipped for airplanes. There were lots of places to go, but there was no place to land once you got there. This created a special breed of flyer: the bush pilot.

Referring to Alaska's boondocks as "the bush" was not an American idea. Credit belongs to Australian visitors at the turn of the century who viewed their own outback as

Territory, Canada; finally he loaded it on a sternwheeler and steamed 800 miles (1,300 km) down the Yukon River, then 100 miles (160 km) up the Tanana and Chena rivers to Fairbanks.

After the boxes arrived in Fairbanks, Martin reassembled the plane. It flew in exhibition for 11 minutes, was taken apart and carted out of the territory; that was Alaska's first taste of aviation.

After World War I, surplus "Curtiss Jennies" were available to anyone for about

the bush and figured the term was appropriate in Alaska as well. The description stuck. Later, a pilot who flew anywhere away from the periphery of a town or village in Alaska became a bush pilot.

Being a bush pilot in the early years definitely lacked glamor. Consider Alaska's first performing flying machine. One James V. Martin contracted with three businessmen to fly an airplane over Fairbanks in honor of the 4th of July in 1913. He loaded his disassembled airplane on a steamship and sailed it to Skagway. There he transferred it to the Whitepass and Yukon Railroad for the 125-mile (200-km) trip to Whitehorse, Yukon

$600. Inevitably some of these found their way to Alaska. The first was *Polar Bear*, flown from New York by Clarence O. Prest in 1922. A year later Carl Ben Eielson lifted this same plane from the ground in Fairbanks on July 3, 1923. This event was the initial appearance of Eielson, a man considered the foremost bush pilot of his era.

Where to land?: For Alaska's early bush pilots, the size of their territory was summed up in the distances between cities, and only four really mattered in 1923: Juneau, Fairbanks, Nome and a small burg on Cook Inlet called Anchorage. From Juneau to Anchorage it's about 600 miles (965 km); Anchorage to Fairbanks, 275 miles (440 km); and Fairbanks to Nome, 450 miles (720 km). These were the business centers of Alaska, and a pilot wanting to fly for a living had to go between them regularly. This created a few problems.

The old Jennies cruised at about 85 mph (135 kph) and carried only four hours' worth of fuel. The only non-stop, city-to-city trip one could manage was between Anchorage and Fairbanks. This meant the baggage compartment on longer flights was filled with

Winter made landings easier. The rivers and lakes froze, snow filled the bumps on the ground, and pilots put skis on their craft. Alaska's winters, however, brought a host of other problems to pilots of open-cockpit biplanes. Noel Wien once took off when it was so cold he didn't know if his engine would stay warm enough to run. At 65 below zero (-52° C) he flew 350 miles (560 km) with the cylinder head temperature steady at 100 degrees (37° C). Normally it's twice that.

Winter weather: Winter stopovers were a

fuel cans. Halfway between stops a pilot landed where he could, stopped, poured in fuel, and took off again.

Finding a place to land was the hard part. A pilot needed a long gravel bar on a river, or a stretch of level ground. Yet fields didn't exist in many places because Alaska had never been plowed. The land was natural, and Mother Nature rarely works in straight lines. In later years planes were equipped with floats for water landings. This eased the problem of selecting suitable landing sites.

Preceding pages: proud pilot. Left, mail pick-up on Kodiak Island. Above, fishing by floatplane.

real joy. As soon as the propellor stopped, a pilot drained the oil and carefully set it aside. He covered the engine with an insulated blanket, tied his plane down to withstand winds of up to 90 mph (145 kph) and then looked to his own comforts.

In the wild, pilots had to fend for themselves. Most carried a wealth of gear for that kind of situation, including a tanned caribou hide. For sleeping in the cold there is no warmer ground cloth available.

Each of the early aviators would have the best sleeping bag he could find, two tents – one slightly smaller so it could be set up inside the other – and a stove of some sort for heating food, water and oil. The oil which had been drained from the plane on landing would be warmed almost to boiling and poured into the frozen engine prior to starting in the morning.

Alaska's menacing weather conditions are often caused by winds and clouds, both associated with mountains and sea coasts. Bush pilot Don Sheldon tells of the time he was flying at 120 mph (195 kmh) into the wind near Mount McKinley; when he looked over the side of his plane, he realized he was going backward. Figuring he wasn't getting anywhere, Don turned around and flew to an alternate, downwind destination.

Harrowing moments: Weather conditions

En route, the leather sack slipped off the board under his feet where he had stowed it; Wien was not sure whether or not it had dropped through a hole in the fabric. As it happened, the poke had lodged under the cockpit deck. Had it fallen out of the plane in flight, Wien would have had to make good the loss, which would have cost him everything he owned and then some. If that poke had disappeared, Wien Air Alaska may not have become one of the major air carriers in Alaska, which it was for several years.

Everything a bush pilot owned or cared about depended on his airplane. This spawned humorous comments on occasion like, "a plane is only overloaded when it won't take

have often placed pilots in unusual roles. Steve Mills was forced down by a blizzard while flying an appendicitis victim from Bethel to Anchorage in March 1937. He nursed the woman all night in sub-zero cold until the weather cleared and he could complete the flight. And Katherine Clark was born in the back seat of Jim Dodson's *Stinson* in 1938. Jim's reward for one-handed flying and one-handed midwifery was to be named the baby's godfather.

Veteran bush pilot Noel Wien describes his worst flight as plagued not by weather but by problem cargo. He was carrying a nine-pound poke of gold to Fairbanks for a miner.

off." Such antics didn't endear pilots to Department of Commerce officials. No matter how businesslike these bureaucrats tried to make their endless hearings, pilots made shambles of them. One flyer, when asked how much money his airline had, counted the bills in his wallet. Because he had some to count, his books were in the black, at least temporarily.

Eventually, regulations did start affecting Alaska aviation. Pilots were licensed, and their cargoes were checked occasionally. They were required to keep records, which most of them despised.

Government rules were sometimes hard to

live with, especially when imposed on a free-wheeling group like the early bush pilots. All recognized the requirements of safety, but the concern of Alaska's aviation pioneers was usually directed more to getting from here to there in one piece than to insuring that the proper federal form was filled out in duplicate or triplicate.

Rescues and heroes: Cargo and passengers paid the bills, but the spectacular rescues – almost always voluntary – made the bush-pilot legends. In 1955 Don Sheldon, one of Alaskan's last flying legends, made what was probably the most harrowing rescue ever attempted. An eight-man Army scout team from Fort Richardson, attempting to

self going backward at 30 mph (48 kmph) as the river swept the plane downstream. He kept the power on so as to slow his backward run and to allow him to steer. Pulling up alongside the exhausted scouts required full throttle to hold the plane against the current. He eased over the bank, and one man jumped aboard for the first trip. For steering control, and to slow down, Sheldon had to keep the plane pointed upstream – and drifting backwards down the canyon. Only after twisting out of the canyon could Sheldon turn around and make a safe, downriver takeoff.

Sheldon made three more trips into the canyon, taking out two men each time. Later he found the eighth man 18 miles (30 km)

chart the Susitna River, was defeated by treacherous Devil's Canyon. Sheldon flew over the Army's proposed route after the team had been gone for two days. First he found pieces of their wrecked boat floating in the river below the canyon. Then, in the middle of the canyon, he spotted seven men clinging to a tiny ledge just above the roaring water. Upstream was a fairly straight part of the canyon and Sheldon carefully guided his plane down through the tricky air currents.

Upon landing, he immediately found him-

Left, a lifeline home. **Above**, landing at Lake Hood near Anchorage.

downstream. Don Sheldon received the standard accolade – a Certificate of Achievement.

That was bush flying. The hazards were many, the pay uncertain, the hours absurd and the conditions unique. Yet from this beginning came the Alaska-based air carriers operating today.

Slowly but surely the planes have evolved, making it possible for passengers to fly in first-class comfort and luxury several miles above the earth. The plane is warm, it flies above most of the weather, and sophisticated electronics guide it almost effortlessly to its destination. It's a far cry from the good old days of the Alaskan bush pilot.

Winter is Alaska's longest season, and its quietest – at least from a tourism perspective. The large majority of visitors explore the state between the end of May and the beginning of September , when daylight hours are long and temperatures warm – though in some parts of the state, warm may translate to 50 or 60°F (10 or 15°C).

By mid-September, most tourists have gone south with the waterfowl. And locals have begun preparing for the season of darkness and cold, a season that in most regions of the state will last from seven to eight months.

Yet Alaska is not some frozen wasteland even in winter. And unlike bears, its human residents do not enter a state of hibernation.

As would be expected, Alaska's Interior and Arctic regions experience the most severe and prolonged winter conditions. Barrow, the nation's northernmost outpost, averages sub-zero temperatures from December through March. Temperatures bottom out in February, which has average daily lows of minus 25° Fahrenheit (-32°C) and highs of minus 12 (-11°C). But Barrow isn't just frigid in winter; it's also very dark. The village's long winter night begins at noon on November 18 and lasts through January 24 – 67 days from sunset until the next sunrise.

Winter in Anchorage: By comparison, Anchorage is downright bright and balmy. The city's shortest day (winter solstice) has five hours and 28 minutes of daylight, plus a couple of hours of twilight. And its coldest month, December, has average daily highs and lows of 20° and 6° Fahrenheit respectively (-7 and -15°C). Even more moderate conditions are experienced in Southeast Alaska. Ketchikan, near the Panhandle's southern tip, has seven hours, six minutes of daylight on the winter solstice and even its coldest month, January, averages above-freezing temperatures (34° F/1°C).

For further evidence of Alaska's winter extremes, consider that the state's record snowfall for one season is 974.5 inches (24.75 meters), at Thompson Pass (near Valdez)

during the winter of 1952–53. The one-day record, also at Thompson Pass, is 62 inches (1.6 meters) in December 1955. Barrow holds the state record for least snowfall in a season: three inches (7.5 cm), in 1935–36.

Not only do darkness and cold tend to keep Alaskans indoors much of the winter, they also produce a variety of malaises, from cabin fever to seasonal affective disorder. To combat winter's woes and help the northland's longest season pass more quickly, residents around the state usually participate

in a variety of activities and special events.

Alaska's winter sport: Among the most popular cures to seasonal blues is sled dog racing, designated Alaska's official winter sport. And the best known of Alaska's mushing events is the Iditarod Trail Sled Dog Race, also known as "The Last Great Race."

The Iditarod is officially billed as a 1,049-mile race (there's no question the race is at least 1,000 miles (1,600 km) long and the "49" is intended to symbolize Alaska, the 49th state), but in reality mushers and dogs travel well over 1,100 miles (1,760 km).

The race trail follows an historic sled dog freight-and-mail route established during the

---

Preceding pages, downtown Fairbanks at noon in January. **Left**, early 20th-century cabin in the bush. **Right**, making the most of the weather.

gold-rush era of the early 1900s; it crosses two mountain ranges, runs along the Yukon River for about 150 miles (240 km) and crosses the pack ice of Norton Sound. And from its ceremonial start in Anchorage – traditionally, the first Saturday in March – until the final musher has reached the finish line in Nome, the Iditarod is given center stage throughout Alaska.

A contest in which men and women compete as equals – by 1994, five of 24 races had been won by women, including four titles by Susan Butcher – the Iditarod not only pits competitors against each other, but also against the wilderness and Alaska's often brutal winter weather. At the same time, it

By contrast, 1994 champion Martin Buser (who also won in 1992), finished in just over 10 days and collected $50,000 in prize money.

The mushers, of course, are the glamor figures in sled dog racing. They get the attention and praise (or blame). The top contenders – people such as Butcher and Buser and five-time winner Rick Swenson – are household names throughout Alaska and, increasingly, in much of the Lower 48. But many would agree that dogs are the true heroes, the athletic stars, of this and other mushing events. They're specially bred, raised, trained and conditioned to race.

Other races: While the Iditarod is unquestionably Alaska's best-known sled dog race,

renews the primal bond between humans and dogs. But most importantly, the Iditarod celebrates Alaska's frontier past and the adventurous spirit in us all. Conceived and organized by musher Joe Redington Sr. of Knik and Wasilla historian Dorothy Page (popularly known as "father" and "mother" of the Iditarod), the first Iditarod took place in 1967, as a two-day event that covered 50 miles (80 km). Six years later, despite widespread skepticism, Redington organized the inaugural race from Anchorage to Nome. Thirty-four teams entered and 22 reached Nome; the winner, Dick Wilmarth, finished in just over 20 days and earned $12,000.

dozens – or perhaps even hundreds – of other competitions are staged around the state. Another major long-distance event is the 1,000-mile (1,600-km) Yukon Quest, staged each February between Fairbanks and Whitehorse, in Canada's Yukon Territory. To date only two mushers, Joe Runyan of Nenana and Jeff King of Denali Park, have won both the Iditarod and the Yukon Quest, and never in the same year.

At the other end of the mushing spectrum are the so-called "speed races," or sprints. People of all abilities and ages compete in limited-class races (most are divided into three-, five-, six- or eight-dog categories), while more serious speed mushers often "graduate" to the unlimited open-class events, which offer greater financial awards and prestige. And challenges.

The two most prestigious speed races are the North American Open, a three-day event staged each March in Fairbanks, and the Fur Rendezvous World Championship, also a three-day affair (teams run 25 miles – 40 km – each day) and the main attraction of Anchorage's annual mid-February winter festival. While Iditarod champions such as Butcher and Swenson have achieved far greater acclaim outside the state, several of Alaska's premier speed racers – George Attla, Charlie Champaine and Roxy Wright-

of sled dogs, many others prefer "iron dogs." Snowmobiles, also locally known as snow-machines and sno-gos, have replaced sled dogs as the primary means of winter transportation in most of rural Alaska, where roads are minimal.

Though commonly used by bush residents for work, or simply "getting from here to there," snowmachines are also popular with recreationists and racers in both urban and rural Alaska. The most challenging snow-mobile race by far is the Gold Rush Classic, a long-distance race along the Iditarod Trail between Nome and Big Lake (in the Susitna Valley). Another intriguing race, one that teams "full-throttle snowmachining" with

Champaine among them – are every bit as famous within the state.

In addition to the well-known titles' there is a potpourri of middle-distance races, ranging from 100 to 300 miles (160 to 480 km). A growing number of Alaskans also run dog teams purely for recreation and several businesses in the state's Southcentral and Interior regions now offer sled dog rides that range from a few hours to more than a week.

Iron dogs: While some Alaskans choose to explore the winter landscape behind a team

Left, the Iditarod starts in Anchorage. **Above**, going to the grocery store in Kotzebue.

speed skiing, is the Arctic Man Ski & Sno-Go Classic, staged each winter in the Hoo-doo Mountains near Paxson.

It's something of a rarity to see skiers and snowmachiners so closely enjoying each other's company in the backcountry. Some recreational areas popular with both user groups – for instance Chugach State Park in the mountains just east of Anchorage, Hatcher Pass in the Talkeetna Mountains and Turnagain Pass on the Kenai Peninsula – have designated snowmobile corridors, to minimize conflicts.

Nordic and alpine skiing: Skiing is especially popular in, and around, Alaska's population centers. Anchorage has one of the nation's premier cross-country ski-trail systems; more than 100 miles (160 km) of trails wind through a variety of terrain, with opportunities for both traditional diagonal striders and skate skiers.

The city's best-known nordic center, at Kincaid Park, has hosted several national championship races, as well as the Olympic Trials. For those who wish backcountry solitude, Chugach State Park – Anchorage's "backyard wilderness" – has dozens of valleys and ridges to explore. Several well-used trailheads are within a half-hour's drive of downtown. Other popular nordic backcountry destinations within a half-day's drive of

ers. The three most popular nordic retreats are Hatcher Pass Lodge, in the Talkeetna Mountains; Sheep Mountain Lodge along the Glenn Highway; and Denali View Chalet – also known as Sepp Weber's Cabin, after its builder and owner – in the Alaska Range foothills. Each of the lodges offers groomed trails, wood-fired saunas, heated rooms, homecooked meals and other amenities. Both Hatcher Pass and Sheep Mountain are road accessible, while Denali View is about 2 miles (3.2 km) from the nearest road.

Though not known as a mecca for alpine skiers, Alaska nonetheless offers a wide variety of downhill ski areas. They range from Alyeska's world-class facility in Girdwood,

Anchorage include the Talkeetna Mountains, Chugach National Forest, on the Kenai Peninsula, and the Peters Hills, foothills of the Alaska Range.

More adventurous skiers seeking longer escapes into remote wilderness often choose the Ruth Amphitheater, located in the Alaska Range only a few miles from Mount McKinley. This area is rarely visited before April because of extreme cold and winter storms; May and June are considered the prime months to visit. Access is normally by air taxi out of Talkeetna.

While most of Alaska's lodges shut down for winter, a few cater to cross-country ski-

about 40 miles (64 km) south of Anchorage, to the single-run volunteer operation at Salmonberry Hill outside Valdez.

Probably the most unique of Alaska's eight downhill sites (including three in the Anchorage area, two near Fairbanks and one on Douglas Island, 12 miles/19 km from Juneau) perhaps is the Eyak Ski Area, near the coastal community of Cordova. This tiny, little-known Prince single-seat lift used to operate at Sun Valley until it was replaced in 1969 by a triple-seat chair. Eventually the lift made its way north to Cordova, where it has operated every winter since 1974.

The Northern Lights: A less strenuous winter-time activity than skiing, snowmobiling or mushing is sky gazing, or aurora watching. Alaska is the best place in the United States to view the aurora borealis, or Northern Lights. Literally meaning "dawn of the north," the aurora borealis is a solar-powered light show that occurs in the earth's upper atmosphere when charged particles from the sun collide with gas molecules.

The Northern Lights occur most intensely in an oval band that stretches across Alaska (as well as Canada, Greenland, Iceland, Norway and Siberia); all of the state, except parts of the Southwest region and Aleutian Chain, are within that "auroral zone," with the best light shows visible north of the Alaska Range.

but may develop vertical bars or rays, that give the aurora the appearance of waving curtains.

Some claim to not just see the aurora but to *hear* it as well. Scientists at the University of Alaska-Fairbanks, who have been studying the northern lights for years, have yet to confirm those reports.

Festivals: Not even auroras, sled dog rides and ski resorts are enough to get all Alaskans through the long winter, so many communities host festivals to chase away mid- and late-winter doldrums. In December, there's the Barrow Christmas Games, followed in January by Kodiak's Russian New Year and Masquerade Ball celebration.

Fairbanks, in fact, has begun marketing itself as an auroral destination, in an attempt to lure winter visitors.

Though occurring throughout the year, the aurora of course cannot be seen except when the sky is appropriately dark; in Alaska that generally means from autumn through spring, with peak viewing in winter. Colors vary from pale yellowish green – the most common shade – to red, blue and purplish-red. Northern Lights often begin as long, uniform bands, stretching from horizon to horizon,

Left, winter skiers near Nome. **Above**, the Northern Lights, photographed above Fairbanks.

Things really begin to pick up in February, with the Anchorage Fur Rendezvous, Wrangell Tent City Winter Festival, Cordova Ice Worm Festival and Valdez International Ice Climbing Festival. March brings the North Pole Winter Carnival, Bering Sea Ice Classic Golf Tournament in Nome and, of course, the Iditarod, which is a sort of statewide celebration.

More information on Alaska's winter festivals, special events, tours, lodges and recreational activities is summarized in a Fall-Winter-Spring Tour Planner available from the Alaska Division of Tourism, P.O. Box 110801, Juneau, 99811, tel: (907) 465-2010.

Some people think of Alaska as a wasteland permanently covered with snow and ice. In fact Alaska is a world teeming with life. From the humblest tundra flower to the mightiest grizzly bear, this land supports a vast array of wildflowers and wildlife. The most exciting part of an Alaskan adventure is discovering the flowers, birds and mammals of the state.

Fascinating flora: All regions of Alaska, from the forests in the Southeast to the tundra on the North Slope, boast brilliant wildflower displays. Mid-June to mid-July is the peak season for flowers; in many areas, the blossoms are so thick it is impossible to avoid stepping on them.

Fireweed is the most common Alaskan flower. The tall stalks grow as high as a person and are topped with clusters of bright pink blossoms. Fireweed lines the shoulders of almost all of the state's highways. Also common is the *forget-me-not,* Alaska's state flower. This 18-inch (46-cm) blue-flowered plant grows in tundra meadows and along streams. Around pools and marshes, watch for *cotton grass,* a type of sedge capped with what appears to be balls of cotton.

The best place to find and photograph a wide variety of Alaskan flowers is on the tundra. Each spring, an explosion of white, yellow, pink, red, blue and violet flowers covers the tundra.

Many of these tundra plants are northern relatives of flowers found in the Lower 48 states. Look for *arctic poppy, Alaska violet, alpine azalea, Siberian aster, wild geranium, Lapland rosebay* (rhododendron family), *arctic lupine, tundra rose, prickly wild rose, northern primrose, rock jasmine* and *whitish gentian.*

Most of these species are dwarf versions of their southern cousins. To survive on the cold, windswept tundra, the plants must hug

Preceding pages: wildflowers from left to right, (top) Dwarf Dogwood, Northern Dwarf Larkspur, Cotton Grass, Lapland Rosebay; (middle) Scammon's Spring Beauty, Diapensia, Bluebells, Bearberry Leaves; (bottom) Shrub Cinquefoil, Pasque Flowers, Low-Bush Cranberry, Northern Anemone. Left, tundra flowers. Right, a hoary marmot from Denali Park.

the surface of the ground, the warmest and least windy zone available to them. When winter comes, deep snow layers efficiently insulate the plants from the extreme cold temperatures. Some species, such as arctic poppy, have developed a flower shaped like a radar antenna. The poppy flower tracks the motion of the sun across the sky, its parabolic design reflecting the sun's heat on the developing seeds. The inner temperature of the flower may be 18° F (10° C) warmer than the prevailing air temperature.

It is difficult to shoot a detailed photo of a field of tundra flowers. The beauty of these flowers is best shown in close-up shots, as near to the flower as your lens will allow. Winds are common on the tundra and swaying flowers may cause your shot to be blurred. Be patient when photographing tundra plants – if you wait a bit, you will probably experience a brief lull in the wind and can take a sharper photo.

If you enjoy learning about tundra flowers, consider purchasing one of the many excellent flower guide books which are available in local bookstores. The photographs, sketches and background information will enhance your appreciation of what you find.

Plants reproduce themselves through their flowering parts and picking a flower defeats this process. If these flowers have given you pleasure, repay them for this gift by not picking them.

Birds: At least 386 different species of birds have been officially documented in Alaska. With few exceptions, these species inhabit Alaska only during spring and summer and then migrate south. They come north to take advantage of the eruption of life which occurs on the tundra each spring. The tundra offers a nearly limitless banquet of food (plants, insects and small animals) to birds attempting to raise hungry young.

Tierra del Fuego, at the tip of South America, is the winter home of the surfbird. The jaeger spends its winters on the open ocean in the central Pacific or near Japan. The arctic warbler resides in southern Asia during winter months.

Alaska's state bird, the *willow ptarmigan*, was chosen not by politicians but by a vote of the state's school children. Along with its close relatives, the *rock* and *white tailed ptarmigan*, the willow ptarmigan lives in Alaska year round. A ptarmigan is brown in summer and white during winter, changing coloration to blend with the surroundings. During extremely cold winter weather, ptarmigans keep warm by burrowing into snow

The *arctic tern* is the world's record holder for migration. These gull-like birds breed and nest on the shore of Alaskan tundra ponds. In late summer, the terns and their young start a migration which will eventually take them all the way to the Antarctic. Summer is just beginning in the Southern Hemisphere as the terns arrive. The round-trip flight from Alaska to the Antarctic and back is approximately 25,000 miles (40,000 km).

Other long-distance commuters include the *American golden plover*, the *surfbird*, the *long-tailed jaeger* and the *arctic warbler*. Some plovers winter on the Hawaiian Islands while others migrate to Argentina.

drifts. The males fiercely defend nesting females: one male was actually seen attacking a grizzly bear which had stumbled on his mate's nest. Look for ptarmigan in willow thickets and on the open tundra.

Eagle habitat: Alaska is the stronghold of the *bald eagle*. More bald eagles live in Alaska than in the other 49 states combined. The white heads, white tails and eight-foot (2.4-meter) wing-spans make them easily identifiable, even at a great distance. Look for them in places where fish are common, especially along coastal areas in Southeast Alaska. The best place to see bald eagles is near Haines in October and November. The

Chilkat River, just north of town, attracts thousands of eagles to feed on dead or spent salmon. A single tree may contain dozens of roosting eagles. Because fish are available throughout the winter in coastal areas, these bald eagles do not migrate out of Alaska.

Golden eagles, the darker cousins of the bald eagle, are normally found in tundra and mountainous areas. They hunt rodents, such as the arctic ground squirrel, rather than fish. The Polychrome Pass area of Denali National Park is an excellent place to watch for golden eagles.

Alaska's birds can be seen and studied by anyone possessing time and a pair of binoculars. While near tundra ponds, look for *loons,*

checklists for the many species in their area.

Mammals: Without question, the premier wildlife area in Alaska is Denali National Park. *Grizzlies, moose, Dall sheep, caribou, red foxes, snowshoe hares, beavers, arctic ground squirrels,* and *hoary marmots* are seen by almost everyone who visits Denali. With some luck, *wolves* may also be spotted. (See the section on Denali for more information). Denali's shuttle bus system is designed to maximize wildlife sightings. Because the buses cause comparatively little disturbance, many animals, including grizzlies, often can be photographed within 100 yards (90 meters) of the road.

Denali and the other great Alaskan Na-

grebes, geese, ducks, yellowlegs, phalaropes and *sandpipers*. On tundra, watch for *long-tailed jaegers, golden plovers, whimbrels, snow buntings, wheatears, sparrows* and *water pipits.* Owls, goshawks, woodpeckers, *gray jays* and *chickadees* are common in forested areas. *Gulls, terns, murrelets, auklets, shearwaters, cormorants* and *puffins* live along the coastlines.

Most National Parks, National Forests, National Wildlife Refuges, State Parks and many communities have developed free bird

Left, stately caribou against a backdrop of fall tundra. **Above**,a standing grizzly in Denali Park.

tional Parks are textbook examples of what National Parks were meant to be. Each of these parks protects an entire ecosystem in a condition nearly identical to its original state. The population levels of wildlife such as Dall sheep, moose and caribou are controlled not by humans, but by the area's natural predators, the grizzly bears and wolves. The vegetation, prey species and predators interact in the same manner that their ancestors did thousands of years ago. If you see a grizzly dig out a ground squirrel from its burrow or a wolf pack chase a caribou herd, you will be witnessing a scene which could have taken place during the last Ice Age.

Wildflowers & Wildlife   79

Alaska's bears: Katmai National Park is the place for *brown bears*. At one time, grizzlies and browns were considered different species but most experts now believe they are the same animal. The brown bears in Katmai and other coastal areas live where large numbers of salmon are available. Partly because of the nearly unlimited salmon, these bears can grow to weights of more than 1,200 pounds (540 kg). The best time to see them is in July, the time of peak salmon spawning.

Much of Kodiak Island is home to a particularly large variety of brown bear, a huge mammal that captures the imagination of any would-be or real hunter. Native to the island group, these bears stick primarily to

the interior highlands except for during the salmon run. Also on the islands are the *Roosevelt elk*, *mountain goats*, *black-tailed deer* and numerous smaller mammals.

Polar bears live along the northern and northwestern coast of the state. They are the largest land carnivore in the world. Some old males have weighed over 1,500 pounds (680 kg). Polar bears live on the ice floes of the Arctic Ocean and can readily swim long distances in the frigid ocean waters. A number have been seen 50 miles (80 km) from the nearest ice or land.

Polar bears survive by hunting seals and other marine mammals. These nomads of the Arctic Ocean are sadly seldom seen by travelers to Alaska.

Reindeer are the domesticated version of caribou, although both animals are considered the same species. The first reindeer were introduced into Alaska from the Old World in 1892 as a dependable source of food and clothing for native people and early white settlers. In 1937, a law was passed which restricted reindeer ownership to Natives. Today, approximately 30,000 reindeer are in Alaska. The largest herd, 5,000 to 6,000 animals, lives near Kotzebue on the Seward Peninsula. Other herds of reindeer are located on Nunivak and Saint Lawrence islands. A small herd can be viewed at the Reindeer Research Station in Cantwell, 27 miles (43 km) south of the entrance to Denali National Park.

Also on Nunivak is grazing for what is perhaps the most extraordinary native animal: the *musk ox*. Looking like one of nature's most ridiculous mistakes, a musk ox is stout, shaggy, and appears to be the result of an amorous encounter between a prehistoric ox and a mountain sheep. Musk oxen are few and far between, and shy in the wild, but they are preserved in research stations, particularly in the Large Animal Research Facility which is part of the University of Alaska Fairbanks.

Sealife is varied and profuse around Alaska's shores. Salmon come in all varieties – sockeye, king, chum, silver and pink – and in the rivers are rainbow trout, grayling, pike, Dolly Varden, whitefish and arctic char, amongst others.

Alaska's wildlife lives in one of the last great wilderness areas of the world. Regardless of how Alaska is developed in the future, the National Parks and National Wildlife Refuges will always be a safe haven for this great assemblage of animal species. The protection and preservation of this wildlife is one of the greater gifts America has made to the people of the world.

If you've never been to Alaska before, a whole world of wildlife and wildflowers awaits you. Your first sighting of a grizzly or a bald eagle and your first walk over the profusely flowered tundra could be the high points of your trip.

Left, a mature bald eagle. **Right**, Dall ewes on the slopes of Mount McKinley.

With one-fifth of the land area of the contiguous United States and more shoreline than all the other states combined, Alaska includes 150 million acres (61 million hectares) of national parks and forests, wildlife refuges and other designated preserves – ample territory for wilderness adventure. Its 38 mountain ranges, 3,000 rivers and 3 million lake, fall within climate ranges from temperate rainforest to arid arctic. Much of this territory is barely charted, let alone touched by the human foot.

Of Alaska's 40 national parks and preserves, only 11 are accessible by road. Glacier Bay National Park (3.2 million acres), for example, can only by reached by boat or floatplane. North America's premier mountain wilderness and its largest national Park, Wrangell-St. Elias National Park and Preserve (13.2 million acres), boasts nine peaks of more than 14,000 feet (including 18,008-foot Mt. St. Elias).

It also has the largest collection of glaciers in North America; the Bagley Icefield, the largest subpolar icefield on the continent; wild rivers; and multitudes of wildlife. Yet only two unpaved roads, best negotiated by four-wheel-drive vehicles, penetrate the park boundaries.

Gates of the Arctic National Park, the northernmost of the state's parks, is a remote and undeveloped 7.5 million acres of crags and sweeping arctic valleys. Without roads or trails, backpacking, mountaineering and dog sled excursions become some of the only ways to access these areas.

When federal geographer Henry Gannett, a founder of the National Geographic Society, surveyed Alaska's expanse in 1904, he set the tone for today's ecotourism: "Its grandeur is more valuable than the gold or the fish or the timber, for it will never be exhausted." Alaska is a land where inhabitants and travelers sense they can do no better.

Low-impact tourism: Alaska is wild to the limits of the term, a place where one encounters wildlife in the profusion of ages past. Grizzlies weighing as much as 1,500

pounds romp about sand flats digging clams or snatching salmon from glacial-fed torrents. Caribou, numbering in the thousands, roam across sweeping tundra, and whales ply turquoise fjords. "Alaska is a wonderful classroom," exclaims Bob Jacobs, owner of St. Elias Alpine Guides in McCarthy. But, unlike school, "you don't need a schedule. In summer you can hike until 2 am and sleep until noon."

On Jacobs' trips into the heart of Alaska's 13.2 million-acre Wrangell-St. Elias National Park, you climb nameless peaks, raft swift,

milky rivers and backpack for weeks at a time, enjoying the rich wilderness traditions that have long typified Alaskans and the Alaskan way of life. Alaska becomes a whole new experience once you've touched the thousand-year-old ice of a massive glacier, rafted a raging river and heard wildlife calling across unpeopled land.

Unfortunately traditional tourism in the state often bypasses its great wilderness areas in favor of organized tours that take visitors by bus, train or airplane to cities, towns and developed parks. The majority of Alaska tourists see sights that are reached by road (such as Portage Glacier, Denali National

Preceding pages: kayaking in Lake Clark National Park. Left, walking into the Harding ice fields. Right, one method of getting around.

Park and Preserve, and cities such as Anchorage and Fairbanks) – but rarely step into untouched wilderness. Only one road goes into 6 million-acre Denali National Park – a 90-mile strip that bars most private vehicle traffic. While this road channels more visitors into the park each year via bus tours, only a meager 33,200 of the park's 500,000 visitors in one recent year registered for backcountry permits.

Guides such as Jacobs feel that visitors to Alaska should see more. Enter an industry labeled "ecotourism," which reveals the quintessential Alaska outdoor traditions such as sea-kayaking, mountaineering and wildlife-watching to travelers.

try has retooled itself toward this new brand of adventure where sea-kayakers, white-water rafters, backpackers and nature photographers commingle with bald eagles, grizzly bears and caribou. The Alaska Division of Tourism estimates that between May and September around 900,000 non resident visitors spend close to $700 million in the state. Fifty percent of them indicated that they did some wildlife viewing – although only an estimated 10 percent strike out away from traditional tourist areas.

Protecting the land: At its heart, Alaska ecotourism uses tourism as a tool to protect and enhance Alaska's natural beauty so that visitors may continue to enjoy the land for

Ecotourism – defined as low-impact vacations that allow travelers to enjoy, learn about and help preserve the natural environment while disturbing the local people as little as possible – is becoming a preferred manner of travel in Alaska.

Ample adventure: Traveling at nature's pace in a land that offers adventure and asks for respect, tourists gain an intimate awareness of life as it was 1,000 years ago. They enter another civilization as privileged guests, where sea lions, loons, moose and whales are constant companions – and that's ecotourism's modern appeal.

In the past decade, the Alaska travel indus-

generations to come. "It's important to understand that we're a part of nature and a part of the plan," says Penney Hodges, administrator of the Alaska Center for Coastal Studies in Homer. "We need to learn how to get back into balance with nature." By opening its doors to travelers in summer and to parties of Alaska schoolchildren in spring and fall, the center works to foster responsible human interaction with our natural surroundings and to generate knowledge of marine and coastal ecosystems of Kachemak Bay through its environmental education and research programs.

Ultimately, ecotourism relies on pristine

country and wildlife as its chief commodity, so there is great motivation to maintain the health of the land. Essentially, it is a clean industry which could well take the place of its dirtier colleagues.

While ecotourism initially was the province of small, independent operators and outfitters that led groups into the outback, the industry mainstream concentrated on marketing developed resort areas. Now many businesses and organizations have developed policies and principles that depart from traditional tourism commerce.

The American Society of Travel Agents' guidelines herald the ecotourism ethos: travelers should leave behind only footprints

bird-watching, whale cruising, wildlife photography safaris and sea-kayaking adventures from easy to strenuous. Some tour operators offer ecotours geared specifically for senior citizens. Although these trips harken back to the days of pioneers, they are most often accompanied by today's amenities. Clients enjoy the experience of skilled guides without having to acquire all the necessary skills themselves, and many of today's backcountry meals can approach the gourmet in quality.

Wildlife viewing is a major draw, especially for those hoping to see the monarch of the land: the grizzly. One of the most notable grizzly areas is the McNeil River State Game

and take away only memories and photographs; support local cultures; avoid littering; walk only on designated trails; support conservation-oriented programs; learn local customs; refrain from disturbing local habitat and from buying products made from endangered animals. Some observers go further, arguing that in sensitive tundra areas, footprints may even be too great an impact.

Options: Dozens of outfitters offer river rafting, tundra trekking, mountain climbing,

Left, grizzlies – such as this one in Denali – are remarkably unfazed by tour buses. **Above,** the *Alpine forget-me-not*, Alaska's state flower.

Sanctuary, where as many as 60 bears have been observed fishing at McNeil River Falls. State Fish and Game officials supervise the area to ensure the bears are allowed to fish undisturbed, and visitors are regulated by permit – which means that if you want to see them you will need to plan ahead.

Renowned grizzly-viewing areas include Denali National Park and Preserve, home to 200-300 grizzlies. Kodiak National Wildlife Refuge, set aside as a bear refuge by Franklin D. Roosevelt in 1941, is home to the largest bears on earth. Perhaps as many as 10 percent of Alaska's grizzlies live on Kodiak Island. "Big bears fill big hotels," notes grizzly activist and photographer Timothy Treadwell. "People go to Alaska to see wilderness, to be part of what Earth used to be like. That's good for tourism. If you protect grizzly habitat, you protect your bread and butter."

Ethical guidelines: Although ecotourism industry operators generally follow environmental ethics, not all operators equally abide by the unwritten code of minimal impact. Some advocate a "green rating" system so that travel industry personnel can distinguish between good and poor operators on an ecological impact scale.

Currently, no such system exists, but Bob Jacobs has some suggestions to enable would-be visitors to pick the right company to travel with. "Do your homework. Look for organizations that go beyond the bottom line of making money. Talk to them. Get a feeling for their philosophy. Ask for references – then call the references. That's the best policy."

Following some general guidelines will help make your trip part of the ecotourism movement. Check to see if an operator limits the number of people it takes into fragile areas – it should. Does the company practice low-impact camping and hiking and vary campsites from trip to trip to avoid scarring the ground in certain areas? Does it supply a reading list about the area and the type of adventure you will be doing?

Top ecotourism companies are staffed by experienced naturalists who always accompany their guests on journeys and offer extensive information along the way. Such specialists help minimize impact on wildlife by keeping the group at unobtrusive, safe distances. The business should also be committed to energy conservation and recycling, as this helps preserve the environment they will help you enjoy.

Solo travelers: Even if you're traveling in Alaska on your own, you can do your part. Follow carefully the guidelines that come with backcountry permits from the Park or Forest Service and write your own code for minimum-impact traveling. It makes sense to keep Alaska's wilderness wild for future generations and preserve the grandeur.

Right, one camper who has done his best to make sure his tent makes as little impact as possible on the ground.

In March 1981, a 35-year-old man was flown into the wilderness to an unnamed lake near the Coleen river, 150 miles (241 km) northeast of Fort Yukon. He planned to camp until August, spending his time photographing wildlife. All preparations had been made for his wilderness experience. He had ample provisions – shotgun, .30-30 rifle, .22 rifle, plenty of ammunition, reliable tent, wood stove, gas lamp and fuel, fishing equipment, plenty of matches and an axe.

On February 2, 1982, Alaska State Troopers found the man's emaciated body in his tent. The camper, starving and suffering from frostbitten limbs, had apparently despaired and killed himself. The victim filled 100 pages of a diary that was found intact when his body was discovered. The diary is a poignant record of an idyllic outing that ended in tragedy.

The victim in this tale made two errors that eventually cost him his life. The first was made before he arrived at the remote lake – he failed to make firm arrangements to return to Fairbanks. The pilot told the man not to count on him for the planned August pickup, a fact confirmed in the diary.

The second error occurred in early fall when an Alaska State Trooper's airplane flew over his campsite. The starving man frantically waved both his arms over his head. When the plane flew over a second time, the victim again waved. The plane flew off. Days later, the man realized his mistake when he studied the back side of his hunting license. He had signaled, "everything OK, don't wait."

Traveling in Alaska need be no more hazardous than elsewhere in the world if proper precautions are observed. Due to the latitude and varying weather conditions around the state, the traveler must have the appropriate equipment and be physically prepared for the activities he or she wishes to pursue. Because there are so few roads and distances are so great, clear and precise communication while travelling is vital. This section is

Preceding pages: climber atop McConnell Ridge in Glacier Bay Park. **Left,** an ice climber carefully negotiates a crevasse.

not an exhaustive discourse on any one topic; its purpose is to cite several common wilderness problems and to offer some simple remedies for Alaska travelers.

WEATHER

Coastal and Southcentral Alaska: The word to remember when selecting equipment for coastal Alaska is rain. If you are going to spend time in Southeast Alaska remember that portions of this area receive up to 200 inches (508 cm) of rainfall annually – a raincoat and an umbrella can be constant companions. Reliable raingear is a must. If you plan to be outside for long periods, a rainsuit (jacket, pants and hat) will be used frequently. Rain is also the prime consideration when selecting a tent and sleeping bag. Tents must be able to withstand long wet spells. Sleeping bags filled with synthetic materials are a wiser choice than down because they retain more of their insulating qualities when wet.

The Interior: The Interior has dramatic seasonal contrasts. Summer temperatures are warm and winter temperatures can dip below –40 °F (-40°C).

Summer equipment and clothing may be lightweight although mountain travellers will face much colder temperatures. A light hat and at least one heavy long-sleeved shirt will be welcome additions to your wardrobe. A mosquito headnet takes little room and will be greatly appreciated if needed.

The extreme cold of winter makes only the best equipment suitable. A good down jacket, a hat, mittens and warm boots are musts. Camping at this time of year is most rewarding (no crowds), but requires a sleeping bag comfortable at –40°F or colder.

The finest time, by far, to ski in the mountains is spring. Temperatures on the snow are so comfortable that people ski without shirts. However, snow-blindness is a very painful reality of spring for unprotected eyes; mirrored sunglasses are best, but dark sunglasses will suffice.

The North Slope: If the password for coastal Alaska is rain, then the key word for the North Slope is wind. The area is technically an arctic desert with less than five inches (13 cm) of annual precipitation. This meager amount of precipitation should not be disregarded as it may fall as snow or freezing rain on any day of the year and be driven by gale force winds. Travelers to the North Slope need clothes that are windproof and warm. Camping equipment must also be able to withstand heavy winds.

TRAVEL

Charter flights: If your destination is a small village, confirm that there is regular service. Several commercial airlines service outlying Alaskan villages and communities. Again, required to locate the missing fisherman.

What happens if the plane crashes while you are in it? There is a legal requirement for all planes to carry emergency equipment. The required list includes food for each person for two weeks, axe, first-aid kit, knife, matches, mosquito headnet for each person, gill net, fishing tackle and a pistol or rifle with ammunition. A sleeping bag, snowshoes and one wool blanket are added to the list for winter travel.

Although most flights carry some survival gear, sometimes the requirements are ignored. Check the survival gear before taking off. If you decide to bring your own, keep as much of it on your person as possible. In

check first to see if there is regular air service – this will save you a lot of money. If, however, you are bound for the wilderness, a charter flight is necessary.

Before departure, be *sure* someone knows where you are going. If you must, inform the Alaska State Troopers of your destination and expected return date. *Make firm arrangements to be picked up.* Be certain that someone besides the pilot knows where you are going. In one case, a fisherman was dropped off in a remote location and the pilot was the only person who knew of his whereabouts. The pilot had a fatal crash while returning to town, and several days of searching were winter fill your pockets; in summer, use a small waist pack. You may have to evacuate the downed craft quickly.

Every plane in Alaska is also required to carry a downed aircraft transmitting device (Emergency Location Transmitter or ELT). Learn how to operate this device before you depart on your journey. If the pilot becomes incapacitated in a crash, you can activate the ELT and be rescued more quickly. Almost everyone arrives at his destination safely, despite all the gloom and doom. The above-mentioned precautions pertain to the less than 0.5 percent of flights during which an inflight problem does occur.

Automobile travel: This can be even more involved than air travel. There is no Alaska law which governs what survival equipment should be kept in a vehicle. Yet the average car is maintained less frequently than an airplane, which means that more cars break down while traveling.

When traveling in sub-freezing weather, a breakdown can be life-threatening as well as inconvenient. The Alaska State Troopers recommend the following survival kit: down coat, boots, mittens, hat, snow-pants, sleeping bag, flare, candles, extra spark plugs, extra belts, shovel, chain, flashlight and high-energy food.

Automobile maintenance is vitally impor-

Winter mandates snow tires or studded tires, an operating engine heater and ample electrical cord to reach a receptacle.

AVOIDABLE DILEMMAS

Mosquitoes: Whatever Alaska missed out on when it didn't get snakes or termites has been more than compensated for with the mosquito. Billed sarcastically as the "Alaskan State Bird," these insects are a wilderness force to be reckoned with. Use the most powerful repellents available, such as the "musk" types or those with a high concentration of DEET. Even in the face of these strong measures (and probably in your face

tant. It is expensive and time-consuming to break down on the road, and towing charges can be costly. Check the car carefully before leaving the city.

Be straightforward with the rental agency when hiring a car. Inform them of your proposed route and confirm that maintenance is available along your way. Most agencies have stringent rules about driving on gravel roads (e.g. the Dalton Highway). Solving problems before travel will avoid misunderstandings later.

Left, crossing the Thorofare River. Above, well-prepared for mosquitoes.

also), the mosquito seems to thrive. Thick clothing will reduce the number of bites per square inch, but sometimes relief is only a headnet away.

Bears: When bears and people cross paths in the wild, only one wins. Many Alaskans have stories about encountering bears at close quarters, but tragic accounts abound. Most bears turn tail and run upon encountering people, and vice versa. However, in some instances, the bear will stand its ground. At this point, advice differs widely on what course of action to take next.

One school of thought preaches stay calm and speak softly to the beast, encouraging it to leave. The second line of thinking contends that you should shout loudly to scare the animal away. Both schools agree that if the bear is a brown (Coastal) or grizzly (Interior), you should climb a tree if available. (Black bears may follow the climber). Should a bear attack, the *only* course of action is to "play dead." Protect your head and neck and try to lie on your stomach, but do not struggle. Bears have been known to walk away if they think the prey is dead.

Three important strategies should be used to minimize the number of chance meetings with bears. Firstly, make plenty of noise while walking in the wilderness. Bears will hear your approach and leave. Secondly, be

and wet clothing. Left untreated, the hypothermic individual may become disoriented, incoherent, unconscious and may finally die. Never ignore shivering, it is the body's way of signaling for help.

The time to prevent hypothermia is during the period of exposure before complete exhaustion. The five following suggestions may help prevent an emergency:

Stay dry. Wet clothing loses most of its insulating value. Functional raingear is vitally important. Ponchos are nearly useless.

Avoid the wind. Wind carries body heat away much faster than still air. Wind also refrigerates wet clothing by evaporation.

Understand the cold. Remarkably, most

TOOT HORN ONLY IF BEAR IN CAMP

careful with food around camp. If possible, do not cook in camp and always store food away from your sleeping area.

The third suggestion seems like common sense, but is easy to forget. If you see a well-worn path in the wilderness – it may even be grooved into the earth – remember the trail may belong to Mr Bear. Be alert if you must walk along the path, make lots of noise, and do not pitch your tent on the trail, or you may have an unexpected tent mate.

Hypothermia: Beware of hypothermia, the sub-normal lowering of the body temperature. Hypothermia is caused by exposure to cold, but aggravated by exhaustion, wind

people die of hypothermia between 30 and 50 degrees F (-1 and 10°C). Most hikers underestimate the severity of being wet in any Alaskan waters. It can be fatal and first aid measures must be taken immediately.

End the exposure. If a member of your party shows signs of hypothermia or if it becomes impossible to keep dry with existing clothing and conditions, make camp or end the trip.

Do not become overly tired. Don't be too ambitious. Make camp before you are exhausted, and bring high energy food to replenish your reserves.

Handle the hypothermic victim gently,

replace wet clothing with dry, and warm the core area of the body. The procedure to warm the core is with a human sandwich: one person on each side of the victim, bare skin to bare skin, inside a warm sleeping bag. Do not give the victim any alcoholic drink as this could prove fatal. Also, do not rapidly warm the victim's extremities, as it takes much-needed blood away from the core and results in unconsciousness.

Avalanches: Avalanches pose a serious threat to winter mountain adventurers. Research has shown that most avalanches are triggered by people skiing through an avalanche zone.

An avalanche zone is a slope in which

Tides: Tidal variations are large in Southeastern Alaska, Prince William Sound, Cook Inlet and Bristol Bay. The extreme diurnal variation occurs in spring in Cook Inlet near Anchorage where high tide can be more than 38 feet (11.5 meters) above low tide. Tides of this size present two dangers for sport fishing: swift incoming tides and strong currents, magnified in island areas.

Obtain a tide book from a fishing tackle shop, a hardware store, bar or gas station if you plan to be on the water or along the shoreline. All too frequently, the fisherman standing on a rock working the incoming tide waits too long to retreat. This can develop into a life-threatening situation. People with

temperatures range between 27 and 45°F (-3 and 7°C). On shallower slopes, the snow usually does not accumulate. The two ways to avoid an avalanche are knowledgeable route selection and careful trip planning. Avoid skiing through a likely avalanche zone – pass above or below it. Spend as little time as possible near the zone. Choose the route carefully to avoid steep mountain faces, especially after a fresh snowfall. And remember, spring is an especially dangerous season for avalanches.

<u>Left</u>, essential repellents. <u>Above</u>, land that looks friendly in sunlight can be fatal to the unprepared.

vehicles travelling along the beaches must be aware of the tides or risk losing their transportation – or more. Large tides create swift currents in constricted areas, such as inlets. Travel by small craft is perilous during these times.

Savor the memory: This section is not intended to deter anyone from enjoying the wilds. Great obstacles were overcome by early expeditions, which by today's standards had no proper equipment. Yet parties with even the best gear have tragedies. Make the wilderness a part of your Alaskan vacation. Experience it, leave nothing but footprints, and always savor the memory.

PLACES

Alaska is, above all else, a land of remarkable diversity. With an average of about 1.2 sq. miles (3 sq. km) of land for each resident, this huge state possesses some very distinct places: the confluence of two tiny streams, the migratory paths of caribou, a rural village, or a few square blocks of a major city.

There's urban Alaska: usually described as Anchorage, but often enlarged to include Fairbanks and, occasionally, Juneau. There's rural Alaska: villages scattered throughout the land, mostly along major rivers or near the coast. And there's wilderness Alaska, vast regions of relatively untouched ground – ground that knows only the whims of nature.

Communities have their attractions to be sure, but it is the wilderness that beckons most travelers to Alaska. Where else in the world can you climb the highest of peaks, tread softly along an unexplored river bank, chill refreshments with ice broken from a glacier, or view hundreds of square miles of untrampled wildflowers, all with little more formality than a passport check when stepping from an airliner?

Almost every city or town has one or more businesses designed to provide access to the wilderness. Charter air services, outdoor expedition ventures and a host of other related industries exist as a means of taking travelers into remote regions, and, not incidentally, to provide methods for earning a living in the wilderness.

Each Alaskan enjoys his or her own "special place," almost all of which are in the wilderness. Visitors to Alaska should make the effort to spirit themselves away from civilization and seek that special place of their own. Ask those who have been to Alaska whether it was a picture of a glacier or a picture of a city that lured them north. From the answers to such questions come the first blushes of wisdom about Alaska – the Great Land, overwhelmingly undertamed.

Preceding pages: a traditional winter train of dogs; a more contemporary train near Denali; cruiseship at sunset; traveling by horse into difficult territory. **Left**, which way to downtown?

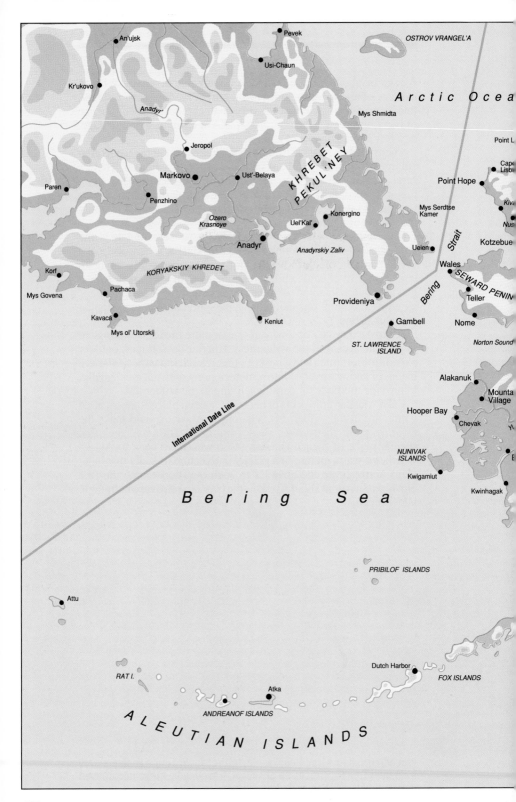

An'ujsk
Pevek
OSTROV VRANGEL'A
Usi-Chaun
Kr'ukovo
Arctic Ocea
Anadyr'
Mys Shmidta
Point L
Jeropol
Cap
KHREBET
PEKUL'NEY
Lisbi
Markovo
Ust'-Belaya
Point Hope
Paren
Kiva
Penzhino
Mys Serdtse
Kamer
Nus
Ozero
Krasnoye
Konergino
Uel'Kal'
Kotzebue
Anadyr
Anadyrskiy Zaliv
Ueien
Strait
Korf
KORYAKSKIY KHREDET
Wales
SEWARD PENIN
Pachaca
Mys Govena
Providerniya
Bering
Teller
Kavaca
Keniut
Gambell
Nome
Mys ol' Utorskij
ST. LAWRENCE
ISLAND
Norton Sound
Alakanuk
Mounta
Village
Hooper Bay
Chevak
Y
NUNIVAK
ISLANDS
Kwigamiut
Kwinhagak

International Date Line

B e r i n g   S e a

PRIBILOF ISLANDS

Attu

RAT I.
Dutch Harbor
FOX ISLANDS
Atka
ANDREANOF ISLANDS
A L E U T I A N   I S L A N D S

Beaufort Sea

Coppermine

Barrow

Wainwright

NORTHWEST TERRITORY

Beechey Point

Tuktovaktuk

Prudhoe Bay

Herschel

Umiat

Sagwon

Inuvik

Great Bear Lake

Colville R

(USA)

Arctic Village

Old Crow

Fort Mc Pherson

Noatak R

BROOKS RANGE

Christian

Norman Wells

Fort Norman

Wiseman

Porcupine R.

Mackenzie

Shungnak

Bettles

Fort Yukon

C A N A D A

Wrigley

iwik

Peel

A L A S K A

Circle

Yukon

MACKENZIE MOUNTAINS

Fort Simpson

Livengood

Alaska Pipeline

YUKON TERRITORY

Tanana

Eagle

Yukon R

Fairbanks

Mayo

Macmillan

Galena

Manley Hot Springs

Chicken

Dawson

Ross River

leet

Delta Junction

Tok

Stewart

Yukon R.

Watson Lake

DENALI NAT. PARK

Northway

Mc Grath

Mt. McKinley
▲
6194

Haines Junction

Whitehorse

CASSIAR MOUNTAINS

Cross

Kuskokwim

A L A S K A   R A N G E

Mt. Blackburn
▲
5036

Glennallen

Atlin Lake

Atlin

Dease Lake

Willow

Palmer

Skagway

Anchorage

Valdez

Cordova

BRITISH COLUMBIA

C.Yakataga

Yakutat

Mt. Fairweather
▲
4663

Haines

Juneau

Iliamna L.

Homer

Seward

ALEXANDER

Hoonah

Illingham

Sitka

Petersburg

Stewart

Gulf of Alaska

KATMAI NAT. PARK

Wrangell

ARCHIPELAGO

Ketchikan

ALASKA PENINSULA

Kodiak

Karluk

KODIAK ISLANDS

Prince Rupert

highnik

Masset

ville

QUEEN CHARLOTTE ISLANDS

Skidegate

P A C I F I C   O C E A N

Alaska

320 km / 200 miles

TOURING THE INSIDE PASSAGE

Ever since it emerged from the melting of the last great Ice Age – some 15,000 years ago, give or take a millennia or two – the great island-studded, 1,000-mile (1,600-km) passage of water that stretches from present lower British Columbia to the top of the southeast Alaska panhandle has been one of earth's treasures. Well, not quite for everybody. The first out-of-towners to visit a portion of what is now called the Inside Passage got an unfriendly reception from the locals, they were taken prisoner by the Indians 248 years ago and haven't been heard of since.

The occasion started out happily enough. In 1741 Alexei Chirikof, captain of the good ship *St Paul*, set sail for Czar Peter of Russia. With his commander, Vitus Bering (who also was captain of the vessel *St Peter*), he left the Russian Kamchatkan Peninsula in Siberia and headed east on a voyage of exploration and discovery.

What Chirikof and Bering were looking for was North America, which everyone knew was out there someplace (after all, Columbus had established that in 1492) but which Bering and his colleagues had only shortly before determined was not connected to Siberia and the European-Asian land mass. Alas for the Alaska-seekers, the two sailors were separated in a storm which struck soon after leaving port. They never saw each other again. Bering, in fact, died after being ship-wrecked on his voyage back home.

To Chirikof goes the prize for seeing North America first. His crew sighted the high wooded mountains of what we now call Prince of Wales Island in southeast Alaska on July 15, 1741. Two days later he dropped anchor probably near the present-day vicinity of Sitka. It was there that tragedy struck – a tragedy recorded by Lt. Sven Waxel, a Swede who served as first mate and pilot aboard the *St Peter*.

The following account is his story: "The ship went to anchor a good dis-

tance from the shore and, being short of water, Chirikov decided to send a boat ashore. To command it he chose an officer called Avraam Demetiev, a very capable man, and gave him a crew of the best men he had. They were all equipped with guns and ammunition and also had a metal cannon with appurtenances. They were also given a signaling system and complete instructions how to behave and act in the event of the unexpected happening. Besides all this, they were supplied with provisions to last several days.

"The boat pulled away from the ship: they watched it disappear around a headland and some while later noticed various signal flashes corresponding with the orders given, so that they had every reason for thinking that the party landed safely. However, two days passed and then a third day, and still the boat did not come back.

"Nevertheless, they could see the whole time that the signal fires continued to burn and so they began to think that perhaps the boat had been damaged

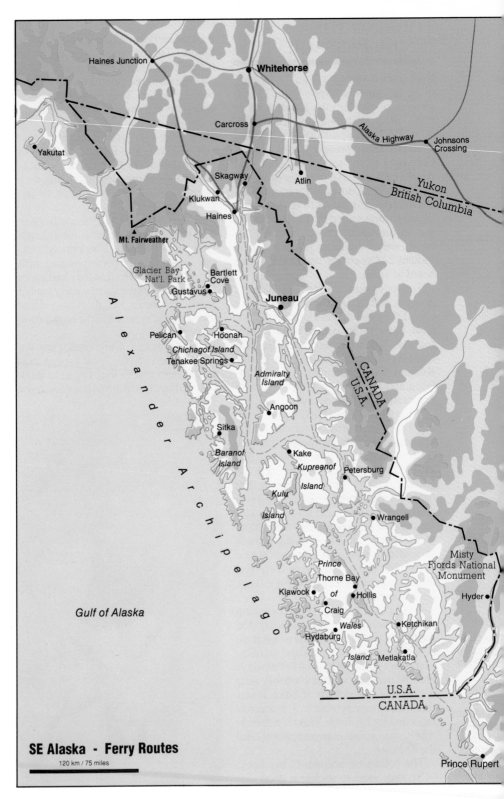

SE Alaska - Ferry Routes

120 km / 75 miles

on landing and that the party's return was being delayed by having to repair it.

"They then decided to send the little jolly-boat ashore with carpenters, calkers and all that they might need, so that the boat could be repaired if that should prove necessary. No sooner said than done. Six men were ordered into the jolly-boat, equipped with guns and ammunition and well supplied with everything else they might need. They were to search out the boat and give all help that might be called for when they found it, after which both boats were to return to the ship immediately.

"Next morning two craft were seen coming out from the land, the one slightly larger than the other. Naturally it was assumed that these were the long-boat and the jolly-boat and very glad they were to see them. They began to get the ship ready to put to sea again... But then, as the two craft drew near the ship, they discovered the truth was the exact opposite of what they had thought.

"These were American boats and they were filled with savages. They approached to within three cable lengths of the ship. Then, seeing so many on deck, they turned back towards land. Those on board the ship had no boat left in which they could have put out after the Americans, and they had just to draw the melancholy conclusion that both the long boat and the jolly-boat were lost along with their entire crews."

Incredible museum: These days, it is rare indeed when a visitor to the Inside Passage fails to return to ship. And on those infrequent occasions when that happens, it is likely the person simply lost track of time in the search for culture at the incredible provincial museum in Victoria, in the quest for adventure on a hike to the top of Deer Mountain in Ketchikan, or in the pursuit of pleasure at the Red Dog Saloon in Juneau.

The sites and sightings along the Inside Passage are never boring – and they are surprisingly varied. One of Canada's – and North America's – largest, most cosmopolitan, cities is located along the way. There are, likewise, tiny Native villages where the food on most residents' tables still depends on the hunter's, trapper's or fisherman's skill. There are two capital cities along the length of the passage, one Canadian and one American, where life and lifestyle revolve largely around lusty politics and bureaucratic doings and the strange machinations of government. There are other communities in both countries where jobs and ways of living depend on the more basic harvest of sea, land and forest.

There are homes and condos and highrise hotels as modern as can be found in any of the communities of the world, and there are tiny, hand-built cabins and camps which may be spotted – briefly, on a cruise or during a fly-by – in isolated wilderness settings far from roads, stores, television stations, or daily newspapers.

The geography and the geology of the Inside Passage varies greatly as well. At its southernmost, the passage is protected by Vancouver Island, a large and elongated landmass that begins near the northern border of the United States and

stretches nearly 300 miles (482 km) northwesterly, nearly half the distance up the British Columbia coast to southeast Alaska. Then comes the seaward protection of the Queen Charlotte Islands, not as large as Vancouver Island but a number of them – especially Graham and Moresby islands – are sizeable nonetheless. And finally, about where US jurisdiction, and southeast Alaska begins, there's the Alexander Archipelago. (For the purpose of this book, only destinations within Alaska's national boundary are covered.)

This is a 400-mile-long (643-km) maze of 1,000 massive and minuscule isles that, along with a 30-mile-wide (48- km) sliver of mainland, makes up the southeast Alaska panhandle.

If the size and national colors of the islands of the Inside Passage vary, there is this commonality all along the way: lush green forests of hemlock, cedar, pine and other conifers cover whole islands and mountains except for snow-capped peaks and gravel beaches. Generous bays and exquisite little coves rival one another for exposure in visitors' cameras and memories. And major rivers course through great glacier-carved valleys, while waterfalls plunge from mountainside cliffs to the sea.

And everywhere along the way are watercraft: seineboats with crews of half a dozen or more; small trollers and gillnet fishing craft with a skipper and, maybe, a single helper; tugs pulling rafts of logs or barges or commercial goods; exotic yachts and simple open boats; cruise-ships; state ferries; freighters; super-tankers; even sailboats and kayaks.

The reason for this concentration of watercraft, of course, is protection from the elements. The same islands which provide near-continuous evergreen beauty to visitors along the way provide buffers from North Pacific winds and weather that could otherwise threaten all but the toughest vessels.

The islands also afford protection and nurture for a wide variety of wild creatures. Ashore, and beyond the gaze of spectators, thousands of animals make their homes within the forests and even

Totems at Ketchikan's Cultural Heritage Center.

atop the mountains of the southeast Alaska panhandle. Charter a light aircraft at Yakutat, near the very top of the panhandle, and you'll likely see moose and perhaps brown bear as well. Near Juneau or Ketchikan or any of the other cities in the region, the opportunity to spot whole herds of glistening white mountain goats is almost assured.

Take one of the kayak excursions in **Glacier Bay National Park**, located also in the northern panhandle, and as you paddle alongside forest or beach you just might see the rare "Glacier Blue" – a subspecies of black bear. Cruise or fly to Pack Creek on **Admiralty Island** during the salmon spawning season and you can easily view and photograph dozens of huge, lumbering brown bears.

Throughout the panhandle, and down the coast of British Columbia as well, Sitka blacktail deer are extremely numerous. Indeed, this is one species of land animal you may be able to see along the beaches from a cruiseship.

Sea mammals are much more easily seen, of course. Humpback and killer whales, cavorting porpoises by the twos and fours, and sea lions by the dozen are frequently seen and always appreciated by vessel-borne visitors along the Inside Passage.

Symbol of the States: And eagles are everywhere – the white headed, white tailed bald eagle which is the symbol of the United States. You see them diving and swooping from the heights to grab unwary fish swimming near the water's surface, you witness the strength of their powerful talons as they rip salmon carcasses to shreds alongside spawning streams, and you view them high in the spruce trees, standing guard over heavy nests which are lodged in the forks of great branches.

Besides the eagles, there are huge black ravens, tiny gray wrens and black-capped Arctic terns (who come each year to the northern climes from as far south as Antarctica), plus hundreds of other kinds of waterfowl, shorebirds and upland species.

And the fishing here is world-class.

Russian dancers at Sitka.

Perhaps your goal is to haul in a lunker king salmon of 50 pounds (23 kg) or more. Or maybe you want to test your skill against diving, dancing and frothing steelhead trout. Whatever your angling heart's desire, the fishing in this region is simply unexcelled anywhere else. In addition to kings and steelheads, there are coho (silver) salmon – considered by many to be, pound for pound, the fightingest, gamest fish in salt water – plus sockeye, halibut, rainbow trout, Dolly Varden and eastern brook trout (these latter two actually chars). With this concentration of fish, furry creatures and scenic beauty, it's not hard to imagine why increasing numbers of people choose to live in this region. Big cities and small can be seen all along the way.

Ketchikan, which Alaskans call "the First City" because it is the first major Alaskan community encountered on a journey north, is famous for at least three things: totem poles (more of them are located here, in fact, than anywhere else in the world); salmon (caught in considerable numbers both by sport and commercial fishermen); and it is the jumping-off place (as well as cruising-off or flying-off place) for **Misty Fjords National Monument**, which in recent years has come to be appreciated as one of the mountain and maritime scenic wonders of Alaska. Ketchikan is also known as a place where it rains a lot, although that is true of almost anywhere along the Inside Passage.

Wrangell is a town bypassed by most cruise boats and most tourists. This is a pity, because it is a small untouristy patch of authentic Alaska. The fishing is excellent and, the people are genuinely anxious to help you enjoy their town. A local museum and an easily accessible totem park (on **Chief Shakes Island**) are well worth a visit. A boat trip up the nearby **Stikine River** is a time-capsule voyage back into Alaska's unspoiled past. The forested scenery around the town is likewise spectacular – except for some big, ugly clearcut logging scars on the side of some mountains, but that's part of what Alaska is all about these days.

Peaceful village at Petersburg.

Petersburg, across the Stikine to the north and just a few minutes by plane from Wrangell, is likewise bypassed by most tour ships and visitors. Again, a pity – for this spick-and-span little city of Norwegian descendents offers still another opportunity for the unstructured visitor who enjoys poking around on his/her own.

There are ancient Native Alaskan petroglyphs to be seen on the beaches, a small but tasteful museum offers a lot of insight into the history and art of fishing, and simply wandering the docks and wharves of the community gives the visitor a view of the largest, home-based halibut fishing fleet in Alaska.

Sitka, as the well-read history buff may know, dates back to 1799 when the Russian trader and colonizer Alexander Baranof established his headquarters there. Actually, Tlingit Natives had been there centuries before, and near the site of present day Sitka were fought two of the bloodiest battles in Alaska's recorded history. The Natives won the first round, but the Russians, utilizing cannons as well as guns, won the second encounter. Today, the city is a pleasurable blend of Tlingit, Russian and American culture. The Russian Orthodox **Cathedral of St Michael**, with its priceless icons and other religious treasures, is reason enough to visit this city. Additional reasons include excellent fishing, the **Sitka National Historical Park** (located at the site of the second battle), and mountain-water-island scenery on a grand scale.

Juneau is a port of call for virtually every cruiseship, ferry and airline that comes to southeast Alaska. (This capital city is covered in detail in the following chapter of this guide.)

Haines, 80 air miles (130 km) north of Juneau, is the northern co-terminus (along with Skagway) of the southeast segment of the Alaska state ferry system. From here you can drive the 150-mile (242-km) Haines Highway to Haines Junction (Canada) on the Alaska Highway to the interior of the state. But do not leave for the Interior until you have seen what this community offers.

istant
acking
ouse near
aines.

Old **Fort William Henry Seward** has massive turn-of-the-century officers' homes and command buildings still surrounding the old rectangular grounds. The biggest hotel in town is located in two of these buildings.

And in the fall the world's greatest gathering of bald eagles – more than 3,000 of the winged creatures, many of them coming from home territories hundreds of miles away – flies to a nearby river and woods to feast on a late run of salmon in icefree waters.

Skagway is the northernmost of all the communities usually visited on a cruise or ferry tour of the Inside Passage. (For more detail about this community, see the chapter on Skagway, pages 134–139.)

In addition to the major communities along the Inside Passage, there are throughout the region countless other settlements, Native villages and fishing camps equally worth a day's or a week's visit. Near Ketchikan, colorful old **Waterfall Cannery** has been converted into what the owners call "the most

civilized resort in Alaska;" it's within easy access to some of southeast Alaska's hottest salmon angling. Similarly superlative fishing can be experienced near the Native villages of **Angoon, Kake** and **Hoonah**, all of which offer modest but tidy tourist accommodations. Small commercial fishing centers, like **Elfin Cove, Tenakee Springs** and **Pelican** – though never touted as tourist towns – nonetheless provide do-it-yourself, arrange-it-yourself visitors with indelible memories of a very happy and contented portion of Alaska.

How to get around amongst all this wonderful wildlife, fabulous fishing, glacier grandeur and mountain-shrouded seaways? It's easy and the options are wide. There are posh cruiseships, for example. Some choose to drive the family buggy aboard ferries of the Alaska Marine Highway System, which runs from the city of Bellingham, in Washington, with a stop at Canada's Prince Rupert, in British Columbia, before hitting all the major ports in Southeast Alaska, terminating in either Haines or Skagway. Passengers can get off and explore big towns and small villages along the way.

Still others jet in from Seattle to Ketchikan, Wrangell, Petersburg, Sitka and Juneau. Those who are really tough and want a true travel experience paddle their own canoe or kayak – but be careful… crossing Queen Charlotte Sound in such little craft can be deadly.

Once you've arrived, the options are even broader. Big and little yacht excursions are available at every turn. Alaska's famed bush pilots, some on wheels and others on floats, will take you wherever you want to go. Hiking trails fan out from every settlement.

Few indeed – with the possible exception of Chirikof's hapless kidnapped sailors of 1741 – are the visitors who are not more than satisfied with an Inside Passage sojourn. And Southeast Alaskans, never hesitant to tout the attractiveness of their place on the planet, speculate that maybe, having sampled life ashore in this lush and bountiful land, those Russian sailors decided they really didn't want to leave.

Left, a line of Dolly Varden trout caught near Glacier Bay. Right, a radio-tagged eagle is to be released.

JUNEAU, STATE CAPITAL CITY

The going had been slow, sweaty, frustrating – plodding leadenly upstream beside the forest-rimmed waterway. Thick entangling underbrush, huge grasping devil's club plants (with thousands of tiny needles on every stalk and leaf), and great boulders in and alongside the stream… these obstacles and more had hampered the party's progress every step of the way.

Then it got even worse, and the five men – two white prospectors who were guided (some would later say all but carried) by three Natives – had to abandon the stream entirely. They were forced to climb the mountain beside them in order to get to the gulch they sought. But as they descended from the mountaintop into the watershed the labor was well worth the effort.

Before they even got to the mouth of the gulch, they took samples from the quartz lodes that cropped out of the mountain. And they were incredulous at what their pounding hammers yielded. One of the men recorded the experience in his journal thus: "We knew it was gold, but so much, and not in particles; streaks running through the rock and little lumps as large as peas or beans… I took the gold pan, pick, and shovel and panned $1.20 to $1.30 to the pan…"

The two men were Joe Juneau and Richard Harris. The year was 1880. The place was Silver Bow Basin. And out of their discovery came a camp that became the capital city of Alaska.

City of gold and government: The delightful and varied city of **Juneau** today is a far cry from the wilderness site that Joe Juneau and Dick Harris encountered. About 30,000 Alaskans – whites, Native Tlingits, other ethnic groups – call the community home. Most of Juneau's folk either live off the government (state, federal or local) or live off the civil servants who do.

The town is as modern as a state-of-the-art computer center in the S.O.B. (for "state office building") and as old-fashioned as the plantation-style, turn-

of-the-century Governor's Mansion a couple of blocks down the street. It is as cosmopolitan as the local World Affairs Council which meets to discuss the weightier matters of international geopolitics and as down-to-earth as the lobby group of Alaskan Mothers Against Drunk Driving who want to get dangerous inebriates off the road.

The town is as sophisticated as its surprisingly talented symphony and as earthy as the Red Dog Saloon or the equally frontierish Alaskan Hotel bar next door. (At either of these two watering holes it would not be out of character, on any given rehearsal night, to find musicians letting down their hair after their music making – arm-wrestling, perhaps, to see who picks up the beer tab.) The town is as urban as its highrise office buildings and high comfort hotels, and as rugged as the northern wilderness of thick, lush forests, glacial ice and saltwater which surrounds it. The wilderness begins literally where the houses stop.

By stateside standards, Juneau is a

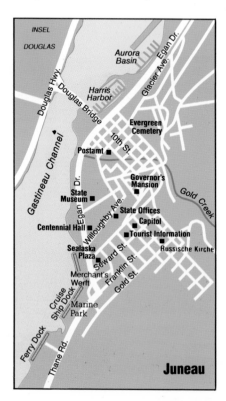

small town in terms of population (about 30,000) – but in square miles it is the biggest town in North America and second biggest in the world. More about that later, but first some additional data about how the city came to be

Gold fever: The town was first named Harrisburg – some say because Harris, unlike his partner Juneau, was able to write and recorded it that way. The name didn't stick, however. After news of the gold strike spread to Sitka and elsewhere, and nearly 300 prospectors swarmed to the scene during the following year, the miners decided to rename the place Rockwell. Shortly thereafter it became Juneau.

By whatever name, the camp was bustling with gold fever and, soon, gold production. It didn't take long for simple goldpans, pickaxes and human labor to be replaced by miles-long flumes and ditches, carrying water to massive hydraulic earth-moving and sluicing operations. Within a decade of the Juneau/Harris discovery, wagon roads penetrated the valleys behind the camp-

turned-town – roads you can drive or hike on to this day.

Juneau is, of course, on the North American mainland. Across Gastineau Channel, on **Douglas Island**, even more furiously paced development took place. By 1882 the world famous Treadwell Mine was operational and expanding. Near it, the proud community of **Douglas** grew up, and indeed rivaled Juneau in population, industry and miners' baseball for a good number of years. Eventually, more than 50 years later, the two towns would merge, but the Douglas community and Douglasites remain distinct to this day, similar to the way Alaska is part of, but somehow set apart from, the rest of the United States.

Early on, politics assumed considerable importance in Juneau. The future state's first political convention was held there in the summer of 1881. The camp became a first-class municipality under the law in 1900 and in 1906 the district government of Alaska transferred there from Sitka.

In 1913, Alaska's first territorial leg-

Juneau's South Franklin Avenue.

islature convened, in what is now the Elks Hall on Seward Street. Near life-size photo murals of that distinguished group can be seen today on the first floor of the state capitol building. The all-male representatives and senators in the pictures look like what they were, rugged frontier types, most of them probably uncomfortable in the stiff collars and ties they were forced to wear on the floors of their respective houses.

As the city grew and prospered, such additional enterprises as fishing, saw-milling and trading became important in Juneau's economic scheme of things: important but never paramount.

Gold was what Juneau was all about. Gold was not only practically everyone's vocation, it was the avocation of choice as well. Miners labored daily in miles and miles of tunnels that honeycombed the mountains both on the mainland and on Douglas Island. For recreation on days off they scoured the wild country beyond the urban centers, digging, panning, hoping against hope that they, too, might strike it rich like Juneau

and Harris. (Juneau and Harris, like many gold locators the world over, never really realized much from their discoveries. Juneau, in fact, died broke in the Canadian Yukon and a collection had to be taken up to send his body home for burial in the city he co-founded).

A frontier government: As the years passed there were ups and downs (definitely down when, in 1917, major portions of the Treadwell tunnels beneath the waters of Gastineau Channel caved in and flooded), but gold remained Juneau's and Alaska's mainstay, until relatively recent times. During World War II, however, the government closed down the massive AJ gold mine and milling operation as a manpower and conservation matter, ending an era.

But even with the mine closure, things didn't go too badly. By the time the 1944 shutdown came about, the city was experiencing something of a war boom, and with war's end there came a gradual but continuous rise in territorial government activity and employment.

By 1959, when Alaska became state

number 49, government had all but filled the economic void left by mining's demise. And in the years since, Juneau has grown from a waterfront community hovering beneath the skeletal remains of the old A J millsites to a gregarious, upreaching, outreaching city spread for miles both north and south.

The city's size was established in the mid-1960s when the then-cities of Juneau and Douglas and the Greater Juneau Borough (county) were unified by a vote of the people into the City and Borough of Juneau. Since then, at least two additional communities in Alaska (Anchorage and Sitka) have consolidated their city and borough governments, but none have come close to ending up with as much territory.

In fact Juneau is spread over so many miles that it is the biggest town, in size, in all of North and South America. In the international bigness sweep-stakes, Juneau's 3,108 sq. miles (8,050 sq. km) are exceeded only by the city of Kiruna, Sweden, which boasts 5,458 sq. miles (14,136 sq. km) within its borders. With that much land under its collective belt, it's little wonder that visitors to Juneau find lots to see and do.

Glaciers – up close: From Juneau, a number of impressive glaciers can be reached by auto, by trail, or viewed by airplane or helicopter. Best known of Juneau's great rivers of ice is the **Mendenhall Glacier** which can be seen, and photographed, quite easily from a US Forest Service information center about 13 miles (21 km) north of town. The center sits on the edge of a frigid lake into which Mendenhall Glacier calves icebergs large and small. The face of the glacier is about one mile from the visitor center, while its 1,500 sq. miles (3,885 sq. km) of ice and snow is called the **Juneau Ice Field**.

Dozens of glaciers flow down from the ice field, creating Mendenhall, Eagle, Lemon and Herbert glaciers, to name only a few. Mendenhall is unquestionably among the most visited and photographed glaciers in the world. (Hint: mornings and late afternoons render the most satisfactory pictures. Dramatic

Inside the Alaska State Museum.

128

shadows which give depth and definition to the blue ice river are missing when photographed near noontime.)

There are several options for exploring the glacier. Choices range from just sitting in a car or bus in the parking lot and taking in the glacier's incredible mass and majesty, to hiking several trails around it, actually hiking on it or floating past it in rubber rafts before "running" the Mendenhall River from the glacier almost to the saltwaters of Gastineau Channel.

Perhaps the most exciting way to savor the glacier and its originating ice field is to take a "flightseeing" excursion with one of several air charter companies or the helicopter carrier that offers 45 minutes or so over the great white deserts of snow. The chopper ride includes not only flying *over* the ice-field, it includes a landing *on* the surface itself. There's time to take pictures, walk around, even kneel down to take a bone-chilling drink from a puddle of very cold water – the temperature of which is only a fraction of a degree or two above freezing.

If Mendenhall Glacier and the Juneau Icefield are, collectively, Juneau's best-known visitor attraction, the **Alaska State Museum**, within walking distance of downtown hotels and shopping, is a close and highly regarded second.

To visit the museum is to visit, in a real sense, all of Alaska. Eskimo culture is represented here in the form of small, intricate ivory carvings and a huge 40-foot (12-meter) *umiak*, or skin boat, of the type which were used for whale- and walrus-hunting on the ice floes of the Arctic Ocean.

Southeast Alaska's ancient Native way of life is reflected in the recreation of an authentic community house, complete with priceless totemic carvings, living utensils, and even a figure of a Native woman busily engaged in weaving a much-valued Chilkat blanket.

Alaska's Interior Athabascan Natives, too, are represented with displays of a birch bark canoe, weapons and bead-decorated moosehide garments. Gold-rush memorabilia, natural history displays (including ancient mastodon and prehistoric musk ox skulls) are on display, as are contemporary mounts of deer, moose, wolves and a rich variety of birdlife. Nor is Alaska's pre-gold-rush Russian heritage ignored. Orthodox religious exhibits include precious coins, priest's raiments and the first American flag to be flown at Sitka when Russian America became American territory on October 18, 1867.

Most notable of all the museum's exhibits is probably the "eagle tree," encountered just inside the front entrance of the building. There, in the middle of a spiraling staircase, a towering spruce tree rises from ground level almost to the ceiling at the second floor. In a natural fork of massive branches, is a huge, flat, very authentic nest on which a young bald eagle – its magnificent 5-foot (1.2-meter) spread of wings outstretched – has just landed. There are other eagles in the tree, and beneath its branches stand two brown bears.

Most of Juneau's other visitor attractions can be encountered in a walking tour along the community's docks and among its meandering, frequently nar-

rospector's mp.

row, streets and alleys. For starters there's **Marine Park**, overlooking the city's dock and wharf area. It's a small, but pleasurable place of green grass, benches and shady trees situated near the ramp where cruiseship passengers land after being lightered from ships at anchor offshore. This is where it seems that half of Juneau eats its lunch, especially on sunny summer days. Street vendors in the vicinity offer entrees, literally *à la carte*, that range from halibut to hot dogs to tacos and Vietnamese spring rolls.

Nearby are shops that feature Alaskan ivory, jade, totemic wood carvings and leatherwork. Nearby, too, are art galleries, bars (yes, the **Red Dog Saloon** and the **Alaskan Hotel bar** really are worth a visit, even if you don't imbibe any of the available refreshments), seafood and regular restaurants, and, of course, the city's standard assortment of merchants and professional offices.

Juneau's visitor information office – a re-creation of the town's first log school, which later became a brewery –

is located on Seward Street, uphill three blocks from Marine Park and on the way to tiny **St. Nicholas Russian Orthodox Church**. This, surely, is one of the most picturesque houses of worship in Alaska.

The onion-domed, octagon-shaped church, located on Fifth Street, was constructed in 1894 at the specific request of Ishkhanalykh, the then principal chief of the Tlingits of Juneau. It is the oldest original Orthodox church in southeast Alaska and one of the senior parishes of the entire state.

Downhill on Fourth Street is the **State Capitol Building** where tours are conducted daily in the visitor season. The capital was built in the 1930s and many of its halls and offices have recently been refurnished to reflect that era. You can see where the Alaska House and Senate meet during sessions; it's well worth a stop, as is a stroll through the sky-lighted great hall of the **State Office Building** on Fourth Street. S.O.B. visitors on Friday, at noon, can enjoy a special treat. A giant old Kimball theater

Left, a curious owl. **Right**, the Mendenhall Glacier near Juneau.

organ, a magnificent relic of Juneau's silent movie days, has been relocated in the atrium of the building; visiting organists and local musicians joyously celebrate Friday evenings by playing its pipes from 12 to 1pm.

Two blocks beyond the State Office Building is the **Governor's Mansion**. Although you cannot enter the house, you can take pictures of its exterior. Recently the state spent $2 million restoring it to the glory of its 1913 opening – when it was built and furnished for just $40,000.

Beyond the Governor's Mansion and across **Gold Creek** – where Joe Juneau and Dick Harris panned their first gold in the area – you come to a cemetery where the two prospectors are buried. Their burial monuments are not overly impressive but the partially wooded cemetery is a popular place for visitors to stroll, for residents to walk their dogs, and for youngsters from the nearby high and middle schools to sneak cigarettes or worse.

Perhaps the most memorable thing about Juneau for outdoorsy folk is the rich variety of hiking trails which can be reached within minutes even from dockside. The **Mt. Roberts Trail** takes off from a trailhead on Fifth Street. The starting point for the somewhat gentler **Perseverance Mine Trail** is only a few blocks further; for the history buff the reward on this path is the chance to see and explore the mountainside ruins of early mining sites.

For the experienced, and thoroughly fit hiker, **Mount Juneau's** steep trail provides perhaps the community's grandest, most panoramic view to be had with two feet planted on the ground. Mainland Juneau and Douglas Island are laid out below – 3,500 rather precipitous feet (1,066 meters) below – and the twisting, glistening channel of saltwater called Gastineau seems to go on and on forever.

The scene is classic Southeast Alaska: woods, water, snowcapped peaks and solitude. As enthusiasts will remind you, it's what visiting Southeast Alaska, and living there, is all about.

magnificent bull moose.

SKAGWAY, THE FUN CITY

The old sounds are everywhere. You hear them all the time in **Skagway**. Especially on a calm midsummer night when the sun has just skipped behind the last peak, you can't help but hear them coming from behind those false fronts as you walk up the boardwalk on Broadway. They're the sounds of a not-too-distant era: ragtime pianos, whooping cancan girls, ringing cash registers, songs and laughter. Happy sounds of gold fever run rampant at the start of the trail. They're still heard in Skagway today nearly 100 years since the great Klondike Gold Rush.

Here you'll find the rollicking past preserved. But if you stop at a corner, let your imagination wander and listen carefully, you can hear other sounds too: horses slogging through mud, whips cracking backs, hammers striking rail spikes, and the faint moans and cries of broken men. These unpleasant sounds of the gold rush aren't really heard anymore nor recreated. They're just sensed when an unexpected gust of wind comes howling around the corner of an old building.

Skagway's rich past: There's no town in Alaska quite like Skagway when it comes to blending history with natural beauty. Situated at the northern end of southeast Alaska's Inside Passage, Skagway was and always will be the natural jumping-off point for anyone taking the shortcut over the Coastal Mountains into Canada's Yukon. In 1897–98 stampeders took to the trail, and a town of 10,000–20,000 sprouted. Today many of the old buildings still stand and the town's 600 residents cater for the needs of more than 150,000 tourists who hit the trail every summer in cars, campers, buses, bikes or, as in the old days, on foot.

When you approach Skagway from the south – by Alaska ferry, cruise ship or air taxi – you see a tiny town at the base of a river valley surrounded by mountains. The mountains range in height from 5,000 to 7,000 feet (1,500 to 2,100 meters) above sea level, rising almost straight out of the saltwater fjord. To look at the closed-in valley, you would not expect to find a pass, but there is one – the White Pass.

The first white man to discover it was Captain William Moore, a member of an 1887 Canadian survey party. Moore, who had captained steamboats on rivers all over the Western Hemisphere, was a professional dreamer. At the spry age of 65, he came across the wooded tideflats of "Skagua" (a Native Tlingit word meaning "windy place") and visioned a lively port with a railroad heading across the pass into the Yukon. The railroad would haul miners in and bring gold out, he dreamed, and he would make the most of it. Moore and his son Bernard staked their claim, built a cabin (still standing) and a wharf, and waited for the rush to come. It was a long wait.

The big strike in the Yukon did not occur until August 1896, and word did not reach the rest of the world until *Portland*, the steamship with the famous "ton of gold," cruised into Seattle's

Preceding pages: participants in July 4 parade, Skagway. Below, one-armed bandit in the gold-rush style.

harbor about a year later. Twelve days later, the first of many hundreds of steamers brought men and supplies in Skagway. Captain Moore was in for a rude shock. The early miners preferred the old name to the one Moore had given: "Mooresville." They added a "y" at the end to make it "Skaguay." The US Post Office later went with a simpler pronunciation, and replaced the "u" with a "w." The change caused quite a stir around town, but the official name exists. However, a few local businesses harken back to the old days and display the "u" proudly in their logos. Skagway boomed overnight in the fall of 1887. Miners literally pushed Moore aside, setting up their own system of streets (one going right through the Captain's home), and "gave" the old man 5 acres (2 hectares) of the 160 he and his son had originally claimed. Moore protested, moved his building and watched the excitement pass him by.

When Skagway's first newspaper was published in October 1897, it reported 15 general stores, 19 restaurants, four meat markets, three wharves, 11 saloons, six lumber yards, eight pack trains, and nine hotels. Three other newspapers would join in the competition by the summer of 1898. The stampeders arrived in Skagway with lots of money to tie up in supplies and in various distractions made available to them by Skagway merchants.

As the town grew, so did its bad reputation. With no law to speak of, Skagway was ripe for con artists. Jefferson Randolph "Soapy" Smith, a master of the shell game who had been chased out of Colorado, set up his gang in Skagway. For nine months under the guise of a civic leader, he won the allegiance of not only prostitutes, gamblers and saloon keepers, but also bankers, editors and church builders. But Soapy's downfall was quick once things got out of hand; one of his men robbed a miner, and Soapy refused to bow to vigilantes and return the gold. He died in a shootout trying to break up the lynch mob.

Skagway was not alone at the top of the Inside Passage in its quest to become

the "Metropolis of the North." **Dyea**, a city on the bay 10 miles (16 km) to the west, sprang up as well. It sat at the foot of the Chilkoot Trail, an established Native route that was shorter but steeper than the White Pass Trail. Dyea and Skagway competed bitterly for every stampeder heading into the interior, each boasting the better trail.

The biggest liars were in Skagway, because the White Pass Trail was far more treacherous, nicknamed "Dead Horse Trail" for the 3,000 pack animals that perished in the canyon. But Skagway won the battle for survival with Dyea. The White Pass and Yukon Route railroad laid its first tracks up the middle of Broadway in May 1898, and by 1900 the narrow gauge line was completed, 100 miles (160 km) to Whitehorse, future capital of the Yukon Territory. An easy route to the gold fields was established, and Dyea subsequently became a ghost town.

The Klondike rush had subsided by 1900, but Skagway was set up for life as the port for Yukon. Its population has fluctuated between 400 and 3,000 in the years since, due to the North's continuous boom-and-bust cycle. Food, fuel, war supplies, minerals and tourists have all been hauled by the railroad in various volumes.

More volume meant more trains running and more people employed. According to the railroad's owners, there was not enough volume of anything, even tourists, to meet rising costs at the end of the 1982 summer season. The railroad "suspended operations" at that time; however, service was reinstated in the summer of 1988.

Riding the narrow gauge train over the White Pass is the best way for visitors to get a feel of what the gold rush was like. Travel in turn-of-the-century parlor cars, pulled by steam or diesel engines, which seem to cling to the small cut in the mountainside. Hundreds of feet below are the still visible remains of the old trails. Excursions are available to White Pass Summit or passengers may book a one-way ticket from Skagway to Fraser, British Columbia,

Rail comes to town...

where they continue to Whitehorse by bus. Visitors can also drive the Klondike Highway, completed in 1978, which climbs the opposite side of the canyon from the railroad. It is paved from Skagway to the junction with the Alaska Highway near Whitehorse.

The three-hour drive gives you much the same scenery as is viewed on the railroad: **Skagway River Gorge, Pitchfork Falls, White Pass Summit** (3,290 feet/1,000 meters), and the beautiful lake country of British Columbia and the Yukon.

The center of activity in Skagway is along **Broadway Street** in the Historic District, where more than 60 gold-rush-era buildings still stand. After its creation in 1977, the Klondike Gold Rush National Historical Park took over ownership of many of these buildings and has since spent millions of dollars in their restoration. Private restoration has also taken place, breathing life into old structures that surely would have fallen down in time.

Occupying the old buildings are curio shops, restaurants, saloons, hotels, art galleries, ice cream parlors, and other businesses creating a carnival-like atmosphere in a gold-rush setting.

It always helps to know what you're seeing, and Skagway has a number of options for the interpretive traveler. Cheapest among them is the free walking tour of the historic district given by the National Park Service. The tours are conducted three times a day and begin at the Visitors' Center in the restored WP & YR depot building. More mobile and entertaining tours of the district are given by pony-pulling hacks and old street cars, which will also take you to the **Trail of '98 Museum**, **Reid Falls** and the **Gold Rush Cemetery**, where Soapy Smith is buried.

Skaguay in the Days of '98 recreates the Soapy Smith tragedy nightly at the **Eagles Hall**. This one-hour historical drama follows an hour of live ragtime music and gambling. The dealers are cast members and the money is phoney, and some of the tables date back to the gold rush. The show's popularity has

.and keeps n chuffing.

kept it going since 1925, and residents affectionately refer to it as "the longest running show on Broadway."

If you're reasonably fit, own a backpack, and have time, hiking the **Chilkoot Trail** is the most adventurous option for tracing the route of the gold seekers. Managed by the park services of the United States and Canada, the trail extends 33 miles (53 km) from old Dyea to Lake Bennett, British Columbia. Most hikers allow three to five days to fully capture the scenery and explore the thousands of gold-rush relics left behind during the stampede.

As you approach the base of the **Chilkoot Pass** and look up at the steps carved in the snow by the day's hikers, one can't help but visualize what passed there before. Fortunately, it was captured in photographs and on paper.

Edwin Tappan Adney recorded the scene for *Harper's Weekly* in September 1897: "Look more closely. The eye catches movement. There is a continuous moving train; they are perceptible only by their movement, just as ants are.

The moving train is zigzagging across the towering face of the precipice, up, up into the sky, even at the very top. See! they are going against the sky! They are human beings, but never did men look so small."

Alaska's fun city: Skagway has the reputation for being a party town, especially in summer. Ask any Yukoner who bolts for the coast on weekends. Skagway people are fun-loving and seem to bask in the attention, but by fall they are ready for the quiet months ahead.

The best weather is in spring. Skies are clear, the sun is hot, and the snow's still deep on White Pass until mid-May. Cross country skiers and snow mobilers drive to the top of the highway, jump on their gear and go all day. Later in the summer after the snow has melted, hundreds of small ponds form on the moonlike terrain. On hot days, the ponds warm up to about 80°F (27°C) – the next best thing to a hot tub!

Other good picnic spots are at Dyea; among the ruins there, **Yakutania Point, Lower Dewey Lake** and **Pullen Creek**

Skagway parade.

Park, where pink and silver salmon run in August and September. When the fish aren't biting, Skagway's saloons are hopping, especially on days when the larger cruise ships are in town. Jazz musicians off the boats frequently jump ship in Skagway for a few hours to attend jam sessions. They say it's the only day of the cruise that they don't have to play "old folks music." If business is good, the bars stay open till 5 am, the official closing time.

Visitors are welcome to join several official town-wide parties in Skagway throughout the summer. Featured in March is the *Windfest*, with its zany chainsaw toss, chili contest and other events. Late June's *Summer Solstice Party* is an all-night event, with bands performing in parks.

A traditional gold-rush style Independence Day is celebrated on 4th July, complete with parades, races and contests of all kinds. Four days later, on July 8th is *Soapy Smith's Wake*, a graveyard party and champagne toast to Skagway's notorious con-man.

The Klondike Trail of '98 Road Relay is held on the second weekend of September. About 100 ten-person teams run 110 miles (176 km) from Skagway to Whitehorse, ending with a party. Skagway also is planning several events to coincide with the Klondike Gold Rush Centennial, which begins in 1996.

Skagway's award-winning Bigger Hammer Marching Band, which won grand prizes in four Southeast Alaska State Fairs, is usually present. Dressed to fit the day and theme, this kazoo-blowing band of Skagway's least-respected civic leaders will parody anything remotely political that is blowing in the wind, be it rail closures or the nuclear age. Bigger Hammer's motto is: "In Skagway, we take humor seriously."

A more direct route to the interior of Alaska from the panhandle is through **Haines**, an hour south on the ferry from Skagway. Haines is a community rich in Tlingit Native culture and is best known for its majestic mountain scenery, king and sockeye salmon-fishing, native art and dance, and the newly created **Chilkat Bald Eagle Preserve**.

The Haines Highway follows the Chilkat River, a rich stream that stays ice-free in late fall and early winter, supporting salmon runs and the world's largest concentration of bald eagles. November and December are the best months to view eagles in the Haines area. Thousands of bald eagles congregate in the area, feeding off the spawned-out salmon in the river.

Since the opening of the Klondike Highway out of Skagway, more and more travelers have opted to drive the "Golden Horseshoe" route to include both Haines and Skagway on their way to or from the Interior. Driving up the Alaska Highway from the south, you can cut off to Skagway on the Klondike, put your car on the ferry for the short ride to Haines, and then proceed north over the Chilkoot Pass till you meet the Alaska Highway again at Haines Junction. Drivers see Haines first, and Skagway second, if they choose this route on the way south. Either way, the two towns and the two mountain passes are worth seeing in one trip.

...ugged ...askan ...aloon-girl.

PRINCE WILLIAM SOUND

Few slide shows present pictures of rain in **Prince William Sound**. Rather, viewers see sunshine flickering in water cascading from the flukes of a breaching humpback whale. Kayakers wearing T-shirts are silhouetted in front of a brilliant white glacier. Sea otters float atop their glossy reflections and munch on Dungeness crab they have plucked from the ocean floor.

But all those pictures are taken on clear days, which many people consider mythical. The cameras are brought out during the times visitors call Prince William Sound a backcountry heaven.

While some may regard a slide show which depicts sunny scenes as meteorologically deceptive, it would be similarly inaccurate, in the wake of the 1989 *Exxon Valdez* oil spill, to limit a presentation on Prince William Sound to pictures of oil-stained beaches, coated sea birds and crews of clean-up workers scouring blackened rocks.

The fact is, most tourists will be hard-pressed to observe any of the 10.8 million gallons of crude which spilled when the tanker ran aground on Bligh Reef between the port cities of Valdez and Cordova in the north end of the Sound.

US Coast Guard authorities, who supervised the massive clean-up operation immediately after the disaster and during the following summer, report that there are almost no signs of the sticky oil which washed along more than 1,100 miles (1,770 km) of Alaskan shoreline.

Those willing to charter boats or floatplanes to isolated locations – primarily the Barren Islands between the Kenai Peninsula and Kodiak Island, hundreds of miles southwest of Cordova – no doubt would be able to return with photographic evidence of the disaster. But most visitors to Prince William Sound will come back with pictures of the aforementioned kayakers in T-shirts and even sea otters and whales.

And each year those pictures, along with stories told by the travelers who took them, draw more people to see the Sound's wonderful natural displays of animals, ice, forest and mountains.

Yet rain is the rule in this watery wild country southeast of Anchorage, where coastal peaks form a cloud-stopping arc from Whittier to Cordova. Here, precipitation is measured in feet, not inches. Much of that moisture, driven into the sound by the Gulf of Alaska's wicked winter storms, pours onto maritime rain forests. Even more precipitation falls as snow and adds substance to the Sound's numerous glaciers. Come summer the rain hardly falls at all. Then moisture, too thick to be called fog, hangs between gray-green glassy salt water and clouds the color of concrete.

Often enough, the clouds seems as durable as concrete, apparently anchored in place by gray, rocky peaks and black, green and gray forests of Sitka spruce and western hemlock. Horizons close in and the spirit of the Sound plays games with visitors. Newcomers camping in this cloud-shrouded funereal world often feel tension build. Many get depressed and sometimes desperate too.

But frequent visitors aren't particularly bothered by the rain. They overcome the weather by laughing a lot. They recognize that rain accounts for much of the Sound's mystique, and they relish telling weather stories.

"I've never had a problem getting wet out there," says Kelley Weavering, a bearded, gangly kayaking guide. "On the other hand, I've had some real problems getting dry."

During one "good weather" summer in the Sound, Weavering took a group through 13 consecutive rainy days. He prides himself that he accomplished the task without having anyone become violent from a build-up of stress. He did it – and kept dry, too – with the help of an umbrella.

"Rough, tough woodsmen might laugh at the idea of carrying an umbrella," Weavering says, "well, let 'em. Laughter's good for the soul."

When the umbrella wasn't keeping rain off his head, it was employed in a Charlie Chaplin routine he'd perfected over many years of practice.

Weavering also is one of the few who,

receding ages: ooking own over ordova. Left, ukes of a umpback hale.

under the protection of his umbrella, has taken pictures in the rain.

Down a brown bear's trail: But it was a geologist new to the Sound, a woodsman who'd never carried an umbrella, who one day conveyed the eerie quality that cloudy, rainy weather imparts to the region. The geologist, Ben Porterfield, and a partner were sitting drinking beer at the Sportsman's Inn in Whittier. They couldn't very well work. Outside, clouds boiled across the glaciated mountains that shoulder up to the community's concrete buildings. Wind grabbed the waterfalls pouring off invisible ice sheets and torqued them up into horizontal jets of spray.

Porterfield told a story about weather and bears. One day he and his partner were working their way down Fish Creek drainage, taking sediment samples from the stream for study by the government. The high overcast was standard cement as they descended through spongy alpine tundra. But the clouds dropped with them as they approached brush line, where they faced dense tangles of alder interwined with thorny devil's club.

The geologists' mood plummeted. They became only a little happier when they found a trail packed by brown bears, the large grizzlies of Alaska's southerly coasts. The trail obviously was well used by brownies commuting to the stream's lower reaches for a steady supply of spawning chum salmon. Still, it was a route through the thickets.

The first paw prints the geologists saw were big as a magazine cover but full of rain water – at least several hours old. The two talked loudly and sang campfire songs. They weren't about to vacate the trail, but they didn't want to interfere with any powerful fellow travelers, either.

A bit farther down they came across a pile of fresh, rank scat. At that point, Ben checked his shotgun. His partner slipped the government-issue .44 magnum from its shoulder holster. The two talked more and sang louder.

The brush finally gave way to hemlock forest. Tall trees formed a leaky canopy over an open carpet of light-

Forest Service cabin in remote Prince William Sound.

green moss that completely covered the ground. Moss covered fallen rotting trees, and even many of the live trees. It hung in tendrils from branches, and it dripped.

Save for the steady drone of the stream, the forest was silent. Only the bear trail wasn't covered with moss. It was almost a trench of slick, soft soil. And on the trail the geologists saw urine steaming in a foot-print that dwarfed the others. The claw marks were now well-defined points far in front of the imprint of the pad.

Around a bend and across a moss-covered deadfall, 50 feet above the stream, a fresh salmon lay on the trail. The strong smell of dead fish came from a clump of nearby trees. Brown bears smell like dead fish when they gorge on salmon. Now, the geologists didn't say anything. Porterfield and his partner stood and held their guns like a couple of cowboys expecting a bandit. But the bandit never showed.

The two tip-toed to the stream. Porterfield stood guard while his partner collected a final handful of gravel. Then they waited in a sopping meadow for their helicopter to arrive.

Only after the geologists were lifted away did they feel silly about the melodrama. It was the gloom, Porterfield says, the Twilight Zone atmosphere of the forest, that got to them as much as the perceived threat of a bear attack.

So too figures Lynn Mitchell, a district ranger for the US Forest Service, the agency that manages much of the land throughout the Sound.

"The bears are very real, but they tend to leave people alone, so long as you don't startle them or bother them," Mitchell says. "It's a rich environment. The bears have plenty to eat without going after campers. Just be sure they don't get at *your* food."

Getting there: Visitors can savor the atmosphere of the Sound simply by crossing it on a ferry or tour boat. Passengers traveling by boat between Whittier and Valdez sometimes see bears and, occasionally, goats balanced on high cliffs. Humpback and killer whales frequent the route, and Dall porpoises

surf the bow wake. Sea lions haul out on rocks, and harbor seals rest on chunks of ice that drift with the wind and tide away from the glaciers.

It's a stop at one particular glacier, the Columbia, that passengers remember most about their boat trips. **Columbia Glacier** is the largest among the 20 that drop down from the Chugach Mountains into the northerly fjords of Prince William Sound.

Fortunately, the enormous sheet of ice is situated almost due north of the spill site, upwind and upstream, so none of the black oil fouled the glacier's dazzling blue-white face. Fed each year by enough snow to bury a five-story building, Columbia Glacier covers an area the size of Los Angeles. It flows more than 40 miles (64 km) from the mountains to Columbia Bay, where its 4-mile-wide (6.4-km) face daily drops hundreds of thousands of tons of ice into the sound.

The glacier's output of ice increased in 1983, when it began a rapid retreat. Now, glaciologists estimate that 50 cu-

bic miles (210 cubic km) of icebergs could possibly be released during the next half century.

So much ice has filled the bay in recent years that boats can't approach the glacier as closely as they could in the past, when passengers routinely were provided with a close-up view of massive flakes peeling from the 300-foot-high (90-meter) wall.

When the flakes come down, the harbor seals resting on bergs in the bay are rocked by the resulting swells. They don't even look up. Meanwhile, gulls and other birds swarm around the glacier face; the plunging ice has stirred the seafood-rich water, bringing shrimp and other delicacies to the surface for their consumption. Thus, the glaciers are an intrinsic part of the life cycle of Prince William Sound.

Earthquakes and tidal waves: The land is also shaped by forces other than slow-moving glaciers. Earthquakes cause sudden, dramatic changes in the lay of the country. On March 27, 1964 – Good Friday – bedrock shifted just west of Columbia Glacier. The shock waves, registering between 8.4 and 8.6 on the Richter Scale, were the most intense ever recorded on North America. In just a few minutes, extensive new beach lines emerged as the land rose. The most dramatic geological adjustment occurred at the south end of **Montague Island**, which actually tilted upward 38 feet (11.5 meters).

But most damage was done by undersea landslides that generated enormous tidal waves. **Valdez**, to the east of the earthquake epicenter, was completely destroyed, and had to be rebuilt at a different site.

Whittier, to the southwest, was hit by three successive waves, one of which crested at 104 feet (32 meters). A lumber mill was demolished and 13 people were killed, but the port was left relatively undamaged.

The worst human disaster was at **Chenega**, a village of 80 on an island south of Whittier near the western edge of the sound. A wave enveloped all the buildings but the school and one house,

Worthington Glacier, near Valdez.

146

and swept away 23 residents. Only recently have the survivors and their offspring returned to rebuild.

Many hard rock and placer claims are buried under rock slides and fast-growing alder and hemlock. In a few places, like the Beatson mine on **La Touche Island**, piles of tailings stand out, along with a few unstable and old buildings, rust-red lengths of steel pipe and pumps, and stripped trucks whose tires have been eaten by porcupines.

The Sound is still rich in copper and gold, molybdenum, tungsten and silver. However, low mineral prices mean those resources will be left in the ground for at least the next decade, according to executives with Chugach Alaska Corporation, a major private land owner in the Prince William Sound basin.

Miners initially came to the Sound at the turn of the century to reach Valdez. From there they intended to take the Richardson Trail to Interior Alaska's gold fields.

The spirit of the Sound is powerful indeed. But perhaps it isn't as powerful as the human spirit. A story is told of a prospector who fell into a crevasse while crossing **Blackstone Glacier** northwest of Whittier. Wedged between the tapering walls, he felt the ice sap his body heat and strength. The prospector realized his partners couldn't rescue him. He called up to them and asked that, some day, they retrieve his gold poke and send it to his wife.

Railroad town: Like Valdez, **Cordova** also became a transportation center shortly after the turn of the century. But there, the important mineral was copper. The deposit, the richest in the world, was at **Kennicott**, 200 miles (320 km) up the Copper and Chitina rivers, and transportation was by rail.

Cordova, still an attractive community of brightly painted, woodframed houses, was turned into a railroad town with the arrival of a shipload of men and equipment on April 1, 1906. The railroad was the brainchild of Michael J. Heney, an engineer who pushed the White Pass & Yukon Railroad through the Wrangell-St Elias Range. Heney

was too well-known for anyone to say it out loud, but quite a few folks considered him an April Fool.

Yet for the next half decade, Cordova was the operations center for the Copper River & Northwestern Railroad construction project. The CR & NW was an undertaking which, along with the oil pipeline, ranks among the greatest engineering achievements in the history of the world.

Heney had to contend with temperatures of minus 60°F (-50°C), a wind that knocked his boxcars off the tracks, drifting snow that buried his locomotives, rampaging floods, and a fast Copper River current that sent massive icebergs crashing into the footings of a crucial railroad bridge.

On April 8, 1911, the first train returned to Cordova with ore from the Kennicott mines. The ore was almost pure copper, and it made the fortunes of the railroad builders. The unfortunate Heney, though, had died of exhaustion a year before the railroad's actual completion. By the mid-1930s the price of copper had dropped drastically and the high-grade ores had been mined. In 1938 the railroad was abandoned.

Fashionable fur: The mineral industry isn't the only one that has declined in the area. Fur harvesting also disappeared early in the century. Foxes, fed on salmon, were "farmed" for great profit on islands in the sound until the fashion industry shifted away from those pelts, particularly as a result of anti-cruelty lobbying.

Sea otters, whose thick, warm fur originally attracted Russian and American colonists to Prince William Sound, were hunted to the brink of extinction. Now protected by law, these animals proliferated until thousands perished in the *Exxon* spill. Clean-up workers collected the bodies of 1,016 sea otters and figure at least that many bodies disappeared at sea.

While wildlife officials have reported seeing the animals back in the sound in 1990, the long-term consequences for the sea otter population are unknown. But commercial fishing remains the ma-

Harbor seals at the Columbia Glacier.

jor source of income for the 6,000-plus people who live along the Sound. In 1994, a record 14 million pink salmon returned to the Port of Valdez.

Some of the Sound's most promising resources are its wilderness and its visitors. Many visitors moor their boats in Prince William Sound's coves and sleep on board. Kayakers and others often pitch tents on beaches, where they can avoid boggy ground.

The increase in requests for cabin-use permits is one sign of a growing number of visitors to the Sound. And after author Rex Beach documented the construction of the Copper River & Northwestern Railroad, in his bestseller *The Iron Trail*, Cordova and its nearby glaciers became one of the greatest visitor attractions in Alaska.

Whittier has recently developed into an important visitor point. Historically, the site of that community was a resting place for Native and Russian traders portaging their wares between the Sound and Cook Inlet. Later, gold miners and mail carriers crossed Portage Pass to reach the Iditarod Trail, which led to Alaska's far-west gold fields (and now better known as Alaska's big winter dog-sled race). But Whittier didn't really develop until World War II, when the army decided to use its ice-free harbor for a strategic fuel dump. Troops blasted two tunnels through the Chugach Mountains to connect Whittier with the Alaska Railroad depot at Portage.

A large marina and residential area are being planned for **Shotgun Cove**, an isolated area east of Whittier. Farther out, near Columbia Glacier, Chugach Alaska Corporation is considering a lodge and other facilities to serve boaters and cruise ship passengers, although the plans are not yet complete. Forest Service Officials and the Alaska Division of Parks are also sitting on plans for a series of parks on land throughout Prince William Sound. It is a sensitive area, and plans need to be laid carefully.

Whatever developments come about as a result of recreational visitors, no doubt they'll be designed to keep rain off and spirits high.

KODIAK, THE CITY AND THE ISLAND

A shift of the wind can change **Kodiak Island** from a desolate, windswept, rain-pounded rock isolated from the rest of the world by fog to a shimmering emerald of grass, spruce trees and snow-capped mountains glowing pink in the sunrise. But while the winds may shift, they remain predominantly from the north. Both the island itself and the city of Kodiak are places whose characters change with the weather, the seasons and the observer.

A popular T-shirt carries the slogan "Kodiak – It's not the end of the world but you can see it from here." At first glance the city of **Kodiak** might seem to be somewhere near world's end, a town of 9,500 people perched precariously on a small ledge of land between ocean swells and mountains. A look into Kodiak's economy reveals a major fishing port (one of the top three in the United States) and the center of Alaska's developing whitefish industry. Kodiak is home to a mult-imillion-dollar fishing fleet which ranges from the Pacific Northwest to Norton Sound.

More than 200 years of recorded history have swept across Kodiak in waves, each wave leaving traces of its passing. Artifacts of the indigenous Koniag culture surface near remnants of the Russian period or World War II bunkers, derelict whaling stations, collapsing herring-rendering plants, or fish-processing facilities.

Just under the top soil is a layer of volcanic ash which covered the town in 1912 and still drifts about leaving a coating of fine, white dust. White spruce tree skeletons guard the salt marshes, monuments to the land subsidence which occurred during the 1964 earthquake and tidal wave.

At the Kodiak International Airport, jets sit on one side of the fence, while eagles ride the wind overhead.

In restaurants residents talk of trips to the Orient to negotiate fish or timber sales, riding out storms at sea and exploring the island on foot or by kayak.

Many residents live simultaneously in the worlds of international business and subsistence hunting and fishing.

From the air Kodiak Island seems an empty wilderness, 3,588 sq. miles (9,293 sq. km) of rugged mountains deeply indented by bays. The north half of the island is covered with spruce trees, the south half with grass. Foresters say the spruce forest is advancing down Kodiak Island at the rate of one mile a century.

Landing in Kodiak can be an adventure. As the jet approaches the airport, it drops lower and lower over the water until its landing gear seems to skim the waves. Just beyond where the runway seems to emerge from the water, the plane sets down. At the other end of the runway sits **Barometer Mountain**, so called because the peak is only visible in good weather.

The airport is about 5 miles (8 km) from Kodiak City. Spruce trees cast shadows across the highway to town, then the road wends its way in sharp turns around Pillar Mountain. In the winter bald eagles, sometimes as many

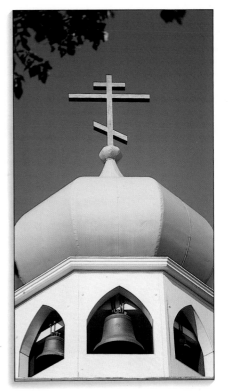

Preceding pages: Steller sea lions, Kenai Fjords. Left, brown bear in the midst of a salmon run. Right, Russian church, Kodiak.

as 10 to a tree, perch in cottonwoods above the highway. The road then dips down and slips into Kodiak's back door.

The sea is Kodiak's front yard. Fifteen fish-processing plants line the city's waterfront. Their names and signs, "We buy halibut" or "Herring wanted," face the sea, visible to passing fishing vessels. Flocks of sea birds bob on the swells and in the spring, bald eagles wheel overhead. The salt-tanged smell of fish announces that this is Kodiak, a fishing port producing fish and shellfish for markets around the world. The blue onion dome of the Holy Resurrection Orthodox Church announces that this is Kodiak, the first Russian settlement in Alaska. Reminders of that heritage can be found everywhere.

The Russian legacy: Drawn by his search for sea-otter pelts, Grigor Ivanovich Shelikof arrived in Three Saints Bay on the southeast corner of Kodiak Island in 1784 with two ships, the *Three Saints* and the *St Simon*. A third, the *St Michael*, left Russia under Shelikof's command, but wintered near Unalaska

Island for repairs. When the *St Michael* sailed from Unalaska it hit a reef and rapidly sank.

The indigenous Koniag did not welcome Shelikof, but proceeded to harass the Russian party. Shelikof, who needed the Koniags to hunt sea otters, responded with what today would be considered appalling force.

"They said Shelikohov [*sic*] loaded two bidarkas [skin boats] with his people," wrote Ivan Peel, acting governor-general of Irkutsak and Kolyvan, to the Russian senate in 1789, "and with the armed band murdered about 500 of these speechless people; if we also count those who ran in fear to their bidarkas and trying to escape, stampeded and drowned each other, the number will exceed 500. Many men and women were taken as prisoners of war. By order of Mr Shelekohov, the men were led to the tundra and speared, the remaining women and children, about 600 altogether, he took with him to the harbor and kept them for three weeks. The husbands who succeeded in escaping the murder began to

Early tribes trading for oil.

TUSKI AND MAHLEMUTS TRADING FOR OIL.

154

come. Shelekohov returned their wives to them, but he retained one child from each family as hostage."

Having established his authority on Kodiak Island, Shelikof founded the first Russian settlement in Alaska on **Three Saints Bay**, built a school to teach the Natives to read and write Russian, and introduced the Russian Orthodox religion.

In 1791 Alexander Adrevich Baranof arrived at Three Saints Bay to take over leadership of the Russian settlement. He moved the colony to the northeast end of the island where timber was available. The location was also closer to the resources of Cook Inlet and Prince William Sound. The site chosen by Baranof is now the city of Kodiak.

Russian members of the colony took Koniag wives and started family lines whose names still continue – Panamaroff, Pestrikoff, Kvasnikoff, Chichenoff… names which now represent clans and families. Russian heritage in the city of Kodiak is also found on its street signs: Baranof, Rezanoff,

Shelikof, Purtov and Delarof. The island's Native culture is also apparent, and can best be observed during a performance by the Kodiak Alutiiq Dancers. The Native troupe, formed by the Kodiak Tribal Council in 1988, includes 50 dancers who dress in brightly colored costumes and perform traditional songs and dances, some of them in English, Aleut and Russian. The troupe performs throughout the state but schedules regular summer events in Kodiak.

Much of the rich culture of the Koniags was absorbed by the Russian culture and can only be guessed at through artifacts and the diaries of the early Russian settlers. The **Baranof Museum**, across from the ferry dock in downtown Kodiak, contains displays of Koniag artifacts and clothing as well as items from the Russian and early American periods. The small, home-like museum is located in the **Erskine House**, designated a National Historic Landmark.

When the United States purchased Alaska from Imperial Russia, the Russian citizens left, but the Russian Ortho-

new eneration of aders.

Officers and Crew
P. A. F. "Kenmore"
Unga, Alaska
9/1/11.

dox church remained. The two blue onion domes of the **Holy Resurrection Church** are the town's most outstanding landmarks. The church is still a significant part of Kodiak's religious community, and the predominant religion in the six villages in the Island area.

In 1974 the **St Herman Orthodox Theological Seminary** was relocated to Kodiak. (The seminary's white buildings stand near the church.) Father Herman was canonized in Kodiak in 1970, the first Orthodox canonization to take place on American soil. Saint Herman arrived in Kodiak in 1794 and settled on **Spruce Island**, where he established a school and became renowned as an ascetic and miracle worker. The Russian Orthodox faithful make pilgrimage every August to his shrine on the island.

The Russian Orthodox Church follows the Julian calendar, making Kodiak a town of two Christmases, December 25 and January 7, and two New Years, January 1 and January 14.

Treasures of the Holy Resurrection Orthodox Church include many brilliantly-colored icons. Visitors are welcome to attend services in the church.

During World War II, Kodiak served as a major supply center for the Aleutian campaign. Military personnel and construction workers changed the city from a fishing village of 500 residents to a boom town of 4,000 people with another 20,000 in nearby areas. The US Navy built a major base on the site, which is now used as a US Coast Guard facility. Residents who lived in Kodiak during the war tell tales of sailors on liberty, submarine nets stretched across the Kodiak-Near Island channel and the difficulty of obtaining fishing supplies. Today all that remains of those years are silent, moss-covered bunkers.

Fort Abercrombie, a state park with limited camping facilities 4 miles (6.5 km) from the city of Kodiak, is dedicated to the memory of World War II. A large bunker and the remains of gun emplacements overlook the sea from a cliff. Other bunkers can be found by walking through an alpine meadow and

The Baranof Museum.

along the cliff edge. There are also bunkers on **Pillar Mountain** behind the city. Hikers working their way through the alders and spruce forests along the tops of shale cliffs often find others.

Kodiak's US Coast Guard facility is the largest in the United States. Its cutters and C-130 airplanes keep track of the foreign fishing fleets working off the coast. For locals, the Coast Guard facility is the home of "angels" who arrive in helicopters to pluck men off their sinking vessels or search the coastline for survivors of marine tragedies.

Natural events have left indelible marks on Kodiak Island. Twice in the 20th century the landscape on the island has been altered, first by a volcanic ash fall in 1912 and again in 1964 by an earthquake and tidal wave.

Humus has covered the ash that fell on June 6, 1912, when Mount Novarupta on the Alaska Peninsula exploded, but where roads have cut into the mountains the white layer of volcanic ash is visible under the soil's surface. Kodiak residents may exaggerate, but they say the volcanic ash still seeps in through every crack. In places the ash from Mount Novarupta's 1912 eruption drifted several feet deep. Small lakes vanished. Wildlife died, and much natural vegetation was destroyed. Five hundred residents were evacuated on the revenue cutter *Manning*, and the town was choked by ash.

The March 27, 1964, earthquake which devastated much of central Alaska also set off a tidal wave which swept into the city of Kodiak and destroyed the downtown buildings, canneries and the docks.

Many Kodiak residents fled up Pillar Mountain and watched helplessly while the sea ran out, leaving the harbor dry, and then rolled back in across the land. Those who didn't reach high ground were swept away.

Although a few fishermen managed to take their boats to sea – and safety – before the tidal wave hit, boats left in the harbor were pushed into town by the wave. The 100-ton power scow *Selief* ended up a half mile inland, still with

diak Island rt and nneries.

3,000 king crab in its hold. Along the shore the land and seabed dropped or subsided by as much as 5 feet (1.5 meters). Forested areas turned into salt water marshes, now identifiable by the still standing skeletal trees.

After the tidal wave, most of downtown Kodiak was redesigned and rebuilt. Fish-processing companies sent in floating processing plants to can king crab and salmon until new plants could be built. Old-timers play their own version of trivia games, pointing out where roads used to be and where buildings stood "before the tidal wave."

Residents who lived through the tidal wave and stayed to rebuild the town have a special bond formed during the difficult post-tidal-wave years. Though the tidal wave was a tragedy, it left behind a feeling of unity which still pervades the community.

A thriving fishing industry: Kodiak's economic dependence on the sea has never changed, but the species of fish and shellfish on which the town's economy is based has changed repeat-edly. The Russians built Kodiak as a base for harvesting sea otters; salmon and herring fisheries gave an economic base after the sea otter trade died.

The city of Kodiak provides moorage and services to more than 2,000 fishing boats a year. Fishermen deliver up to $100 million worth of fish and shellfish annually. Small skiffs, medium-sized salmon seiners, big shrimp trawlers, crab boats and 100-foot (30-meter) midwater draggers steam in and out of the harbor bringing king crab, snow crab, Dungeness crab, shrimp, red salmon, pink salmon, chum salmon, silver salmon, herring, halibut, black cod, Pacific cod, pollock, flounders and flat fish.

Ask a Kodiak resident what season it is and, if it is summer, he's likely to answer, "Salmon season." Fall is king crab season; winter is season of the Tanner crab, marketed as snow crab. Spring is herring season, and halibut and black cod are harvested in spring and summer. Whitefish species are harvested most of the year.

Kodiak's fishermen proudly call **Bear mural.**

themselves diversified fishermen – fishermen who work year round, switching from fishery to fishery as the seasons change. Between seasons the waterfront throbs with activity. Crane trucks and flatbeds move 500-lb (230-kg) steel crab pots from storage to the boat and back to storage. In spring, herring seines and gillnets are stretched out on the docks where crew men with shuttles can attach float and lead lines.

A truck goes by loaded with fluorescent pink balloons? No, crab buoys that mark where a crab pot has been dropped to the sea floor, baited to attract crabs into its funnel-shaped opening. The buoy is attached to the pot by a line long enough to reach the surface.

Visitors are welcome to wander down the ramp behind the **Harbormaster Building** and walk along the floats in **St Paul Harbor**. Across the channel is **St Herman Harbor**, on **Near Island**.

In St Paul Harbor there are two loading docks where skippers load gear onboard their boats – crab pots may swing at the ends of booms or seines may be lifted to the deck. Just before a fishing season it seems there are more boats in a hurry to load than dock space for loading. Fishing boats line the loading docks – the ferry dock, the city dock and the Sea-Land dock where a huge crane lifts Sea-Land vans off barges.

At any time a vessel may be sitting on the harbor grid, a sloped ramp. At high tide the skipper runs his boat up the ramp and when the tide goes out the vessel's hull is exposed for painting or repairing. When visitors wander down the floats, skippers with time to talk may nod "hello" which is an invitation to stop and visit.

On processing-plant docks, heavy cranes lift bathtub-sized totes filled with fish or shellfish out of a vessel's fish holds. Forklifts carry the totes into the plants where machines peel or fillet or skin products for cookers or freezers. The plants are not open to visitors. However, it is possible to watch a boat being unloaded by standing on the southwest corner of the ferry dock and looking across to the All Alaskan Seafoods dock.

All Alaskan Seafoods operates out of a World War II ship, *Star of Kodiak*, which was converted for fish processing and run aground.

Visitors expect to come to a major fishing port and eat seafood. But most of Kodiak's fresh seafood is in refrigerated vans waiting to be loaded onto barges for shipment. Kodiak's fishing industry is geared to large volume production and sales, which has made it difficult for small, local buyers to establish a steady source of supply. The local supermarkets offer fresh seafood in season and some restaurants include fresh seafood on the menu.

Like its fishing industry, Kodiak's population is diversified. Filipinos began coming to Kodiak to work in the processing plants in the 1970s, and stayed to establish a strong community. Japanese and Korean technicians are assigned to processing plants to oversee the preparation of products destined for their countries. The southern drawls of fishermen, who found Alaska a better place than the Gulf of Mexico, mix with the accents of Oregon and Washington, Maine and Massachusetts.

Touring Kodiak Island: The populated portion of Kodiak Island is confined to the road system, less than 100 miles (160 km) of road. The six coastal villages on the island are accessible only by plane or boat. (If you want to visit one of the villages, it is a good idea to make prior arrangements.)

The rest of the island remains a mountainous wilderness belonging to bears and foxes, rabbits and birds, muskrats and otters. Two-thirds of Kodiak Island is a national wildlife refuge.

Most visitors find all the wilderness they want along the road system. It takes about an hour to drive to the end of the road at Fossil Beach. The road heads out of town past the **Buskin River** where the headquarters for the Kodiak National Wildlife Refuge is located. (The headquarters includes a visitors' center.) The Buskin River is a popular sportfishing stream for salmon and steelhead. The road continues past the airport, the Coast Guard base, the fair-

Kodiak salmonberries.

grounds, the community of **Bells Flats**, and then climbs headlands, curves around bays and crosses rivers.

In summer salmon can be seen jumping in the bays and swimming up the rivers. July and August are the best months for salmon-watching or fishing. Occasionally sea lions come into the bays to feed on salmon. It is tempting to stop at every twist of the road and perfectly permissible to explore the beaches, walk in the forests, climb the mountains and smell the wildflowers.

Eventually the road comes to a "T." To the left is the community of **Chiniak,** like Bell Flats a "suburb" of Kodiak. To the right the road travels through cattle country where Kodiak's ranchers run about 2,000 head of beef cattle.

Ahead the ocean comes into view again by **Pasagshak**, a popular river for fishing silver salmon. The road continues past a sand-duned, surf-beaten beach and ends at **Fossil Beach** where fossil shells lie loosely in the clay and rocks. During the fall, gray whales pass Pasagshak and Fossil Beach on their migration to California from the Bering Sea. In spring, the whales pass the island again as they migrate to their northern summer feeding grounds.

Kodiak's bears are legendary – the largest grizzlies in the world. There are three safe ways to see them. Most charter plane companies on the island offer half- or full-day flightseeing tours – and some guarantee bear sightings. Several wilderness lodges on the island have day or overnight bear-viewing packages. And a program within the wildlife refuge offers four-day trips between July and September. Wilderness hikers, however, should walk noisily through Kodiak's backcountry to reduce the chances of any confrontations.

During the salmon season, bears appear along the streams and beaches. As well as berries and salmon, the Kodiak bear enjoys calves, much to the dismay of local ranchers, and deer, much to the dismay of hunters.

A visit to Kodiak is rich in history, particularly of Alaska's Native traditions and the area's Russian settlers.

ossil Beach.

KENAI PENINSULA

It's often said that Alaska is too big to see and do in a single lifetime, let alone a single vacation. But there is one place where one can sample most of the best of Alaska, and do it in a few weeks. That place is the **Kenai Peninsula**.

The entire peninsula is within easy driving distance of Anchorage. In fact, people in the "Big Town" like to refer to the Kenai as their backyard. But please, don't use that line on the peninsula. That one phrase is more likely than any other to dry up local hospitality.

Assuming that critical *faux pas* is avoided, visitors will find that most peninsula residents are quite friendly. And they are the best source of information when it comes to getting the most out of your visit.

On a map of the state, the Kenai Peninsula looks deceptively small. It's worth remembering that the peninsula covers 9,050 sq. miles (23,000 sq. km), making it larger than the combined areas of Rhode Island, Connecticut and Delaware. It is bordered by Prince William Sound and the Gulf of Alaska on the east and Cook Inlet on the west, and attached to the mainland of southcentral Alaska by a narrow mountainous neck of land at the north.

The peninsula is home to one of Alaska's more artistically inclined cities, Homer, and a thriving school system that's considered a standard-maker for the nation. For every development-minded resident, you'll find another who belongs to an environmental group. Some belong to both camps, which is part of what makes the peninsula such a lively place.

The peninsula's history is also one of many contrasts. Kenai, the largest city, is also its oldest, founded by Russian priests in the late 1700s.

Kenai's next door neighbor, Soldotna, is number two in size, but is a relative newcomer in terms of its age – it was founded by homesteaders after World War II.

Seward, founded in 1903, was for years the leading port city of Alaska. It was eventually eclipsed in that role by Anchorage, and the 1964 earthquake devastated the economy. Twenty years later, it began to regain its financial legs and is once again a thriving port.

The peninsula was originally home to Dena'ina Indians, a branch of the Athabascan family, and to Eskimos. Their descendants still live here, mostly in small, remote villages, and today they account for something less than 10 percent of the borough's population. Western ways have long since replaced those of the Natives; they speak, dress and have a lifestyle similar to that of their white neighbors, donning their traditional dress and customs only on special occasions.

The Russians were the first whites to establish permanent communities on the peninsula. From their base on Kodiak Island, they sent out missionaries to found churches all along the eastern shore of Cook Inlet. The town of Kenai began as a Russian settlement in 1791. Other Russian-founded communities include Seldovia, which also dates to the 18th century, and Ninilchik, founded in the early 1800s. Seward didn't yet exist as a town, but the area around Resurrection Bay was used as a shipbuilding site for the Russian-America Company. Early Russian influence is still to be seen in the onion-domed churches, and heard in the Russian names of places and people.

Driving from Anchorage, one crosses into the peninsula just south of **Portage**, a town which sat at the eastern end of Turnagain Arm, the thin finger of Cook Inlet that separates the peninsula from the Anchorage Bowl. Portage was completely destroyed by the 1964 earthquake, and only a few ruins remain. Almost immediately after passing the wreckage of Portage, one begins to climb through the Kenai Mountains, with a maximum elevation about 3,500 feet (1,050 meters).

Mileage along the Seward and Sterling highways is measured from Seward. At about Mile 70 is the summit of **Turnagain Pass**, elevation 988 feet (296 meters). It's a popular spot for winter

eceding
ges:
rved
kimo
ures at
chemak
y. Left,
g crab at
mer.

recreation, primarily cross-country skiing and snowmachining.

The pass and much of the area along the highway are part of the **Chugach National Forest**. Creeks, lakes and campgrounds are scattered through this area. The camps' opening dates vary with the weather, but generally they are open from Memorial Day through Labor Day. Fees are charged for camp use. Facilities often include tables, fire grates, tent pads and some type of water and sanitary facilities. While fires are usually allowed in these sites, one might want to consider carrying a small camp stove instead. If you do decide to light a fire, you must take care to extinguish it properly, and try to restore the area before moving on.

The Forest Service does operate some cabins on the peninsula, most of them located along the **Resurrection Trail**. Cabins must be reserved in advance. Most have bunk space for six and wood stoves. If a cabin is on a lake, it usually has a row boat and oars. Campers must bring their own food, utensils and sleeping bags.

The first town one encounters on the peninsula is **Hope**, a mining town of about 200, founded in the late 1890s. A trip to Hope requires a 16-mile (25-km) detour onto the Hope Cutoff, Mile 56 of the Seward Highway, but it's well worth the time.

Hope is the site of the oldest school house in Alaska – a red, one-room school still in active use. Other facilities in Hope include two stores, two cafes, a bar and two lodges.

An ideal site for pink salmon fishing, moose, caribou and black bear hunting, Hope also is the head of the Resurrection Trail, one of the most popular hiking areas on the peninsula.

The trailhead is located at Mile 3.5 of the Resurrection Creek Road. The entire trail is 38 miles (60 km) long, and hikers emerge at **Schooner Bend**, Mile 52 on the Sterling Highway. An option is to turn off the Resurrection Trail at Mile 20 and take the 10-mile (16-km) **Devil's Pass Trail**, which emerges at Mile 39 of the Seward Highway.

Because of the route's popularity, it is wise to make cabin reservations well in advance. Reservations can be made up to six months in advance by writing to: United States Forest Service, 201 East Ninth Avenue, Suite 206, Anchorage, AK 99501. A payment of $15 per night is necessary to confirm reservations and hikers should provide alternative dates.

Depending on the endurance and interests of the hikers involved, the Resurrection Trail takes from between two to four days to cover. Trout fishing is possible in the several lakes along the trail. It also provides spectacular scenery for the photographer. People who don't want to hike the entire route can take a wonderful day hike, starting at either end.

The Seward Highway: Upon leaving Hope and rejoining the Seward Highway, the next decision for the automobile traveller is whether to go west or south at the Seward Junction at Mile 40. To the south lie Moose Pass and Seward; to the west lie Cooper Landing, Kenai, Soldotna, Anchor Point, Ninilchik, Seldovia and Homer. There are several

Windsurfer is dwarfed by a passing cruiseship.

smaller towns as well, including Clam Gulch and Kasilof.

Heading south, the first community is **Moose Pass**. This is a quiet village of less than 400 people. Residents enjoy hiking, fishing and biking – the town has one of Alaska's few bike trails. One of the highlights of the year is the annual Summer Festival, held to celebrate the solstice. The date changes from year to year, but is always held on the weekend with the most total hours of sunlight. Activities include a barbecue, carnival, softball games and an auction.

To the south, a few miles outside of Seward, is Exit Glacier Road. The glacier is part of the **Kenai Fjords National Park**, and is the most easily accessible point of the **Harding Icefield**, a remnant of the Ice Age that caps a section of the Kenai Mountains.

The glacier itself lies about 2 miles (3 km) past the car parking area at the end of the road; cross the bridge at the parking lot and head up the trail.

It's possible to hike to the face, although the approach up the loose moraine below the glacier can be tricky. The park staff schedules ranger-led hikes and campfire programs. It's also alright to hike in on your own. The elderly and handicapped can also visit the glacier via a shuttle on the last Sunday of each summer month. For further information, contact the park office in Seward at (907) 224-3874.

Turning back onto the highway after a visit to the glacier, one heads south into **Seward**. The city has about 2,000 residents and offers a full range of sights and services, including a hospital.

One of the main attractions of the area is **Resurrection Bay**. Charter boats for sail or power excursions on the bay are available at the city harbor. Boats can be hired for sightseeing or fishing. The state ferry system also has a dock in Seward, offering trips to Kodiak and the Prince William Sound areas.

Visitor information is available at the Chamber of Commerce railroad car, located at Third and Jefferson streets, or at a small center in the Seward boat harbor. Other sites downtown include the city museum, located in the basement of city hall, and the town library. The museum is dedicated to Seward's past and features displays re-creating rooms from early settlers' homes, old copies of newspapers, and equipment from ships which operated in the area. The library features a film of the 1964 earthquake in Seward. Hours at the museum and library vary with the season and day of week. Information on operating hours is available at the Chamber of Commerce.

Another interesting stop is the **Institute of Marine Science**, operated by the University of Alaska. Tours are available week day afternoons, except on holidays.

Seward is the southern terminus for most cruiseships crossing the Gulf of Alaska. These ships bring almost 180,000 visitors through Seward on their way to or from Alaska. The city is also the gateway to Kenai Fjords National Park, home to porpoises, sea otters, sea lions, humpback and orca whales, puffins, bald eagles and other animals. Several local tour operators offer daily wildlife cruises into the park.

Iceboating on Kenai Lake.

The highlight of the year in Seward is undoubtedly the annual 4th of July celebration. This festival includes an all-town barbecue, a parade, acrobatic fliers, fireworks and the Mount Marathon foot race. Racers make a mad scramble up one side of a mountain located behind town, and then take a wild slide down the mountain's back.

Another special event is the annual Silver Salmon Derby, a week-long fishing contest that offers more prize money than any other fishing derby in Alaska. The derby begins on the second Saturday of August.

Driving north out of Seward, it's time to head west on the Sterling Highway. Turn left at the junction; the road is marked as Alaska Route 1.

Out west toward **Cooper Landing**, one enters an area that's been closed to Dall sheep hunting. As a result, it's a good area to spot them. But looking for sheep while driving causes traffic pile-ups – literally – every summer, so pull off at one of many designated stops before peering up to see the white specks high up on the peaks. A spotting scope or powerful zoom lens is a big help.

Cooper Landing is a community of about 300, spread out along the headwaters of the Kenai River. Here the river is a beautiful turquoise color, and in the winter the open stretches of water are a prime feeding ground for bald eagles.

Fishing, hunting and tourism are the area's main industries, although the town began as a mining area. The mining legacy lives on at the **Charley Hubbard Museum**, open during the summer. Watch for a sign on the highway that points the way to the museum.

At nearby **Kenai Lake**, one can fish for Dolly Varden, lake trout, rainbow trout and whitefish. In the Kenai River are trout, king, silver and red salmon. Trophy rainbow trout – some weighing as much as 20 lbs (9 kg) – are often caught here by spin- and fly-fishing enthusiasts, and catch-and-release fishing is widely practiced. Rafting is another popular activity on the river, and several local businesses offer fishing and float trips.

Hunting and fishing regulations vary with different areas and with the species. Complete game regulations are available free from the state Department of Fish and Game. Many sporting goods shops and tourist businesses also offer copies of the regulation manuals.

Continuing west, just outside of the Cooper Landing area, is the turnoff to the **Russian River Campground**. The campground is easy to spot in the summer, as it's usually overflowing with visitors. The Russian is the largest freshwater fishery in Alaska, and it draws about 60,000 fishermen, each year, all hoping to catch a red salmon.

Heading west past the Russian, one leaves the Chugach National Forest and enters the **Kenai National Wildlife Refuge**, which has different regulations and is in a different state game management area. Refuge regulations, as well as information about things to see and do in the refuge, are available from the unit's Soldotna headquarters, phone (907) 262-7021.

Among the major recreational areas in the refuge is the **Skilak Lake Loop**, which intersects the Sterling Highway at two points. This road not only takes you to **Skilak Lake**, but also provides access to several other smaller lakes, streams and trails in the area.

Skilak itself has a surface area of 24,000 acres (57,600 hectares). It is prone to sudden and violent storms – boater warning signs should be taken very seriously. The lake offers fishing for salmon, trout and Dolly Varden.

Sterling is a community of about 2,000, based at the confluence of the Kenai and Moose rivers. It's a very popular salmon fishing area, and is the main access point to the Swanson River oil field and an endless string of lakes that are excellent for canoeing.

An unusual attraction of the area is the **Izaak Walton Recreation Site**, which contains an archeological dig. It is believed the area was an Eskimo village more than 2,000 years ago. Several depressions mark the sites of ancient houses.

Sterling is also the site of the Moose River Raft Race, an annual event that is on the weekend after the 4th of July.

Area businesses construct rafts in a variety of categories, then race down the Moose River to the Kenai River.

Heading on past Sterling, one comes to **Soldotna**, seat of the borough government and home of 3,600 people. With its central location at the intersection of the roads to Kenai and Homer, Soldotna has become the hub of the central peninsula. Here one will find a hospital, a detachment of the Alaska State Troopers and the headquarters of the Kenai National Wildlife Refuge.

Soldotna is a popular spot to meet up with professional fishing guides, most of whom specialize in helping their clients find king salmon.

The amount of traffic on the Kenai River has become the subject of statewide controversy. Twenty-five years ago, only a handful of locals fished on the river for sport. Now the Kenai River system is the most popular fishing area in the state. A special panel is studying the use of the river and may recommend some major changes to protect it. Consult local Fish and Game or State Parks officials for the most up-to-date information on river use.

Information is available from the Visitors' Center, at the corner of the Sterling Highway and Kalifornski Beach Road, which also houses the offices for the local chamber of commerce. The center has many colorful photographs of the area, as well as the World Record King Salmon, weighing 97 lbs (44 kg).

Soldotna's festivals include Progress Days, held the last weekend in July, a winter sports festival and the state sled dog racing championships in late February. Because of its location near the coast, Soldotna doesn't receive enough snow to cover the sled dog course. For that reason, the city usually stockpiles snow scraped off the city streets, saving it over the winter to spread over the course a few days before the races.

Located on the southwest edge of Soldotna is the **Kenai Peninsula College**. Among its major programs is petroleum technology, reflecting the area's tie to the oil industry.

Heading west from Soldotna on ei-

good catch Homer.

ther the Kenai Spur Highway or Kalifornsky Beach Road, one comes to **Kenai**, the oldest permanent settlement on the peninsula, and its largest city.

Kenai is home port to a good share of the peninsula's drift-net fishing fleet. In the summer a parade of boats can be seen coming in and out of the mouth of the river in their quest for red salmon.

In 1990, there was a record salmon catch in Prince William Sound to the north of Kenai, but fishermen who ventured up the Lower Cook Inlet or off Kodiak Island came back with sparse catches. During the spring, the flats along the mouth of the river are temporary nesting ground for thousands of snow geese. They stay in the area for about two weeks and are a popular subject for early-season photographers.

Kenai is also home of the peninsula's largest airport and has the most regularly scheduled flights. Airlines also fly in and out of Soldotna, Seward and Homer, and charter flights can take you almost anywhere else.

One of Kenai's main attractions is the Kenai Bicentennial Visitors' and Cultural Center. The center features exhibits and displays of Kenai's rich and diverse culture, from its Native and Russian history through the industries that currently fuel the area: oil and commercial fishing. It is open daily from May through August.

Special events include the 4th of July parade and the "Christmas Comes to Kenai" celebration on the weekend following Thanksgiving. That fete includes a fireworks display at about 4pm. Since the peninsula has very long days during the summer, the people of Kenai hold off on fireworks until November, when they can easily be seen against the black afternoon sky.

Continuing north of Kenai on the Spur Highway, you come to the **Nikiski** industrial area, with a large chemical plant, two oil refineries and a natural gas liquification plant. The plants aren't open to the public.

The area north of Kenai has several names. Some call it simply "North Kenai," while others say "Nikishka,"

The port of Homer, with its mountain views.

170

"Nikiska," or "Nikiski." The latter name won a popularity vote in the area, but when discussing "that place" with a local, listen carefully to what he calls the area, and use that term.

North of the refineries is the **Captain Cook State Recreation Area**, a popular spot for hiking, camping, fishing, and snowmachining.

Much of the view across the inlet is part of the **Lake Clark National Park**. Charter flights to the park can be arranged in Kenai. Drive the Bridge Access Road and connect with Kalifornski Beach Road to return to the Sterling Highway. An interesting stop at Mile 111 is the **Crooked Creek Salmon Hatchery**. This state-run hatchery is open to the public.

Farther south, the highway begins to parallel Cook Inlet and runs by some fine clamming areas in the aptly named **Clam Gulch**. Clamming requires patience, practice, a fishing license and a current tide book. But for those who like to eat the mollusks, a day in Clam Gulch could well be one of the highlights of their visit.

At Mile 135 is **Ninilchik**, a fishing village founded by the Russians more than 100 years ago. Fishing is still popular here today, with many visitors coming in search of halibut or salmon. The town's 750 residents mostly live in recently constructed homes along the highway. The original village, open to visitors, sits on the inlet at the mouth of the Ninilchik River. On a hill above the old village is the town's Russian Orthodox church, not open for tours but still used by the parish. The modern community of Ninilchik hosts the Kenai Peninsula's fair grounds. The fair is held on the third weekend in August.

Continuing south, one comes to **Anchor Point**, the most westerly point in North America that is accessible by continuous road system. The 2,000-member community hosts a king salmon derby from Memorial Day weekend through the third weekend in June. In addition to kings, the area is a popular fishing spot for silvers, steelhead, halibut and trout.

Still farther south is **Homer**, the south-ern terminus of the Sterling Highway. Homer sits on the shore of **Kachemak Bay**, which is famed for the variety of its marine life. Homer may be best known for its natural spit, which extends five miles out into the bay. Major visitor attractions are boat tours and halibut-fishing trips.

Another attraction in town is the **Pratt Museum**, a natural history museum that focuses on Kachemak Bay. The museum is surrounded by a flower garden, and among the exhibits are skeletal remains of a whale and a live octopus.

In Homer, visitors are impressed by its six art galleries, symphony orchestra, year-round theater company and artists galore. This is also the jumping-off point for trips to the other side of the bay, including Kachemak Bay State Park, Halibut Cove – where there are more artists and galleries – and the town of **Seldovia**. The state ferry service links Homer to Seldovia, Kodiak and Seward during the summer.

Seldovia is accessible only by air and water. One can bring a vehicle on the state ferry, but a car isn't really necessary; all of the town is within easy walking distance.

Seldovia is home of yet another of the peninsula's historic Russian Orthodox churches. Like its sisters around the peninsula, it is also still the home of an active parish. Seldovia's Russian history predates the church, however. It was the site of one of the Russians' first coal mines. By the 1890s, it had become a fishing and shipping center.

Unfortunately, much of the town's boardwalk area was destroyed during the 1964 earthquake. Town residents can show visitors where things were before the ground dropped. Seldovia also has a winter carnival, which brightens up a peaceful, quiet winter. With the bulk of visitors gone and with plenty of nearby trails for hiking and cross-country skiing, winter is one of the nicest times to venture over to the southern shore of Kachemak Bay.

Whether you're searching for trophy-size halibut, Russian history or wildlife-viewing, the peninsula offers it all within an easy drive from Anchorage.

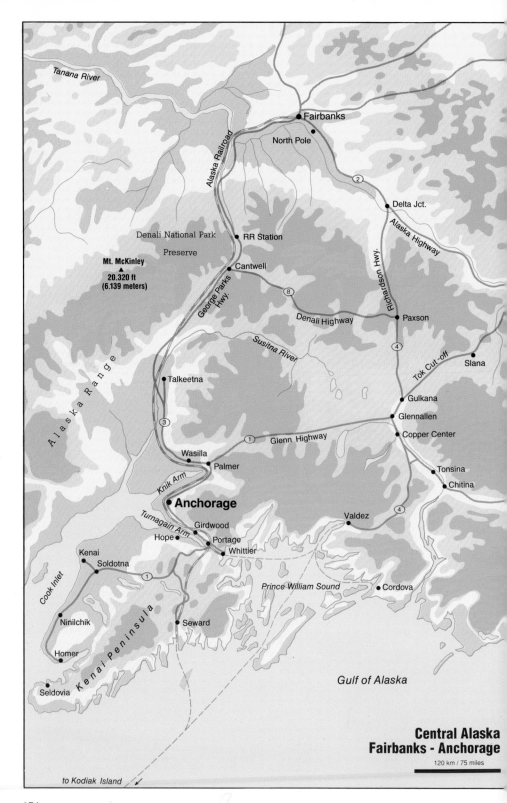

Central Alaska
Fairbanks - Anchorage

120 km / 75 miles

ANCHORAGE

Imagine you're a passenger aboard one of the many domestic and international air carriers serving **Anchorage** daily. About three hours out of Seattle, the pilot announces you'll be landing in Anchorage in a few minutes. You've been peering out of the window ever since your plane took off from the Seattle-Tacoma airport and, except for when you flew by the coast of British Columbia, you've seen darn few signs of civilization. Just as you're beginning to wonder if the pilot has lost his way, you see Anchorage.

Plopped down on a point of land that sticks out into Cook Inlet, with Turnagain Arm bordering the southwest shore and Knik Arm the northwest, the city of Anchorage sprawls out over a 10-mile (16-km) length, seeming to spread over most of the available land between the inlet and the Chugach Mountains to the east.

With almost a quarter of a million residents, Anchorage is the largest metropolis and the commercial center of the state. This port city didn't get a good purchase on life until 1915, but in the 70 years since, has grown from a railroad tent camp to one of the fastest-growing cities in the nation.

The broad peninsula between Turnagain and Knik Arms was probably used by Eskimos from about AD 1000 until the 17th or 18th century, when they were driven out by the Dena'inas, a tribe of nomadic Athabascan Natives. It was the Dena'ina Natives who traded furs and fish with Captain James Cook, the British explorer who sailed into Cook Inlet in 1778. Cook, who was looking for a Northwest Passage to the Atlantic, noted the Natives carried iron and copper weapons, evidence of trade with the Russians who had set up trading posts in lower Cook Inlet and at Kodiak.

Other Russian influences can be seen today at Eklutna, a Dena'ina village inside the northern boundary of the municipality of Anchorage.

When Cook found no way out of the arm of Cook Inlet to the south of Anchorage, he ordered his ships, the *Resolution* and the *Discovery*, to turn around, hence the name "Turnagain." Knik Arm gets its name from the Eskimo word for fire, *knik*, which was used in reference to the Dena'ina people and their villages.

After Alaska was purchased from the Russians in 1867, gold seekers worked the land along Turnagain Arm and at Crow Creek and Girdwood, which is now the southern boundary of the municipality. The gold rush rapidly spread north and across Knik Arm. The old mining supply center of **Knik** is located across the inlet from downtown Anchorage.

During its short history, Anchorage, where half the state's residents live, has reverberated from the sounds of several major construction booms: laying track for the Alaska Railroad, building two adjacent military bases during World War II, discovery and development of the Cook Inlet and Kenai Peninsula oil fields, and construction of the 800-mile

(1,290-km) Trans-Alaska oil pipeline from Prudhoe Bay to Valdez.

Three other events have had significant impact on Anchorage. The first was the federally-sponsored agricultural colonization of the Matanuska Valley by 204 families from the Midwest. Anchorage residents met the newcomers in 1935 with typical frontier hospitality: they threw a wild-game dinner with all the trimmings. Statehood in 1959 opened up new vistas for the territory that had long been under federal dominion.

The earthquake: The Good Friday earthquake of 1964, which is now believed to have measured 9.2 on the Richter scale and was the most powerful earthquake ever recorded in North America, brought Alaskans together to work for a common cause. While the quake devastated many homes and businesses in Anchorage and in other communities, the reconstruction generated a mini boom and Anchorage emerged a new city.

Quakes still shake Anchorage and South Central Alaska occasionally. Reporters in the old *Anchorage Times* newsroom used to have a guessing game every time the building shook. The contest was to see who could forecast the correct Richter magnitude – before the official word came from the Alaska Tsunami Warning Center in nearby Palmer.

During the past decade Anchorage has strived to overcome the consequences of its boom-and-bust economy – unemployment, out-migration, poverty, to name a few. The city experienced another bust in the mid 1980s, which many residents said could have been avoided had the state spent its oil monies wisely; one bumper sticker read, "God, if you give us another oil windfall, we promise not to piss this one away." Today the economy is similar to that of other North American cities.

Rugged individualism: During the booms, Alaska's population was highly transient, with few people making it home for more than three years. The majority were lured by the promise of high paying jobs. The days of the Trans-Alaska pipeline (the 1970s) saw salaries

for construction workers in six-digit figures. More recently, people flocked into the state when they heard that Alaska was willing to share its oil profits with residents. Since 1982, the state has paid an annual dividend from oil revenues. The first year of the program resulted in $1,000 to each man, woman and child. And subsequent years have seen the dividend range from $300 to $800. Average salaries in Alaska are still higher than those in the Lower 48, but services and goods tend to cost a little more here as well.

A few people move to Anchorage, because they want the adventure of living in the "last frontier." This is a city where one needs only to walk out of the backdoor to find the wilderness. Many residents find no need to jump in the car to get away for the weekend – especially when it is common to view a moose right out of a living room window or see a bald eagle fly overhead. Wildlife is so abundant that no one even blinks when they see a moose grazing on the median between the lanes of the Seward High-

Merrill Field Airport.

176

way. The Anchorage president of the Safe Home Program for school children recently cited the only hazardous incident she could recall for the year: one morning a Safe Home mother looked out of her window and saw a moose and calf approaching 10 children waiting at the bus stop. The woman quickly threw on her housecoat and led the children into her house. Her main concern was not that the moose would attack, but that the children would try to pet them.

Discovering the city: Most visitors to Alaska find their way here. Anchorage is the air crossroads of the world with 17 major airlines offering direct flights from 39 cities. Anchorage is as close to Houston as it is to London or Tokyo. About 230 flights arrive daily at the Anchorage International Airport.

Like most American cities, the best way to see Anchorage is to rent a car and explore it on your own. There are several car rental firms in town: Avis, Hertz, Budget and Rent-a-Wreck. There is a bus system, the People Mover, although its routes cater to the local residents versus the visitor. The transit center is located on Sixth Avenue between "G" and "H" streets.

Local tour companies offer half-day and full-day tours of the city and surrounding area. Try Alaska Sightseeing Tours or Gray Line of Alaska.

If you are staying downtown, you can easily explore this section of the city on foot. Start at the **Visitor Information Center** at 546 West Fourth Avenue. Built in 1954, the log cabin is surrounded by flowering foliage in the summer. Here visitors can get information and talk to volunteers who are representing the Anchorage Convention and Visitors Bureau.

Next to it is the **Old City Hall**, a classic 1930s construction. A gallery on the main floor features a changing display of historic Anchorage photographs.

This is the older section of Anchorage, but the city itself is in its infancy compared to other cities in the world. Anchorage's first wood frame house, on Second Avenue near Elderberry Park, has been completely restored and is

e log cabin
sitor
ormation
nter.

open to the public. It belonged to **Oscar Anderson** and his family and was built on one of the first lots sold by the Corps of Engineers in 1915.

Also near Elderberry Park on Second Avenue is the start of the **Tony Knowles Coastal Trail**. The municipality has more than 120 miles (190 km) of bike trails through downtown and the outskirts of the city. The paved Coastal Trail is 11½ miles (19 km) long and parallels Knik Arm, continues past Westchester Lagoon, ending at Kincaid Park. Bicycling is a unique way to experience the city, and offers great views of the city and waters of the inlet, where migrating beluga whales are often seen at the surface. Ask at the log cabin about bicycles that are on free loan during the summer. Maps of all trails are also available here.

For a better understanding of Alaska and its history, stop at the **Anchorage Museum of History and Art**. The museum has recently been renovated and expanded with money from Projects 80s. There is an excellent permanent collection of Native art displayed in skylit galleries, and artifacts from Alaska's past. The museum shop sells books, prints and Alaska Native crafts.

Another Projects 80s site is the **Alaska Center for the Performing Arts**. This building is viewed by some as a monstrosity and by others as architecturally innovative, richly adding to the beauty of the downtown area. It is sandwiched between the glass-towered office buildings and ground-level older, wooden frame houses, which are sporadically placed on high-value land.

The Alaska Center is a hub of activities for the arts. Performances by the Anchorage Symphony Orchestra and the Anchorage Concert Association begin in the fall. The Concert Association each year presents five series in music and dance of world-class performers. Check the local newspapers and visitors' guides for a schedule of events.

Around the corner from the arts center is the **Alaska Experience Theater and Museum**. The theater features the film, *Alaska the Greatland*, shown on a 180-

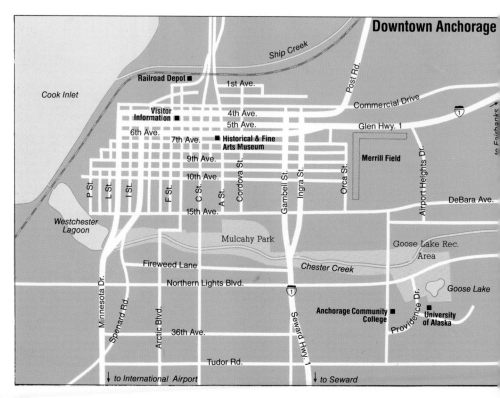

Downtown Anchorage

degree screen. For a firsthand look at the effects of the quake, visit **Earthquake Park** on the west side of the city. Here you can view an interpretative display of the 1964 quake. The park, now deserted land, was a residential neighborhood before the quake.

Downtown also has several shopping malls and major department stores that feature sections selling Alaskan souvenirs. Alaskan jade and gold nugget jewelry are popular buys. Or pick up an Alaskan T-shirt at **Petee's Quality Alaskan T-shirts** on Sixth Avenue.

For Alaskan art, visit the non-profit **Alaska Native Arts & Crafts Association** located in the Post Office Mall at 333 West Fourth Avenue. Other shops also carry Alaskan Native art, which is generally purchased directly from the artists. Works include an array of carved walrus ivory, soapstone and horn. Native women are known for their excellent basket-weaving skills, so look for their intricately made works. Authentic Native-made handicrafts are identified by a tag. There are two different designs: one has a silver hand and the other states "Authentic Native Handicraft." All other Alaskan artists' works are usually identified by a tag with a "silver map" symbol.

Local artists specialize in Alaskan-influenced paintings and photographs. Galleries offer a variety of these artists' works. Try **Artique, Ltd. Gallery** on "G" Street, or **Stephan Fine Arts Gallery** on Sixth Avenue for Alaskan-influenced paintings and photographs.

Downtown has several outstanding restaurants. However, you need to be aware that wherever you eat prices are steep. Services in Alaska are costly and most foodstuffs must be flown in.

For excellent seafood and a view of the inlet, try **Simon & Seaforts**. The neighboring **Elevation 92** also has a view and good food. **Sacks Cafe**, offers an intimate atmosphere and good lunches and dinner. Don't miss trying the Alaskan specialities like baked halibut or salmon and steamed crab.

For an evening out, try **The Marx Brothers Cafe** or the **Corsair**. The

chorage
seum of
story and
.

Crows Nest at the top of the Captain Cook offers gourmet cuisine and a formal atmosphere.

Anchorage has a variety of plush accommodations. The **Sheraton**, the **Anchorage Hilton**, **Hotel Captain Cook** and the **Westmark** are among the largest. There are also many smaller hotels and motels. The **Voyager Hotel**, located in the heart of downtown, has a quaint atmosphere and is economical. There are also over 100 bed and breakfast facilities. For more details contact **Alaska Private Lodgings**, 1236 W. 10th Avenue, Anchorage, AK 99501, (907) 258-1717.

Organizations and businesses planning conventions will be pleasantly surprised to find two excellent facilities in the city. Funded by the Projects 80s money, the **William A. Egan Civic and Convention Center** is located downtown on 5th Avenue. This 10,000-sq. feet (930-sq. meter) facility has a capacity of nearly 3,000. The lobby is decorated with Native art, including "Eskimo Spirit Carvings" and "Volcano Women" sculptures. The **George M. Sullivan Sports Arena** on Gambell Street hosts larger affairs such as major sporting events and entertainers on the concert circuit.

For a taste of nightlife in the last frontier, you can try **Chilkoot Charlies**. Don't bother with a coat and tie; this is where Alaskans go in their boots and jeans. The **Fly By Night Club** and **Midnight Express** also offer a taste of what life is like for the hardy. All clubs are located in Spenard, known to attract the adventuresome.

Around Anchorage: If you want to experience the Alaska outdoors, try fly-in fishing or a flightseeing trip. Excursions can easily be arranged by flight operators at **Lake Hood** or at **Merrill Field**. Not far from downtown near the international airport is **Lake Hood Air Harbor**, the busiest seaplane base in the world. On most summer days there are an average of 800 take-offs and landings. Channels on Lake Hood and Lake Spenard provided the runways for these seaplanes. Alaskans fly into the bush for fishing, hunting, hiking and a myriad

other activities. It is almost as common for an Alaskan to have a pilot's license as it is to have a driver's license – one out of 45.

On the southern edge of town, visitors can view a variety of waterfowl at the **Anchorage Coastal Wildlife Refuge** (locally known as Potter Marsh). The area is the nesting ground for migratory birds during the summer months. Bald eagles, arctic terns, trumpeter swans and many species of ducks are commonly spotted. Canada geese and mallards raise their young here. From the boardwalk above the channel, huge red salmon are visible from mid-July to September as they return to spawn in nearby Rabbit Creek.

Not far from Potter Marsh on the Seward Highway, visitors have a chance to view larger wildlife. During spring and summer it is common to see Dall sheep peering over the rocks of the adjacent cliffs at passing motorists. Several turnouts on this road allow visitors to watch the waters of the Turnagain Arm for white beluga whales. Stop at

One way around town.

Beluga Point Interpretive Site in spring and fall. Here you will find spotting scopes, benches and interpretive signs describing the surrounding area.

And if you want to contemplate the beauty and absolute mammoth size of Alaska, you can grab a takeout lunch in town and picnic at nearby **McHugh Creek Picnic Area**, located just a few miles down the road from Potter Marsh. Here you can see miles and miles down the inlet and view the majestic mountains located on the other shore. Or you can take a short hike on the trail.

At Anchorage's backdoor to the east is **Chugach State Park**; the park headquarters are located across from Potter Marsh in the **Potter Section House Historic Site**. Here you will find a railroad museum and an old rotary snow plow on the track behind the house.

The park covers 495,000 acres (200,500 hectares) and offers visitors a wide variety of opportunities to experience the Alaska outdoors without being too far away from civilization. Between June and September, the park rangers

along the Glenn Highway.

lead nature walks to various parts of the park. Each walk is about two hours and focuses on a specific activity, such as wildflower observation or bird-watching. For a recorded message call: (907) 694-6391.

The park also has a second headquarters at nearby **Eagle River**, north on the Glenn Highway from Anchorage. Only a 20-minute drive (14 miles/23 km) from downtown Anchorage, Eagle River is a popular suburbia. The drive through the lake-dotted valley is worth the trip itself, and once at the center you are likely to see Dall sheep and possibly a bear or two. During August the berries are plentiful and cross-country skiing is a popular winter activity.

Winter activities: Winters are long in Alaska, but this is a special time of the year for visitors. On Thanksgiving weekend, the University of Alaska, Anchorage hosts the **Great Alaska Shoot-Out**, an invitational college basketball tournament. Eight major college basketball teams from across the United States come to Anchorage to compete in the annual tournament. The tournament has gained national prominence and is televised via satellite.

The university is located on several acres of wooded land in the city. The four-year-old institution merged with the community college and now enrolls more than 10,000 each year.

After the holiday season, Anchorageites prepare for their own 10-day carnival in February – **Fur Rendezvous** or, as the locals call it, "Fur Rondy." (It is rumored no one could spell rendezvous!) It starts on the second Friday and ends on the third Sunday. This annual festival celebrates Alaska's frontier past, when fur trappers met to sell and trade their goods. Many came by sled dog over miles of frozen terrain to trade furs, tell tales and have a little friendly competition.

Today Anchorage's Fur Rondy features more than 150 events, ranging from the famous World Championship Sled Dog Race to the annual snowshoe softball tournament on the downtown Ninth Avenue park strip. Competition is held for the best snow sculpture (which draws competitors from as far away as Japan) and the fastest canoe in the Downhill Canoe Race. Other events include the traditional Eskimo blanket toss and the largest outdoor public fur auction in the United States. The highlight of the carnival is the **World Championship Sled Dog Race**. For three days competitors run heats totaling 75 miles. The racers start on 4th Avenue downtown, and continue on the city streets to the outskirts of town where they circle back. Dog mushing is the official state sport and competitors come from all over.

At the conclusion of Fur Rondy, the **Miners and Trappers Ball** is held. This is not a black-tie affair and everyone in the city is invited. Tickets must be purchased in advance. It is held in a huge warehouse and, people arrive in every conceivable attire. There is even a contest for the most unusual costume.

Fur Rondy is a great time to experience what life is *really* like in Alaska. It is a time of camaraderie among the local people and they welcome the chance to share the love of their land with visitors.

As the event is becoming more popular with visitors, it is best to book reservations well in advance. The Anchorage Convention and Visitors Bureau can be contacted for the date of the festival.

The last great race on earth – the **Iditarod Trail Sled Dog Race** – starts on the first Saturday in March. From downtown Anchorage competitors race to Nome, a distance of 1,049 miles (1,750 km). Generally the race takes about two weeks, but Martin Buser, who won in 1994, set a record-breaking time of 10 days. Mushers compete with teams of 12 to 18 dogs against themselves, each other and the wilderness. The success of four-time winner Susan Butcher originated a T-shirt which reads, "Alaska, where men are men and women win the Iditarod!"

The race started in 1973 to commemorate the 1925 event, when 20 mushers rushed life-saving serum to Nome, which was fighting a diphtheria epidemic. Today, the race receives television coverage and residents line the streets to cheer on the competitors.

Blanket toss at the Fur Rondy.

The **Knik Museum and Sled Dog Mushers Hall of Fame** is 40 miles (63 km) from Anchorage in Knik. Open between June and September, the museum displays the history of the Iditarod Trail and Alaskan mushers.

In Girdwood visitors can join the **Glacier Valley Tour** and experience the excitement of riding in a dog sled. The run passes scores of ancient, hanging glaciers and stops in the wilderness for a homemade lunch. Visitors even have a chance to "mush" the dogs and snowshoe during the lunch break.

Downhill and cross-country skiing in Anchorage can be found in **Russian Jack Springs Park** and **Centennial Park** – both have gentle slopes and rope tows for beginning skiers. **The Hilltop Ski Area** has a chairlift and is an excellent facility for beginning skiers. It also has night skiing and is accessible by public bus. For advanced skiers, **Alpenglow** at **Arctic Valley Ski Area** offers more challenging slopes. Two chair lifts, T-bar and three rope tows service the area which has over a 1,000 feet drop. Trails can be very steep and maintenance is sometimes questionable.

Alaska's largest and most popular ski area – **Alyeska Resort & Ski Area** – is 40 miles (64 km) southeast of Anchorage in Girdwood. With a vertical drop of more than 2,800 feet, it caters to all levels of skiers and is a full-service resort with both day and night skiing. The area recently installed a high-speed gondola that whisks passengers to the top of the slope and has a quad chair lift as well as four doubles. The new seven-story Alyeska Prince Hotel opened in early 1995, offering more than 300 rooms, formal and informal dining, an indoor pool, a health club and meeting facilities.

For the cross-country skier, Anchorage offers 141 miles (230 km) of trails. **Kincaid Point** in Campbell Park on Raspberry Road has 18 miles (26 km) of Nordic ski trails, five of them lighted. **Russian Jack Springs Park** has 4 miles (7 km) of lighted trails. Near Service High School and Hilltop Ski Area, another trail is lit for skiers.

In Chugach National Forest more than 200 miles (234 km) of hiking trails which extend from Anchorage to the Kenai Peninsula are open to the cross-country skier. The trail at the top of Upper Huffman Road offers breathtaking views of the city and is manageable for skiers of any level. To get to it take the Seward Highway to the O'Malley turnoff going east, continue towards the mountains turning on to Hillside Drive, and making a left on Upper Huffman to the trailhead.

Each year the **Nordic Ski Club of Anchorage** offers several one-day ski train trips beginning in February. The train leaves the Alaska Railroad terminal in the morning and heads south past Portage into the Chugach Mountains and Grandview Glacier, where it stops and skiers head out over unspoiled snow. The train heads back at 5pm. On the way back weary skiers make a comeback in the polka car which gyrates as wall-to-wall bodies bounce to the rhythm of the live band.

An hour's drive north of Anchorage is an excellent cross-country ski area

og team rosses nchorage uring the litarod.

with a historical flavor. **Hatcher Pass** is at the heart of the majestic Talkeetna Mountains off the Glenn Highway on Fishhook Road. At the turn of the century **Independence Mine** was a hub of gold-mining activity. Today it is a state historic park and its abandoned buildings and old mining machinery have become landmarks of the past. The area has miles of treeless groomed ski trails and on a clear day you can see all the way down the valley to the city of Palmer (20 miles/134 km). Accommodations are available in the small lodge at the entrance to the area. For more information call: (907) 745-5897.

Heading south: With only two roads leading in and out of Anchorage, selecting a day trip is easy. You either head north or south.

Heading south on the Seward Highway, pay a visit to Girdwood, Crow Creek Mine and Portage Glacier. The drive parallels the **Turnagain Arm**, an extension of the Cook Inlet. Numerous turnouts along the 40-mile (66-km) drive to Girdwood offer spectacular views of both scenery and wildlife. Look out for Dall sheep, moose and beluga whales.

Girdwood is a quaint community which sees an influx of tourists in the summer and skiers in the winter. A ride up the Alyeska Ski Resort chairlift on a clear day provides an incredible view of the surrounding mountains and the inlet. The town has a variety of shops worth wandering around, which offer traditional Alaskan souvenirs.

Outside of Girdwood, three miles up Crow Creek Road, is **Crow Creek Mine**. The placer mine and its eight original buildings are listed on the National Register of Historic Sites. They represent the first non-Native settlement in the area. Visitors can pan for gold in this scenic setting. For the robust type, nearby Crow Pass Trail climbs through beautiful mountain valleys. Be sure to have some basic hiking gear before attempting any hike. Weather in Alaska can change dramatically and hikers should always be prepared.

Continuing down the Seward Highway, at **Twenty Mile River**, visitors

Skiers at Turnagain Arm.

184

can see arctic terns, bald eagles, mew gulls and moose from the observation platform. Plaques on the platform have information on the various species.

About 10 miles (16 km) past Girdwood is the turnoff for Portage Glacier. On the right side of the road is **Explorer Glacier**. The turnout has an excellent photography vantage point. Stop at the bridge over Williwaw Creek to observe salmon spawning from late-July to mid-September. At the end of the road is the **Begich Boggs Visitor Center**. Be prepared for a highly dramatic view, as Portage Lake with its mammoth floating blue icebergs seems to appear out of nowhere.

The center has an interpretative display on how glaciers are formed. It even has an iceberg on display so visitors can touch the ancient ice. (Due to the slow formation of the glacial ice, it also melts very slowly.) During the summer, it is common to see campers pluck out ice chunks for their coolers. At the center, you can view a film on wildlife and the geology of the surrounding area.

There are several glaciers in Portage Valley with many trails where visitors can view numerous glacial features, including wild flowers and plant life. Take the short walk into **Byron Glacier**. Signs near Portage Glacier Lodge mark the road to the trailhead. Black bears are commonly seen in the area. Portage Glacier is the turnaround point for this trip to the south. However, visitors with more time may want to head for the Kenai Peninsula and Seward or Homer. Seward is about a three-hour drive from Anchorage and getting to Homer takes four to five hours by car (see *Prince William Sound, pages 143–149,* and *Kenai Peninsula, pages 165–171*).

On the way back to Anchorage stop at the **Bird House Bar** (near Bird Creek), a small sinking log cabin with its walls plastered with business cards and some unmentionables. Ptarmigan, the state bird, are commonly seen, so be sure to ask the bartender to point one out.

Heading North: Traveling on the Glenn Highway north of Anchorage on a day trip, visitors have an opportunity to ob-

Kayak racers.

serve the cultural remnants of Alaska's past and also to enjoy several scenic areas in Palmer and the fertile Matanuska Valley. In Eagle River, you should stop at the **Eagle River Visitor Center** in Chugach State Park. Continuing on the Glenn Highway, you will see beautiful **Mirror Lake Wayside** area on the right. Here if you're brave you can swim in the icy water on a warm day or ice fish in the winter. A mile further takes you to the entrance of **Thunderbird Falls Trailhead**. This is a pleasant 1-mile walk to the rushing falls.

Eklutna Lake is Anchorage's largest. There is a campground and several trails to **Eklutna Glacier**, whose waters feed the lake, and good wildlife-viewing and berry-picking in the area.

Anchorage's oldest building may be the **St. Nicholas Russian Orthodox Church**, part of Eklutna Village Historic Park, on the Eklutna turnoff, off the Glenn Highway. It was built with hand-hewn logs and the surrounding spirit houses represent the interaction between the Natives and the Russians.

This was the site of the first Dena'ina Indian settlement east of the Knik Arm, around 1650. The "spirit" houses show how the Native beliefs were mixed with Russian orthodoxy. Spirit houses were placed over traditional graves and contained personal items to help the spirit in the next world. A three-bar orthodox cross was placed at the foot of the grave. Small spirit houses indicate the resting place of a child and a large house with a smaller one inside means a mother and child were buried together. A picket fence around a spirit house means the deceased was not a Dena'ina.

Further down the Glenn are the **Eklutna Flats**. Moose are often spotted grazing in the area. This is the entrance to the Matanuska Valley, the breadbasket of Southcentral Alaska, where wheat, barley, oats and other grains are grown. Local markets sell Mat-Su Valley carrots, cabbage and potatoes. Here you will find the fabled cabbage weighing more than 80 lbs (37 kg) displayed at the Alaska State Fair. Large-sized produce is a result of the territory's maximum

Experimental Farm near Palmer.

19½ hours of daylight in the summer.

To really get a feel for the valley and a unique Alaskan experience, visitors can take a horseback ride and savor the beauty of the area while riding through the Bradley-Kepler Lakes system.

In Palmer stop at the **Visitor Information Center and Museum**. More than 200 local artists have their works on assignment here. This small town of 3,000 residents is located in a majestic rural setting reminiscent of what many visitors visualize Anchorage to be. Palmer is the site for the **Alaska State Fair**. The fair features the famous valley produce and the largest cabbage wins the blue ribbon – a cabbage must weigh at least 75 lbs (34 kg) to enter the competition.

Displays also include farm animals and locally handmade items. A carnival operates and foodstalls line the runway so visitors can literally eat their way from one end to the other. The 11-day event attracts more than 200,000 people a year and shouldn't be missed.

North of Palmer is the turn off for Hatcher Pass and Independence Mine. A mile after the turn off is the **Musk Ox Farm** with the world's only domesticated musk-ox. In the summer, visitors can watch the newborns romp with their parents in the pasture. The coats of these shaggy animals produce *qiviut* – a rare musk oxen wool. The material is used by the Alaska Natives to hand-knit hats, mittens, gloves and scarves in traditional patterns. The *qiviut* is sent to villages around the state and then returned as finished articles to be sold. It is believed that *qiviut* is the warmest material in the world. The **Oomingmak-Musk Ox Producers Co-op** in downtown Anchorage on "H" Street, also sells *qiviut* products.

Beyond Anchorage: For visitors wishing to get off the beaten track, a day trip on the **Alaska Railroad** is just the answer. The railroad offers excursions to Talkeetna or Seward and longer packages to Denali National Park and/or Fairbanks. The depot is located on the northeast corner of Second Avenue and "E" Street.

The Alaska Railroad has been operating for more than 65 years and runs from Seward on the Kenai Peninsula to Fairbanks in the Interior. Traveling by railroad takes the visitor through areas that are not accessible to other modes of transportation. Besides carrying fee-paying passengers, the railroad brings goods from food and fuel to sled dogs and building materials to those living in the isolated bush.

The Alaska Railroad is the only one in the United States to provide flag stop service. This means passengers may flag down the train anywhere and also alight anywhere along the line. This is an invaluable service for people living in the bush, and it also offers the visitor a unique opportunity to see the Alaskan outback.

Packages include a day trip to **Talkeetna**, a three-hour ride through valleys and spectacular gorges. A 10-minute walk will get you from one side of town to the other. Stop at the **Fairview Inn** for a drink with the locals and hear some great Alaska tales. Talkeetna is the jumping-off spot for climbers to Mount McKinley in the summer. Women may want to peruse the "bachelors' book" to see the local offerings. Or better yet, single women can attend the annual bachelors' ball held the first weekend in December where eligible men auction themselves off to the highest bidder for an evening of dancing.

Another one-day excursion offered by the Alaska railroad is to **Seward**. This four-hour trip parallels the Turnagain Arm for 60 miles (100 km) and then cuts into the heart of the mountains. The tracks traverse deep valleys and come to within a half a mile of both Spencer and Trail Glacier before descending to Seward on Prince William Sound. Overnight trips which include a cruise of Kenai Fjords National Park and lodging are also available.

Visitors with a few days to spare can take the railroad trip to Mount McKinley or Fairbanks. Packages are available for a minimum of one overnight which includes round-trip rail transportation from Anchorage, lodging in Denali National Park and a bus tour of the park. Extensions to Fairbanks can be made.

FAIRBANKS AND THE INTERIOR

"Gold!" The cry has lured men and women to the Interior for nearly a century. At first, the passionate quest, the lust, the hunger was surfeited by a stampede and a handful of valuable nuggets. The golden never-dreams are history now, but the Siren of the Interior still summons the adventurer. It whispers yet of gold; those who listen to it and enter the Interior are forever haunted, because they have found truth in these promises.

There *is* gold in the Interior, gilding every aspen leaf in the autumn explosion of color, glancing off the wingtips of geese, shimmering in the river current as it flows into a blazing sunset. Gold? It splashes across the midnight sky as the aurora and dances as moonlight over the hulking white shoulders of mountain peaks. And for a few days each spring, this gold lies strewn like nuggets, captured for a moment in a carpet of wildflowers. It is gold to the eye of the beholder.

Those who linger, even momentarily, in the Interior find that even its people are a part of this extraordinary wealth, possessing what can only be called "hearts of gold." Many an ill-equipped gold miner would have suffered horribly had it not been for the Athabascan Natives who unquestioningly provided food and shelter for these sometimes unruly explorers, then quietly moved on themselves as the rush for riches intensified. Folks in the Interior carry on this tradition of caring and generosity, and their warm-heartedness welcomes the traveler back again and again to the edge of the frontier.

Land of great contrasts: The Interior of Alaska, that one-third of the state north of the Alaska Range and south of the Brooks Range, is an area of stark contrasts. Denali (Mount McKinley), "the Great One," 20,320 feet (6,195 meters) and snow-capped year-round, towers above the Tanana and Yukon river valleys where summer temperatures can

Preceding pages: Fairbanks in winter. Below, at the airport.

reach 100°F (38°C). The Alaska Range is girdled with miles of glaciers, while in the valleys below rolling hills of white spruce, birch and aspen fold into scraggly stands of black spruce, willow tangles and muskeg.

Three hours and 42 minutes of sunlight is a meager wage for those who winter in the Interior. Temperatures plummet to –30 and –40°F (–40°C), with the average December temperature registering –14°F (–26°C) in Fairbanks. An unpleasant side effect of temperatures below –20°F (–29°C) is ice fog, which hangs in the still air. The fog results from a temperature inversion trapping ice crystals, smoke and exhaust in a blanket of cold air which stays close to the ground.

But then there's summer, with daylight lingering for up to 22 hours. In July, when the average temperature in Fairbanks can be more than 61°F (16°C), it is hard to recall the cold winter nights when the aurora borealis screamed across the clear, crisp sky and everyone huddled by the wood stove for warmth and reassurance that he was not alone in the dark.

Fairbanks International: You are likely to arrive at **Fairbanks International Airport**. Before descending the escalator to claim your luggage, study the series of nine paintings titled "*Our Heritage*" by Rusty Heurlin. This history of the Eskimos was first sketched by Heurlin in 1946. The complete set of 19 paintings was completed in the 1970s in Heurlin's home in Ester.

The Fairbanks Airport offers all standard airport services but you should be prepared to handle your own luggage; there is no porter service. Don't be dismayed; it is only a short scrape to the doors and transportation to town. Take a moment to survey the other luggage being off-loaded in Fairbanks. Backpacks, bicycles, folding boats, dogs, dry fish and the old Alaskan travel favorite, the cardboard box, will all be present.

Many hotels and motels offer free transportation for their guests and will send a vehicle if called. Taxis are usually plentiful and limousine (actually

ft, ngsters at e Malemute loon. ght, bars, rbers and keries.

usually a van) service is also available.

At the heart of downtown Fairbanks: Now that you are settled, where to begin? Without hesitation, head for the site from which **Fairbanks** erupted, near the corner of what is now Cushman Street and First Avenue. This is the heart of downtown Fairbanks, the center of a borough that includes 77,000 people and the towns of North Pole, Fox, Ester and Salcha.

If you are visiting the Interior in summer, try conjuring up an image of winter, low light reflecting blue off the snow-covered riverbed. Summer weather is glorious, with temperatures as high as 96°F (36°C). (No, this is not a misprint.) Travelers may even experience some difficulty sleeping with all the light. The most practical advice is don't sleep until you're tired, but enjoy the late evening light – this is the season that makes the cold dark winter worth enduring.

You will also discover that the later evening is a wonderful time for photography. Light of this quality is experienced at lower latitudes for only a few moments around sunrise and sunset. In Alaska's Interior, the special glow hovers for hours, casting gigantic shadows and ethereal reflections.

The founding of Fairbanks: On August 26, 1901, E.T. Barnette had just been deposited, along with 130 tons (130,000 kg) of equipment, into the wilderness, on a high wooded bank along the Chena River. How did this river boat captain, dog musher and aspiring entrepreneur manage to become marooned on this desolate piece of real estate? The answer has all the ingredients of a true Alaskan story...

Barnette journeyed to the Klondike in 1897, taking what was considered the rich man's route. He sailed from Seattle to St. Michael, then was to travel by sternwheeler to Dawson. But when he arrived in St. Michael, the sternwheeler had already departed. Undaunted, Barnette and several others bought a dilapidated sternwheeler, elected Barnette captain, and set off for Dawson. Barnette piloted the craft to Circle and finally arrived in Dawson via dogsled, **Early river transport.**

after freeze-up. He prospered that winter selling much-needed supplies to men in the gold fields, but the Klondike was too tame for the likes of this man.

During the winter of 1901, Barnette traveled south to Seattle, arranging the coup that he speculated would make him a rich man. He and a partner purchased $20,000 worth of equipment to outfit a trading post, not in the Klondike but at the half-way point on the Eagle-to-Valdez trail. Barnette considered this to be a strategically sound location upon which to create the "Chicago of the North," the industrial hub of the territory. At this point, the trail crossed the Tanana River, and he planned to accommodate the overland, as well as the river, traffic.

Barnette shipped the equipment to St. Michael and departed for Circle to purchase a sternwheeler. He arrived in St. Michael without incident, but there Lady Luck abandoned the entrepreneur. The sternwheeler struck a submerged rock, and the bottom was torn from the boat. At this point, Barnette was more than

1,000 miles (1,600 km) from his destination with 260,000 lbs (120,000 kg) of equipment, including a horse and food, no ready cash and a worthless sternwheeler. It was time for another partner. He convinced the customs agent in St. Michael to co-sign notes and made him a full partner.

Barnette struck a deal with the captain of the sternwheeler *Lavelle Young* to take him to Tanacross (Tanana Crossing). The fine print on the contract stated that if the *Lavelle Young* went beyond the point where the Chena joined the Tanana River and could go no farther, Captain E.T. Barnette would disembark with his entire load of supplies, no matter where they were.

As destiny would have it, the *Lavelle Young* could not float through the Tanana shallows called Bates Rapids, so the captain steamed up the Chena River, convinced by the desperate Barnette that it would join again with the Tanana River. It did not.

The scene was set on August 26, 1901. Captain Barnette off-loaded his

ore recent ansport aving for awson.

full kit on a high bank with a good stand of trees. It seemed that his string of ill-luck could get no worse.

No-credit purchases: Two down-and-out prospectors watched the progress of the sternwheeler in the Chena from a hillside, now called Pedro Dome, about 20 miles (32 km) north of Fairbanks. The miners had found some "color" but no major strike, and were faced with the frustration of a 330-mile (530-km) round-trip hike back to Circle City to replenish much-needed supplies. The prospectors, Felix Pedro, an Italian immigrant, and Tom Gilmore eagerly set off for the stranded boat, hoping to purchase necessities.

Barnette was shocked to see the prospectors but pleased to sell them anything but the transaction didn't much improve his mood. Still possessed by his wild scheme to establish a trading post at Tanacross, Barnette sent for Frank Cleary, his wife Isabelle's brother, in Montana. Frank was to guard the cache of supplies while Captain and Mrs. Barnette returned to Seattle to obtain a boat capable of traveling the remaining 200 miles (320 km) up the Tanana to Tanacross. Cleary's orders were simple, "No credit." The Barnettes departed for Valdez and points south in March 1903, braving the –40°F (–40°C) temperature.

Upon arriving in Seattle, Barnette began with single-minded determination to raise the necessary cash to buy a boat and more supplies. Meanwhile, back at camp, his brother-in-law Cleary broke the only rule, "No Credit." He decided to outfit Felix Pedro again, on credit this time because Pedro had no collateral. Cleary's decision proved wise and changed the history of the Interior; just three months later, Pedro quietly announced to Cleary that he had struck pay dirt.

The Barnettes returned to the Chena camp six weeks later and immediately abandoned all thoughts of moving to Tanacross. Here was Barnette with two shiploads of supplies in the midst of the next gold rush. There was money to be made. The rush was on!

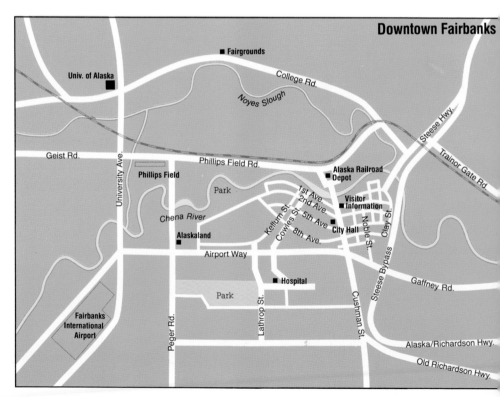

Hundreds of gold-hungry prospectors swarmed out of Circle City, Dawson and Nome, scurrying to the new and, they were told, the richest gold fields in the north. By the time they arrived, much of the promising land was already staked, most of it by "pencil miners" like Barnette who secured the claims only for the purpose of selling them later. These clever businessmen staked as many as 100 claims of 20 acres (8 hectares) each, thus controlling vast amounts of potentially rich ground. And still the stampede continued.

On the return trip from Seattle, Barnette had spoken with Judge Wickersham about naming his little settlement. The judge offered his support to Barnette if he would use the name "Fairbanks," after Senator Charles Fairbanks from Indiana who later became Vice President under Teddy Roosevelt. So Fairbanks it was.

The community of Fairbanks in 1903 consisted of Barnette's trading post, numerous tents, a few log houses and wooden sidewalks where the mud was particularly deep. What a fine tribute to the senator from Indiana.

Past meets present: A stone monument near the **Fairbanks Convention and Visitors' Bureau** at 550 First Avenue, tel (907) 456-5774 or (800) 327-5774 marks the place where the town of Fairbanks was born. This is an appropriate beginning for present-day explorers also.

The well-constructed log building is open 8.30am–8pm every day during summer, and Monday through Friday during the off-season. Besides offering hundreds of brochures on Alaskan attractions, there is a visitor information telephone number, (907) 456-INFO. The recorded message is available at any hour, is updated daily, and may include information on events as diverse as an evening opera performance or the starting time of a dog race. The bureau also provides a free, comprehensive visitor's guide to the Interior and a brochure for a self-guided tour of town.

Stroll through town: Several commercial sightseeing outings of Fairbanks' downtown area are available, but why

gh-noon
d sub-zero
downtown
irbanks.

not design your own personal itinerary?

Start at the Visitors' Bureau on First Avenue. Here you should notice the monument to E.T. Barnette and the obelisk that marks Milepost 1,523 (2,450 km) of the Alaska Highway. The milepost is hidden behind posing tourists most of the summer. Even with the completion of the Dalton Highway to Prudhoe Bay, Fairbanks has, since World War II, been touted as the end of the highway. Fairbanksans like to say that this is where the road ends and the wilderness begins.

Amble west along the **Chena River** for a walking tour of Fairbanks, crossing Cushman Street at the lights. The first stop is **St. Matthew Episcopal Church** at 1029 First Avenue. The land between Cushman and Cowles was the site of E.T. Barnette's trading post, sawmill and home. The log building on the corner of Cowles and First Avenue was built in 1909 as the first library in Fairbanks.

The altar of St. Matthew was carved from a single piece of wood, but no one is quite sure of the origin of the huge chunk. The stained glass windows are of special interest; they portray images of Jesus, Mary and Joseph with dark hair and Alaskan Native features.

Retrace your steps for a scant two-and-one-half blocks and turn onto Wickersham, continuing south until Fourth Avenue. Wickersham Street is named for Judge Wickersham, who "suggested" the name Fairbanks to E.T. Barnette. Turn left on Fourth Avenue, walk one block, then cross Barnette Street. It's a congested thoroughfare now, but perhaps Barnette's sighs can still be heard above the whir of his city.

The next block of Fourth Avenue between Barnette and Cushman was known as **The Line**. To ensure that no one unwittingly wandered into this sinful area, the booming city of Fairbanks erected tall, Victorian, wooden gates at both ends of the avenue. Both sides of the scandalous boulevard were lined with small log cabins housing prostitutes. The Line is sadly gone now, replaced by the less-colorful downtown

Contestants in a "Pedro look-alike" contest.

post office, Woolworths, the Elks Club and a parking lot.

Cross Cushman Street again and continue on Fourth Avenue for one more block to Lacey Street. And if you haven't guessed where the names originated, Judge Wickersham, always alert for an opportunity to win political friends, requested that the streets be named for Congressmen Francis Cushman of Tacoma and John F. Lacey of Iowa.

The Ice Palace: On the block bounded by Lacey and Noble streets and Third and Fourth avenues towers the "Ice Palace." Officially the **Northward Building**, it is the first steel-girded skyscraper built in the Interior, and became the inspiration of Edna Ferber's novel *The Ice Palace*. The Ice Palace in the novel is a modern skyscraper built by a ruthless millionaire named Czar Kennedy. Fairbanks's locals also recognized in Czar Kennedy the reflection of prominent businessman, developer and politician, Captain Austin E. Lathrop.

Turn north (toward the river), walk two blocks to Second Avenue, turn left,

and head toward Cushman Street. Urban renewal has taken its toll here, with the remaining storefronts protruding like the teeth of a Halloween Jack o'lantern.

The next stop is **Co-op Plaza** at 535 Second Avenue. Of 1927 vintage, this building was Captain Lathrop's gift to the people of Fairbanks. Before then, the structures in Fairbanks were constructed of wood because, it was believed, no other material could withstand the test of a −60°F (−51°C) winter. This concrete affair was originally the Empress Theater, outfitted by Captain Lathrop with 670 seats and the first pipe organ in the Interior. A common cry in Fairbanks is "Meet me at the Co-op," so be sure to take a look. People visiting Fairbanks from the villages often eat at the diner and visit the specialty shops.

During the mid-1970s, while the Trans-Alaska Oil Pipeline was under construction, Second Avenue was the scene of incessant activity. Bars were packed at all hours, and the reputation of the avenue rivaled The Line of gold-rush days. Workers flew to town during rest periods from remote construction camps only to spend most of their time (and money) along Second Avenue.

Venerable institutions: The **Old Federal Courthouse** is just south of the intersection of Second Avenue and Cushman. When Judge Wickersham officially moved the Federal Court to Fairbanks in 1904, he built the courthouse on this piece of real estate, donated by E.T. Barnette, securing the future of the young settlement. The original wooden structure burned, and the present building was completed in 1934. It included the first elevator in the Interior. Federal offices soon required more space and were relocated, leaving the building open for tasteful remodelling into office space and shops.

The **Key Bank** at the corner of First and Cushman was started as a First National Bank on that very site in June 1905. Square Sam Bonnifield and his brother John founded the bank, now the oldest national bank in Alaska. "Square Sam" was given his nickname because he had been an honest gambler in Circle City, and miners could turn their backs

e true
ginals.

while he was weighing a poke of gold.

Turn toward the river and stroll across the Cushman Street Bridge pausing perhaps for a momentary glance into the Chena River. The **Immaculate Conception Church** stands directly across the river from the Visitor Information Center. The church, interestingly enough, originally stood on the opposite side of the river at the corner of First and Dunkle. In 1911, Father Francis Monroe decided it should be closer to the hospital on the north side of the Chena. Many good Catholics pitched in to move the building across the frozen river. Visitors are welcome inside to enjoy the stained glass windows and the pressed tin ceiling paneling.

One-half block north on the opposite side of the street is the *Fairbanks Daily News Miner* building at 200 N. Cushman Street. The *News Miner* publishes seven days a week, carrying on a long newspaper tradition. Judge Wickersham published the first newspaper, headlined the *Fairbanks Miner*, on May 9, 1903. All seven copies sold for $5 each, making the first edition one of the most expensive in the world.

Fairbanks offers a cornucopia of perfect gifts for the traveler. Gold-nugget jewelry, always a favorite, is priced by the pennyweight (dwt) with 20 dwt equal to one troy ounce (1 dwt = 1.555 grams). Remember, nuggets used in jewelry command a premium price which is above raw gold.

Native handicrafts from the Interior are also treasured souvenirs. The Authentic Native Handicraft Symbol assures visitors that they are buying the genuine article. Favorite items include beaded slippers, beaded mittens or gloves, birch bark baskets, porcupine quill jewelry and fur dolls.

The Alaskan Interior produces some of the finest lynx, marten, wolverine, fox and wolf fur in the world. Fairbanks is the place to purchase raw or tanned furs and fur coats, jackets and hats. Be aware of customs regulations if you are taking these items out of the United States – and of potentially very strong moral disapproval in your home town.

The Chena River in downtown Fairbanks.

A wildlife trail: Save a little shoe leather for a very special wildlife trail situated within the city limits of Fairbanks. **Creamers Field** at 1300 College Road was originally a homestead until Charles Creamer set up a dairy farm in 1920. The 250 acres (101 hectares) remained in active production until the land was purchased by the state and was set aside as a waterfowl refuge in 1967. While hiking the nature trails you can see many species of animals, including diving ducks, shore birds, cranes, fox or even a moose. The real show, however, is in late-April/early-May and again in August/September when the sandhill cranes, Canadian honkers and ducks congregate in the field.

Alaskaland, a 44-acre (18-hectare) city park at the corner of Airport Way and Peger Road, is a snapshot of life in the Golden Heart of Alaska. The park is open year-round with summer hours from 11am–9pm daily. For information write or call PO Box 71267, Fairbanks, AK 99707, tel: (907) 459-1087.

The **Mining Valley** on the west end of the park contains many machines used in the hills around the area to extract gold. Sluice boxes, dredge buckets, a stamp mill and other equipment lend an air of authenticity to the display.

Be sure to stroll through the **Mining Town**, which includes an assortment of original structures rescued from the boom-town period. Every building is a piece of history, including Judge Wickersham's home, the first frame house in Fairbanks which was built by the judge in 1904 as a surprise for his wife. It is a rather melancholy reminder of life in early Fairbanks, as the bedridden Mrs Wickersham spent most of that summer sleeping in a tent; fresh air was thought to aid the cure of tuberculosis.

Even the building now housing the **Park Office** had a spicy past as a brothel in Nenana. The **Gold Rush Town** is packed with small shops containing a delightful array of unique crafts.

The **Sternwheeler Nenana** is listed in the National Register of Historic Places because so few of these vessels remain. It was a classic paddlewheeler

with a colorful history on the waterways of the Interior. Imagine leaning back in the captain's chair, the stack belching sparks, and the crew scurrying about the deck as you maneuver the craft through the Yukon River.

Along the Chena River within the park you'll find the **Alaska Native Village** display, with artifacts as well as demonstrations of crafts still used in remote parts of the Interior.

If you get hungry, follow your nose to the **Alaska Salmon Bake** (5pm–9pm daily, mid-May through mid-September), great value for a tasty Alaskan meal. King salmon, halibut and ribs are grilled over an open alder fire for that special flavor. After dinner, saunter over to the **Palace Saloon** and enjoy your favorite beverage accompanied by can-can girls.

University pursuits: The **University of Alaska Fairbanks** (UAF) is located on a bluff overlooking Fairbanks and the Tanana Valley. Established in 1917 as the Alaska Agricultural College and School of Mines, UAF is the main cam-pus for a system that operates four-year satellites in Anchorage and Juneau. Emphasis on high latitude and Alaskan problems have earned UAF an excellent reputation.

The 2,500-acre (1,000-hectare) campus is a town unto itself, complete with its own post office, radio station, TV station, fire department and the traditional college facilities. A trip to the UAF campus is worthwhile if only to relax at the turnout on Yukon Drive and absorb the view of the Alaska Range in the distance. The large marker, complete with mountain silhouettes and elevations, assists you in identifying all those splendid peaks fringing the southern horizon – yes, including Denali.

The **Otto William Geist Museum** on the UAF campus is a must for visitors to the Interior. Displays include prehistoric objects extricated during mining operations from the permanently frozen ground. One recent addition is a 36,000-year-old bison carcass found near Fairbanks, preserved in the permafrost, complete with skin and flesh. The Na-

Left, local delicacy. **Below**, chain saw carving a wooden miner.

tive Cultures displays are an educational introduction to the Athabascan, Eskimo, Aleut and Tlingit cultures. The collections date back to 1926 when the president of the school assigned Geist the task of amassing Eskimo artifacts.

During summer, free guided tours of the museum are available Monday through Friday; telephone (907) 474-7505 for information. Tours are also provided at the **Geophysical Institute** during which a spectacular film of the aurora borealis is shown.

A free UAF off-campus tour is offered on Yankovich Road about one mile (2 km) from Ballaine Road at the **Large Animal Research Facility**, formerly known as the Musk Ox Farm. These woolly prehistoric creatures graze in research pastures together with moose, reindeer and caribou.

Wheel into the past: Riverboats have never been far removed from the history of Fairbanks, since E.T. Barnette's load of supplies was put ashore. Jim and Mary Binkley continue the tradition with river tours aboard the *Discovery III*. The four-hour excursion begins at 8.45am and 2pm each day, covering 20 miles (32 km) on the Chena and Tanana rivers. The Binkleys' narration brings history to life along the river banks. To reach the sternwheeler's port of departure at the landing off Dale Road, take Airport Way toward the airport, turn onto Dale Road, and watch for the signs. Reservations are recommended.

As you float by the **Pump House Restaurant**, take note for later. Excellent family-style meals, mining decor and turn-of-the century atmosphere combine to create a noteworthy dining experience. This historical site was built by the F.E. Company to supply water to diggings in Ester.

The gold dredges in the Fairbanks area have been mute since 1966 and now stand like aging, silent dinosaurs, with necks outstretched, waiting. The dredges, like so many pieces of Fairbanks history, are strewn about the hills waiting for some new purpose.

The easiest gold dredge to visit is **Gold Dredge No. 8**, rusting at Mile 9

oung musk
x at the
nimal
esearch
acility.

(15 km) Old Steese Highway, ironically only 200 yards (183 meters) from the Trans-Alaska Oil Pipeline. The five-deck ship is more than 250 feet (76 meters) long and displaced 1,065 tons as it plied the gold pay dirt of Goldstream and Engineer creeks. Tours of the dredge are available all summer. The $10 admission fee includes gold panning; keep what you pan.

You may want to visit Mile 28.7 (46 km) Steese Highway. Walk on the easy trail through the dredged tailings (piles of crushed rock) opposite **Chatanika Lodge** for a topside view.

Only the true dredge aficionado will care to explore the other three dredges in the area. The one on **Nome Creek** off Mile 57 (92 km) Steese Highway requires a long hike before reaching the dismantled piece. The site resembles a complete inventory of the disassembled behemoth spread over about 3 acres (1.2 hectares). The second dredge is off Mile 2 (3.2 km) Murphy Dome Road, but on the other side of the valley. The final apparatus is off Mile 6 (9.7 km) Murphy Dome Road on **Nugget Creek**. Prepare for a strenuous hike made even more difficult by blood-thirsty mosquitoes.

The big ditch: Large-scale mining demands water, lots of water. J.M. Davidson, to bring water from the Chatanika River to the diggings on Fox, Cleary and Goldstream creeks, proposed building an 80-mile (130-km) water system composed of 72 miles (116 km) of canals and seven miles (12 km) of huge pipes that created siphons to raise the water over the hills. A 5,000-kilowatt power plant was erected, as well as six or seven dredges, and shops and camps to maintain the equipment and house the crews.

During construction of the **Davidson Ditch**, portions of the Steese Highway were built to facilitate access. The "Ditch" was completed in 1930 and was capable of carrying 56,000 gallons (254,500 liters) of water per minute. After the dredges were put to rest, this system continued to generate electricity until the Flood of 1967 destroyed it.

Remnants of the Davidson Ditch are visible along the Steese Highway in

Gold dredge at Nome.

several places. One of the most accessible is at Mile 57 (91 km), where a turnout guides you within a few feet of a decaying siphon.

Over the river and through the woods: Outdoor adventure is the glue that binds people to the land in the Interior. The mountains, rivers and valleys offer unparalleled opportunities for hiking, canoeing, hunting and fishing.

Three excellent sources of information you should not ignore when planning a hike in the Interior are the State Division of Parks, the Bureau of Land Management (BLM) and the United States Geologic Survey map distribution center in the Federal building in Fairbanks. Armed with these sources, hikers can head for the hills well-informed.

One stimulating trek, the **Pinnell Mountain National Recreation Trail**, a 24-mile (39-km) spine connecting 12 Mile Summit and Eagle Summit on the Steese Highway, is a challenging example. The trail is defined with rock cairns along mountain ridges and high passes.

Caribou migrate through here in summer, and an occasional moose or bear may claim the path. The trail promises stunning vistas of the Alaska Range, the White Mountains and the Tanana Hills. Due to the elevation, 3,600 feet (1,100 meters) at Eagle Summit, hikers are treated to nearly 24 hours of daylight during the summer solstice.

The usually blue skies of summer coupled with hundreds of miles of wild and scenic rivers make water travel a natural pastime. Canoeing offers an idyllic opportunity to observe game animals undisturbed as the boat slips silently past. You couldn't manage to cram your canoe into the suitcase? Never fear. Several rental establishments have anticipated your needs. In Fairbanks, try Canoe Alaska, Beaver Sports, Independent Rental or 7 Bridges, Boats and Bikes.

With the entire Interior river system at your paddle tip, deciding where to explore depends on ability and time. The Chena and Chatanika rivers offer a multitude of easily accessible possibilities for day trips. If time can be stretched,

Fur for sale at a trading post near Fairbanks.

one might attempt the clear waters of the **Birch Creek** at Mile 94 (150 km) Steese Highway or a five-day sojourn on the broad sweep of the **Tanana River** from Delta to Fairbanks.

Those fortunate enthusiasts with a month or more could paddle away from Fairbanks and float into the Tanana and Yukon rivers. This expedition is more than 1,000 miles (1,600 km) of wilderness river without a portage. Portions of the easily accessible **Nenana River** contain Class IV and V rapids (not suitable for an open canoe), and should be reserved only for experienced kayakers able to perform the Eskimo roll. If contemplating the Nenana, select one of the many guided raft tours available at Mile 239 (385 km) on the Parks Highway.

The water level of the Nenana varies with the temperature. It is a glacier-fed river and will run in torrents if several days of warm weather produce ideal melting conditions.

The aforementioned rivers are all conveniently accessible by road. If the traveler owns a collapsible kayak, myriad remote rivers can be reached by airplane.

Happy hooking: The Interior is a fisherman's promised land, and the Arctic grayling its manna. The flash of the strike and the fight of the silver streak on light tackle is a treasured memory – not to be hauled out again and again when swapping fishing tales, but to be savored nonetheless. All clear-flowing creeks and rivers in the Interior are suitably grayling inhabited. The Clearwater, Salcha, Chantanika and Chena rivers are superior grayling producers and are accessible by road. Northern pike, rainbow trout, burbot and lake trout abound in the clear, cold waters throughout the Interior.

Chartered airplane operators can be contacted in Fairbanks, North Pole, Delta and Tok. Fly-in fishing is an expensive proposition, but the spectacular scenery and bountiful catches make it good value.

The fall hunts in August and September attract avid trophy hunters to the Interior. Guided hunts are available into the Alaska and Brooks ranges, with most hunters hoping for a Dall sheep, moose or caribou. Make arrangements for guided hunts far in advance.

Special events in Fairbanks: The winter festival spirit has been revived in Fairbanks and is now called the **Winter Carnival**, celebrated during the second and third weeks of March. Fairbanks has traditionally hosted the **North American Open Sled Dog Championship** during this time. The North American, as locals refer to it, is not to be missed. The sprint race is run on three consecutive days, with the start/finish line in downtown Fairbanks on Second Avenue. It attracts the finest sprint dogmushers from the States, racing teams of up to 20 dogs.

Another sled dog race, not a sprint, is the **Yukon-Quest**, a grueling 1,000-mile (1,600-km) race between Whitehorse, Yukon Territory, Canada, and Fairbanks, ends in Fairbanks in odd-numbered years and runs in the opposite direction in even-numbered years. The Quest challenges the sturdiest of long-distance mushers.

A full slate of events continues

Leaping skills in the annual Eskimo Olympics.

throughout the festival including, of course, ice carving. The Festival of Native Arts takes place in February, along with Native-style potlatches.

Fairbanksans do not allow the Summer Solstice to slip by uncelebrated. The Fairbanks Gold Panners baseball team plays a game at Growden Field with the first pitch crossing the plate at 10.45pm – under natural light.

Boating fanatics endure competition of another sort. Sleek racing boats propelled by twin 50-horsepower outboard motors zoom down the Chena, Tanana and Yukon rivers to Galena, returning at breakneck speed to Fairbanks and the finish line at Pike's Landing. The Yukon 800 tests both machine and man.

Felix Pedro sported a beard. And so does almost everyone else during the third week of July when Fairbanks celebrates Golden Days. One event is a Felix Pedro look-alike contest, so men allow facial hair to grow unchecked. The largest attraction of the week-long celebration is a parade through downtown Fairbanks complete with antique cars, clowns, marching bands and Felix Pedro himself dragging his reluctant mule through the streets. Beware of the roving jail, for those not true of heart and dressed as early miners could be incarcerated for the short time it takes to bribe the jailkeeper.

For those in Fairbanks during July, the **World Eskimo-Indian Olympics** is a must. Among Alaskan Natives, great value and respect have always been awarded to physical fitness. The wide variety of games and contests have become traditional Native pastimes. Many of the games require excellent coordination, quickness of hand and eye, and great personal strength.

The list of games includes the expected and also some surprises. The blanket toss competition is fun to watch, as is the Native Baby Contest. The Knuckle Hop, Ear Pulling and Ear Weight competitions are what they say, and seem excruciatingly painful. The *muktuk* (whale meat) -eating, fish-cutting and seal-skinning competitions are opportunities to learn more about the Native

Malemute waits for the Sled Dog contest.

cultures. The World Eskimo-Indian Olympics is a time for Natives to display crafts for sale, including beadwork, baskets, mukluks, skin garments, masks and carvings, and a unique opportunity for travelers to buy arts and crafts directly from Native artisans.

Although officially called the **Alaska State Fair** on even years and the **Tanana Valley Fair** on odd years, most everyone uses the latter name every year. The fair, held at the College Road fairgrounds during the second or third week of August, has grown to be the most popular event in the Interior, with attendance of more than 100,000. The prime attraction for travelers is the Harvest Hall filled with colossal vegetables. See what the long days can produce in the Interior, including huge radishes and 70-lb (32-kg) cabbages.

The fringe: The sawdust floor and sourdough bartenders pushing beer across the bar mingle in a frozen moment when past and present swirl into one, as the deep-voiced rendition of Robert Service's *The Shooting of Dan McGrew* silences even those vivacious *cheechakos* (newcomers to the north) near the door:

So the stranger stumbles across the room, and flops down there like a fool.
In a buckskin shirt that was glazed with dirt he sat, and I saw him sway;
Then he clutched the keys with his talon hands – my God! but that man could play.

To enjoy this trip back in time, head for the settlement of **Ester**, 7 miles (11 km) from Fairbanks off the Parks Highway. To the outsider, Ester is just another faded mining community, but during summer months, the **Malemute Saloon** swings open its doors to evening readings of Robert Service and vaudeville shows. Locals hang around the **Red Garter**, and everyone enjoys the **Ester Gold Camp Restaurant**. The rest of the year, the 200 residents of Ester sink into the solitude of small-town Alaska.

Home of Santa Claus: Yes, there is a Santa Claus. His home is located 14 miles (22 km) east of Fairbanks in, of

Left, Santaland. Below, refinery at North Pole.

course, **North Pole**. Other people have moved in around him; a few were even there before Santa handhewed the logs for his first **Santa Claus House**. With urban renewal and all, Santa had to move closer to the highway, where he's situated today. **Santaland** is a thriving commercial enterprise on the Richardson Highway, and perhaps it gives the visitor an idea of the enterprising types who homesteaded this area during the 1930s and 1940s. They were a new wave of pioneers who found Fairbanks already too crowded and who didn't mind living in this low-lying basin where winter temperatures are severe enough for the nickname "North Pole" to stick.

Presently, North Pole, an incorporated city within the North Star Borough, is home to 940 folks and a surrounding population of 13,000. Land parcels are still available, and some of the homesteads remain intact, although most have been subdivided to ease the craving for land and for housing. No longer a little sister to Fairbanks, or that swampy outpost between the city and Eielson Air Force Base, North Pole operates with its own utilities, brand-new shopping malls and thriving real estate businesses.

There's no mad stampede, no gold rush. But there is a bit of black gold flowing through North Pole. Daily, 45,000 barrels of crude oil are diverted from the Trans-Alaska Pipeline to North Pole Refining. Fifteen thousand barrels of home-heating oil and jet fuel are distilled and the rest returned to the main pipeline.

Another form of refining is going on in North Pole, at the sod-roofed KJNP (King Jesus North Pole) radio and television station on Mission Road.

With its 50,000 watts of broadcasting power, KJNP sends messages out to Bush Alaska. This service, aptly labeled *Trapline Chatter,* has saved lives, ended relationships and eased the loneliness for many a bush dweller.

One young trapper, after tuning in to 1170 AM night after night at 9.20 sharp to eavesdrop on his northern neighbors, fell so deeply in love with the soothing

eparing for
'-mile
owmobile
ce.

voice of the announcer that he returned to civilization in spring and married her.

Trails, like the threads of a spider's web, spun into Fairbanks from every direction in the early 1900s. The more popular routes were eventually transformed from dogsled tracks to the paved and gravel roadways that now link the rest of Alaska to Fairbanks, the commercial hub of the Interior. The first trail-cum-highway in all of Alaska, the **Richardson**, was originally a pack trail between the then-bustling mining settlements of Eagle and Valdez. Following the gold rush, the trail was extended to Fairbanks, linking the Interior to an icefree port. E.T. Barnette and company made many a trip on this path. Today, the Richardson joins with the Alaska Highway for the 98 miles (157 km) between Fairbanks and Delta Junction.

As surely as there is gold in the hills, there are buffalo and barley in **Delta Junction**, or is that buffalo IN the barley? The **Tanana Valley** is one of the largest agricultural areas in the state, with most of the farming centered in the Delta area. Despite the typical Interior winter climate, the valley supports the Delta Barley Project, a state-sponsored attempt to introduce large-scale grain production to the Interior. Now at 90,000 acres (36,450 hectares), this farming venture, begun in 1978, is another example of the exuberant pioneering spirit in the Interior.

But what of hirsute bearded beasts? Although they could be the spirit watchers of the shaggy bison who ranged the Interior millennia ago, this herd was actually imported from Montana and introduced to the area specifically as a game animal. The original 23-member herd now numbers as many as 400, and is the largest free-roaming buffalo herd in North America.

These woolly wanderers have even been granted their own 90,000 acres (36,500 hectares) which in no way discourages them from haunting the barley patch. For a glimpse of the Delta buffalo, most people pull over at Mile 241 on the Richardson Highway and scan the country across the Delta River. **The interior.**

Fairbanks or bust: "Once is Enough" declares the mud-splattered bumper sticker. Inside the vehicle is another *cheechako*, as a first-time visitor to Alaska is called, and this one is probably fresh off the **Alaska Highway**, that infamous 1,500-mile (2,400-km) stretch of road paved with curses and windshield chips. Bulldozed through the wilderness in 1942 as part of the war effort, the "Alcan" (Alaska-Canada military highway) literally rose from the permafrost and slid down mountainsides as the US Army Corps of Engineers frantically battled mud, mosquitoes and time. The road from Dawson Creek in British Columbia, Canada, to Fairbanks is now paved, easing the perils of the odyssey, but not diminishing the thrill of arrival.

State Highway 3, alias the George Parks Highway – alias the Anchorage-Fairbanks Highway, and referred to locally as the "Parks" – does, strangely enough, lead to Denali National Park, although the roadway was named in honor of a governor, not the park. While still in the rolling hills of the Tanana

Valley, the Parks passes through the town of **Nenana**, located 64 miles (103 km) southwest of Fairbanks.

Railway town: Nenana, an Athabascan word meaning "between two rivers," is situated at the confluence of the Tanana and Nenana rivers. Always one of the main river-freighting centers in Alaska, life in Nenana changed with the completion of the Alaska Railroad in 1923.

Folks in Nenana remember the stifling hot day of July 15, 1923, when President Warren Harding drove the golden spike signifying completion of the federally owned railroad. The original tracks stretching from the seaport of Seward to Nenana were later extended to Fairbanks. During construction, Fairbanks breathed softly. It appeared in 1920 that Nenana would become the major city of the Interior. All danger has apparently passed, as the population currently hovers around 500.

The railroad, constructed with excess equipment from the Panana Canal Project, made headlines again in January 1985 when it was purchased from the

US government by the state of Alaska. As in 1923, the celebration was held in Nenana, with the townspeople serving up moose stew for the dignitaries, sightseers and old-timers on hand to witness or relive a bit of Alaskan history. Losing its status as the only federally owned railroad in the country has not changed the Interior's love affair with this slow-moving apparatus. The train chugs along at about 50 mph (80 kph) and still makes flag stops. Travelers can board in Fairbanks for the rolling trip south.

Nenana is also the terminus port for tug and barge fleets that still service the villages along the Tanana and Yukon rivers, loaded with supplies, fuel and tons of freight. For a closer inspection of an old tug, look up the refurbished **Taku Chief** which is behind the Visitor Information Center.

Although not yet the Monte Carlo of the north, Nenana is known far and wide for the **Nenana Ice Classic**, one of those annual events held only in the land of snow and ice and cabin fever. Cash prizes are awarded to the lucky souls who guess the exact time – to the minute, mind you – of spring break-up on the Tanana. Break-up is that moment when suddenly there's more water than ice on the river, when massive blocks of ice rip and surge, grind and groan against one another. But at that exact moment, ticket holders are more concerned with the time than with the spectacular release of winter energy.

The Tanana River again becomes the focal point a month or so later with **River Daze**, celebrated during the first weekend in June. One event is the raft race down the Tanana from Fairbanks to Nenana. Not an ordinary race, it's permeated with typical Alaskan inspiration and humor of latter-day Huck Finns who create a variety of floating contraptions and boldly enter them as "rafts." Anything goes, providing it floats and utilizes only "natural" power. All in good fun.

Whether one arrives in Nenana by highway or railroad, one will ultimately be drawn by the wide sweep of the river to stand close to the bank, fix an eye on

The pipeline raised to allow animal life across.

the river, and listen for the imagined slap of a sternwheeler or the swish of a canoe paddle.

Off to the gold fields: To drive the **Steese Highway** is to travel with the spirits of the miners who worked the many creek beds prospecting for gold. The road angles to the northeast for 162 miles (260 km) before ending at the Yukon River. First stop is on Hagelbarger Road at Mile 3.6 (6 km) for a wide-angle view of Fairbanks and the Alaska Range.

Back out on the Steese, don't accelerate too much. The best look at the **Trans-Alaska Pipeline** is right up ahead at Mile 8.4 (13.5 km). Resting on vertical support members (VSMs) and bound in a sleeve of insulation, the pipeline parallels the Steese Highway above the permafrost-rich ground. Farther on at Mile 11 (18 km) is the community of **Fox**, an early mining encampment which took its name from a nearby creek. The community is most famous now for its excellent spring water. The symmetrical piles of gravel surrounding Fox are the dregs of the mighty earth-eating

hard-hatted
il worker.

dredges. The piles lie like great loaves of bread, browned on top and awaiting the next course.

The **Monument to Felix Pedro** at 17 Mile (27 km) is a modest reminder of the Italian immigrant who was the first to strike it rich in these valleys. Gravel in the creek on the opposite side of the road has been known to show some "color," so practice panning here.

The next 3 miles (5 km) of road gradually ascend to **Cleary Summit**, which was named for Frank Cleary, Barnette's brother-in-law. The summit offers a magnificent panoramic view of the Tanana Valley, the White Mountains and the Alaska Range.

The story of a bandit: Back in 1905, the legendary "Blue Parka Bandit" found this encompassing lookout quite handy for his trade. Charles Hendrickson, engineer-turned-robber and terror of the trails, haunted these bold granite crags, pinching the pokes of unsuspecting gold miners. Armed and masked, he demanded gold, occasionally tarnishing his ignominious reputation with Robin Hood tactics; like the time when he detained the Episcopalian Bishop and his entourage and the Bishop managed to persuade him to hand over all the stolen gold pokes.

Fans of Alaskan gold-rush lore will not want to miss **Fairbanks Creek Road**. Leave the Steese Highway and Cleary Summit and travel south along the ridgeline for eight miles (13 km) to Alder Creek Camp. Beyond this, be prepared for a 1-mile (1.6-km) walk to **Meehan**, an abandoned machine shop area where maintenance was done on mining equipment. History hangs heavy in the air here; rusted equipment can be found strewn along the trail.

Fairbanks Creek Camp is an additional two miles (3.2 km) below Meehan. Dredge Number Two met an untimely end in 1959 along this creek when a deck hand decided to use dynamite to open an ice-blocked hole. The dredge quickly sank.

Fairbanks Creek relinquished many tusks, teeth and bones of Pleistocene mammals during stripping operations. One of the most famous fossils is a well-preserved baby Woolly Mammoth found in 1949.

Hot baths for the miners: The old Circle District is not yet devoid of gold or the miners who search for it. Some of them live in **Central**, a small mining community strung out along the Steese Highway and described by locals as "three miles long and one block wide." An active winter population of 100 swells to more than 800 during the summer months when miners and vacationers return. With the addition of a permanent school in Central in 1981, more and more "summer people" are staying on late into fall. A worthwhile detour on your way to the hot springs (eight miles/13 km up the road) is a stop at the **Circle District Historical Society Museum** located in Central. The museum's grand opening was celebrated in July 1984 with the unveiling of a mining equipment attraction, a display featuring the hardy alpine wildflowers found on Eagle Summit, and a period cabin containing authentic artifacts. The museum is open noon–5pm in summer and upon request in winter. Overnight accommodations, camping facilities and general "pitstop" services are available in Central.

Gold nuggets weren't the only pleasures that warmed the miners' souls during the rush. Imagine the heartwarming experience of William Greats, who, back in 1893, crept into a small valley for a closer look at the steaming witches' cauldron he had spotted. He must have been a popular fellow for a time, leading colleagues to the mineral springs he'd discovered.

Many areas are abandoned after a rush, but never a hot spring. Visitors do not have to re-enact days of old when ice was chipped from tent flaps to enter the bathing houses. **Circle Hot Springs** has been spruced up and now offers a 1930s hotel refurbished with Victorian decor, an ice cream parlor, family-style restaurant and the Miners' Saloon. The hotel offers an upstairs hostel, as well as comfortable hotel rooms and cabins, and a campground with hiking and skiing trails. But those are places and activities to investigate after your body

Mining techniques remembered in Circle District.

has withered beyond recognition and your rubbery legs can no longer propel you to the edge of the open-air pool. There's really nothing quite like dangling from an inner tube in 109°F (43°C) mineral water, completely enveloped in a cloak of mist as the water condenses in the –40°F (–40°C) air.

The summer experience is equally pleasurable after the 130-mile (210-km) trip up the Steese. Scheduled commercial flights are available since 1984; the Steese Highway is maintained daily during winter. Call ahead for overnight reservations and road conditions, tel (907) 451-5204 in winter. No advance notice is necessary to use the pool.

Road's end: All roads end some place. For the Steese, it's all over at **Circle City**, a small community 50 miles (80 km) south of the Arctic Circle, poised along a bend in the Yukon River. This is the same Circle of gold-rush days, which had a population of 1,000 in the 1890s. Today that has dwindled down to 71 friendly folks.

Once the largest gold mining town on the Yukon, Circle was nearly abandoned after the gold strikes in the Klondike and Fairbanks areas. Gone are Jack McQuesten's two-story log store, two dozen or so saloons, eight dance halls, theaters and the music hall that earned Circle City the name "Paris of the North." In their places reign a modern-day trading post with a motel, cafe, general store, bar and gas station. Tourist facilities are definitely geared for the summer visitor. Chartered "flightseeing" trips are available, but boat rentals are not.

There's usually plenty of waterfront activity in this popular "take in" and "take out" place for canoeists and rafters traveling the Yukon River. One popular river trip begins in either Eagle or Circle and terminates at Fort Yukon or farther downstream under the pipeline bridge.

Circle, so named because early miners thought they were camped at the Arctic Circle, still teems with activity. Fishwheels smack the water as they turn in the current, flat-bottomed boats zoom up and down the river and barges still make their way to points upriver. River travelers could easily miss all of this; the "land" in front of Circle is actually an island concealing another channel of the mighty Yukon.

Gamblers gained notoriety in the saloons of boom and bust towns like Circle City. One who went on to national fame was Tex Richard. He was 24 years old in 1895 when he trekked into Circle and found a job in "Square Sam" Bonnifield's gambling saloon. Impressed by the honesty of his boss, for the rest of his life, it is said, he gambled "as if Sam Bonnifield were looking over his shoulder." His claim to fame was not made in Circle City, however, but a bit later when he built Madison Square Garden in New York City. He was also well-known as a promoter for the heavyweight boxing champ of the world, Jack Dempsey.

Historic Eagle: "Joe. We left 'round midnight. Dried out, canoe patched. Meet ya in Circle or Fort Yukon. Gene and Doreen."

The above is a typical message to be left fluttering on the bulletin board outside the US Post Office in **Eagle**, a popular jumping-off place for Yukon River paddlers, as well as an official stop for river explorers floating from Dawson City. As the first city on the US side of the silty Yukon, Eagle's Post Office is where river travelers check in with US customs.

Life in Eagle has all the pleasurable ingredients of a river village as well as the advantages of an "end-of-the-road" community. It is situated 161 miles (260 km) from Tetlin Junction at the terminus of the Taylor Highway, a mixed blessing since the road closes when winter snow isolates the community.

"People of the River," or the Han Athabascans, were the original inhabitants of this area. Chief John, of legendary fame for crushing the cheap glass beads which were offered to him by early white traders, left his impression; and, for quite a time, Eagle was known as John's Village.

Perhaps the spirits of those first white traders still linger in the back streets of Eagle, whispering revenge on John's ancestors. An uneasiness has settled over Eagle, most perceptibly in the white community and Native populations separated by a 3-mile (5-km) gravel road and an invisible barrier not yet completely hurdled by either group.

The Eagle visited by travelers today had its beginnings in 1874 when the far-reaching and powerful Northern Commercial Company (NC) stretched its commercial fingers along the Yukon River and established a trading post at this site. Gold seekers followed fur traders and, within 24 years, Moses Mercier's tiny outpost was transformed into a brazen mining town of 1,700. Seized by gold fever, thousands more, digging in every tributary of the Yukon, swept through Han territory.

By 1898, the city was renamed for the eagles who stake their claim on the bluffs along the riverside. A post office was established, along with an army post, a saloon and a dressmaker; and entrepreneurs flourished, including a piano player.

History was being made at the turn of the century, and Eagle was host to its share. Judge Wickersham wintered here in 1900. The incredible Valdez-to-Eagle telegraph line spun out a most interesting message in 1905 when Roald Amundsen, passing through after his successful expedition into the Northwest Passage, made his announcement to the world from Eagle.

Eagle paid its dues in the boom-and-bust cycle of the gold fields. By 1910 the muckers had vanished, trekking after even richer dreams near Fairbanks. They left behind 178 people, about the same population as today. But the buildings still stand and Eagle has undertaken a program to restore many of its fine older structures.

During summer, the Eagle Historical Society conducts a free walking tour which includes **Judge Wickersham's Courthouse**, built by fines he imposed quarterly on gamblers and prostitutes in the rowdy mining town. Inside are the judge's desk and an early map of the country constructed of papier-mâché and moose blood. Also open for inspection **Church in Eagle.**

214

is **Fort Egbert**, established by the US Army, but abandoned in 1911.

Summer visitors will find the basic necessities – laundry, restaurant, lodging, groceries, gas station, gravel airstrip and mechanic shop. For those who are inclined to go further "upriver," a daily commercial cruise motors between Eagle and Dawson City. Gone, though, are the sternwheelers plying the muddy Yukon between Dawson and the Bering Sea, bringing to Eagle the gold dust and sweeping away discarded dreams. Today, Eagle "feeds" the Yukon in another way. The insatiable appetite of the river current crumbles the high bank, devouring chunks of the city's real estate with each season and causing a stir each time the "river viewing" bench is moved back a few feet.

Another hot one: A jog to the right at Mile 3 (5 km) and the Steese Highway sends you rollercoasting through the countryside on Chena Hot Springs Road. This paved beauty is only 56 miles (90 km) long, passes through the middle of the 254,000-acre (103,000-hectare)

Chena River Recreation Area, and terminates at the gates to the privately owned and publicly adored **Chena Hot Springs Resort**. The place is commercially equipped with all the necessities for an extended visit, but more alluring are the steaming hot-water ponds scattered throughout Monument Creek Valley, and the indoor swimming and soaking facilities.

The four major highways in the Interior extend out of Fairbanks like the arms of a lopsided windmill. To the northwest is the **Elliot Highway** and, continuing beyond, the Dalton Highway. The Elliot branches off the Steese 11 miles (18 km) north of Fairbanks and winds through 152 miles (245 km) of gold-mining country trimmed with broad valleys, bubbling creeks, blueberries and poppies, homesteads and mining camps.

Livengood, near the junction of the Elliot and Dalton highways, once held the "end-of-the-road" position. Here, a jog to the left terminates in either the Athabascan Village of **Minto** on the

ackcountry
wboy.

Tolovana River or at **Manley Hot Springs**, another mining center, farther on. Livengood, however, experienced an invasion in the mid-1970s when it was transformed from an isolated "mind-your-own-business" neighborhood to a pipeline construction camp.

Black gold: Three million man-hours, five months of intensive labor, and millions of tons of gravel equal one 416-mile (670-km) service road paralleling one of the most ambitious projects ever undertaken in the North American Arctic – the Trans-Alaska Pipeline.

This service road-cum-state highway, which is officially dubbed the **Dalton Highway** but known simply as the "Haul Road," opened up thousands of acres of wilderness territory which can now be explored from the comfort of a vehicle. The road is maintained from Livengood to Prudhoe Bay, but privately owned vehicles are allowed only as far as **Disaster Creek** near Dietrich Camp, about 280 miles (450 km) north of Fairbanks and 200 miles (322 km) south of the Arctic Ocean. Travel beyond the Dietrich checkpoint is reserved for industrial traffic, by permit.

A journey north on the Dalton, above the Arctic Circle, through the land of sheep, bears, wolves and foxes can be the ultimate coup of your trip. Several tour companies offer excursions to the Arctic Circle and Prudhoe Bay. But if you choose to do it alone, beware: rental cars cannot be driven up the road. Conditions are hazardous; the roadway is rough and dusty in summer and slippery in winter. Because this is primarily a service road, heavily loaded 18-wheelers rule the route.

If you can't resist going, plan as you would for a wilderness camping trip, but take your wallet – automobile towing charges on the Highway can cost up to $5 a mile. Service station facilities and emergency communications are available at only two locations, the Yukon River crossing at Mile 56.6 (91 km) and Coldfoot at Mile 173.6 (280 km). For road conditions, telephone (907) 451-2294.

Into the bush: What is beyond Pedro

Fish camp on the Yukon River.

216

Dome, Cleary Summit and the White Mountains? What is it that the Chena, the Chatanika and the Tanana rivers are all drawn toward? Not unlike explorers of yesterday, visitors to Fairbanks often feel a gentle urge to soar over the mountain peaks or float with the river current right to its mouth. Beyond, north of Fairbanks, is the **Yukon River**, seemingly with a magnetic force of its own. If Fairbanks is the heart of the Interior, then the Yukon River is surely a life-supporting artery.

Centuries before European explorers spread out over the land, the Yukon River and its many tributaries were a common link in the survival of the nomadic Athabascan tribes living in the Interior. Ironically, the Yukon then became the means of intrusion as sternwheelers labored upriver from St. Michael on the Bering Sea to the fur country and gold fields.

When explorers, missionaries and fortune hunters penetrated this wilderness, the Athabascans were living as they had for generations, subsisting on salmon, moose or caribou, berries and water birds. They were survivors in a harsh and unmerciful land. With the arrival of outsiders, the Natives congregated into small communities.

Along the Yukon, scattered like knots on a kite string, are the Athabascan river villages. Dozens of tiny settlements still exist, sharing this inhospitable northern country with the rivers. The historical perspective of each community varies, but, remarkably, they remain part of 20th-century Alaska, silent tributes to the Athabascans of the past.

Present-day village lifestyles: It would be naive to believe that the villages exist in a totally virgin state, untouched by the modern world; conversely, it would be presumptious to assume that the villages continue to provide a viable existence due only to space-age technology (e.g. satellite telephones). Generally, villagers maintain a subsistence lifestyle, hunting, fishing, trapping, gardening and gathering berries. Daily life embraces the rhythm of the seasons; and often survival demands adjusting to weather conditions and the unpredictable cycles of wildlife.

Elementary schools, many containing the most modern educational equipment available, are a part of every village. Since 1976, many villages have offered a high school education to their young people. The typical village teenager, however, carrying all the dreams of his ancestors, is spiralling into the 20th century, often at a crossroads both personally and culturally.

The village elders, those keepers of the culture, go on dispensing wisdom daily as did their grandmothers and grandfathers a century ago. Village pride seems to have deepened in recent years, as influences from the "outside" pressed an ever-tighter fist into the core of Athabascan strongholds. Almost forgotten dialects now roll easily from the lips of youngsters. Ancient drumbeats and dances are as popular as are the howls of today's "rockers." The village is a microcosm of contrast, evoking a strong sense of the past and surging into the present, welcoming the traditional and grappling toward the future.

ood
ackcountry
ansport.

NOME AND THE REMOTE WEST

"I've never been to Nome and not had a good time," says one Alaskan who has visited the city six times in the past dozen years. His is a sentiment that captures the spirit of this most remote of Alaska's major cities. **Nome** has long been known as the city that wouldn't die, although it has had more than enough reason to disappear many times since its founding in 1899.

Nome has been burned to the ground; pounded by relentless gales (including one that left the city looking like it had been "shelled by a hostile fleet," according to a survivor); decimated by flu, diptheria and other maladies; and almost starved out of existence. Yet, through it all, the city has always rebuilt and always struggled on.

It was gold, discovered in 1898, that brought men, and later women to this wind-swept, wave-battered beach on the Seward Peninsula, 75 or more miles from the nearest tree. Of all the Alaska gold-rush towns, Nome was the largest and the rowdiest. The year 1900 was the big time in Nome. Best estimates put the population in excess of 20,000 people by the end of the summer, but nobody knows for certain – there was no way to make an accurate count.

By the time gold-bearing creeks around the area were discovered, claim jumping and other less-than-ethical mining practices were well advanced in Alaska. Claim-jumping was so rampant that it probably took a dozen years or more before everything was straightened out. By then the boom was dying and Nome boasted little more than 5,000 residents. Over the years the permanent population has shrunk to as low as 500. It has more or less stabilized in recent years at about 4,000 residents in the immediate area.

Nome hosted a whole series of gold rushes, each almost blending into the other. The first gold came the traditional way – it was found in the streams flowing into Norton Sound. The thousands who rushed to Nome set their tents on

the beach and explored the nearby gullies, little realizing that all they had to do was sift the sand that was their floor for the precious yellow metal.

The famed black sand beaches of Nome count as the "second" gold rush. Since nobody could legally stake a claim on the beach, a man could work any ground he could stand upon near the shoreline. The sands were turned over dozens of times and yielded millions of dollars in gold.

Then geologists pointed out that Nome had more than a single beach. Over the centuries, as rivers carried silt to the ocean, the beach line had gradually extended out to sea. These geologists predicted early on that under the tundra a few yards back from the water, miners would find an ancient beach and, with it, more deposits of gold. And so it was that later years saw yet a third gold rush as ground behind the sea wall was dug and redug to extract the gold.

Today, fortune seekers still sift the sands in front of Nome. During the summer of 1984, a Nome resident out for a walk along the beach reached under a piece of driftwood and picked up a gold nugget weighing over an ounce. Such are the rewards of fresh air and exercise.

The beach at Nome is still open to the public. Anyone with a gold pan or a sluice box and a tent to camp in can search for gold along the waterfront. It's hard, back-breaking work, but then riches have never come easy for miners. Perhaps the only ones who found easy money were the gamblers and the tricksters who made their living relieving miners of their hard-earned gold.

The shifty-eyed characters who learned their crafts in the boom towns of the Wild West converged on Nome as practiced, professional con artists – men like Wyatt Earp, famed frontier marshal, who arrived in Nome as a paunchy, 51-year-old saloon keeper. (In Nome he was frequently at odds with the law.)

Yet Nome's gold rush years spawned a hero or two amid the unscrupulous. Shortly after Earp arrived, a family named Doolittle moved to town. One boy, Jimmy, never very tall, delivered newspapers for the *Nome Nugget*, the oldest continually published newspaper in Alaska. Jimmy grew up to lead "Doolittle's Raiders," the daring group of army pilots who launched their over-sized, overloaded bombers from the pitching decks of a Navy aircraft carrier in the darkest days of World War II.

Energetic celebrations: The ability to face all comers, whatever the odds, is what makes Nome the rollicking place it is today. Nomites bring a special energy to almost every project they take on. After all, in western Alaska you sometimes have to make your own fun.

The Midnight Sun Festival is a good example. Held on the weekend closest to summer solstice (June 21), the two-day festival includes a late-night softball tournament, a street dance, a barbecued chicken feed, food and carnival booths (selling such items as reindeer hot dogs and cotton candy), a dart tournament and the taking of the town photo.

Less than two weeks later, Nome gets ready to party again with the 4th of July celebration. This event includes street games, a big raffle, free ice cream (provided by the fire department) and the Anvil Mountain Run. Runners are required to run up the mountain on the road, but are allowed to take any path they want on the way down; through the tundra is a shorter route, but it's not as smooth going.

As with most civic celebrations, each event has its own parade. There are hardly any spectators: most of the local residents are in the parade. If you walk down to the starting point, you'll find those scheduled to march last in the parade watching the leaders start out. At the finish line, all those in the early part of the parade get to watch the stragglers finish. Thus everybody gets to be part of the parade and watch part of it too.

The Nome River Raft Race is part of the Midnight Sun Festival. Its only rule seems to be that there are no rules. In truth, however, there are five stipulations: rafts must be home made; each raft must be half as wide as it is long; a flag or banner must be displayed; at least four crew members must be on

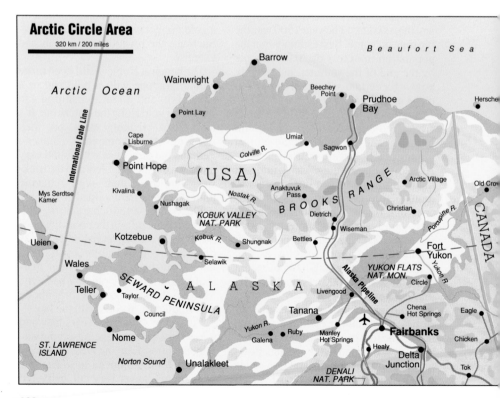

board; and all crew members must be wet when they cross the finish line.

And what would the 4th of July be without fireworks? In the early 1980s Nome's city council wanted to stop such devices within the city limits because of the fire hazard – burning down the whole town gets old after you've done it a few times. This particularly affected the mayor at the time, one of the largest fireworks dealers in the area. He solved the problem by setting up his firework stand a few steps outside the city line and gleefully sold all manner of pyrotechnics to the people, who then immediately took the goods to their homes in town. Thus there was still plenty of noise, fire and smoke for the 4th of July, and the mayor didn't need to worry about being jailed for breaking the law.

Nome loves to party – almost any excuse will do. Take June of 1981, when a US Coast Guard icebreaker with a crew of about 150 men anchored offshore. Early that afternoon the skipper made his way into Nome's police department to warn the cops that he was giving half his crew liberty at 4pm. He was worried lest any of his men be jailed, and offered the services of his officers should any problems arise.

News travels fast in rural communities and by the time the Coasties hit the beach a few hours later, Nome was ready. Local artisans and craftspeople brought out their wares for sale. The bars were doing a booming business and Front Street was jumping all night.

And the cops filled up the jail. But when things calmed down and the jailer took a head count, there were no Coasties behind bars. All those incarcerated were locals caught trying to show the Coast Guards how to party. So much for the rumors about sailors on liberty. And, mysteriously enough, few of those jailed saw a judge the next morning. When they sobered up the doors were opened and the party-goers made their way home. There are advantages to living in a remote frontier town.

Those advantages show themselves in other ways. Nome is a close community, with almost anyone available to

elcoming ords to lar Circle sitors.

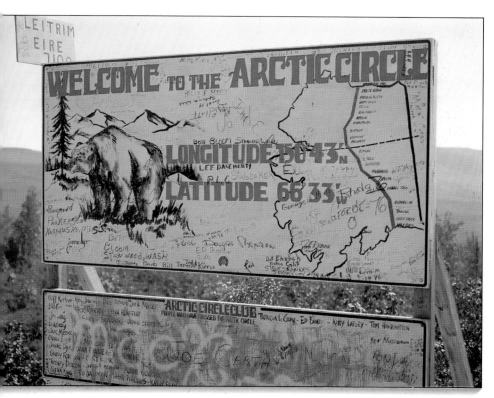

lend a hand. Consider Christmas. Christmas trees are traditional decorations in local homes just as elsewhere in the United States. The problem with this arises because the last ship of the season usually departs in October, just before Norton Sound freezes. Trees can be flown in, but that's expensive.

However, about 80 miles (129 km) to the east is a convenient forest, and in the weeks before Christmas residents band together and dispatch truckloads of volunteers along a bone-crunching road leading to the forest. The trucks are then filled with small spruce trees, enough to ensure that every household can have one. These aren't the magnificent Douglas firs which are favored in the Lower 48. Instead, they're scraggly tundra spruce trees, but they are adequate for the task.

After the holidays, residents take their old trees out to "Nome National Forest" – a stretch of ice outside town – and "plant" them. The trees generally stay there until spring, tended by a self-appointed "ranger" who stands them up when they get blown over, and sometimes visitors to Nome are fooled into thinking there really is a forest here.

The Great Race: After Christmas, there's one more high point in the long winter, the combined Spring Carnival and Iditarod Trail Sled Dog Race. The Iditarod commemorates the frantic race to get diptheria serum to Nome in 1925. The town was teetering on the verge of an epidemic and the only possible way to get the cure through was overland by dogsled. The serum was taken by train to Nenana and from there experienced mushers ran their sleds and teams in relays, round the clock, to get it to Nome. A trip that normally took a month or more was therefore completed in a matter of days.

Today, the Iditarod is a sporting event billed as "The Last Great Race on Earth." About 65 racers bring their teams to the starting line in Anchorage on the first Saturday in March. The winners reach Nome about two weeks later, having traveled an actual distance of more than 1,100 miles (1,760 km) on the grueling **Early dogsledders**

DOG-DRIVING NEAR THE VESOLIA SOPKA.

224

trail. All manner of hostile terrain – and the elements – batter the racers from start to finish.

In the 1985 race, Susan Butcher, leading the pack a couple of days out of Anchorage, tangled with a moose. Before things were sorted out in the dark, the moose had stomped and kicked her dog team out of the race. Later the race was halted twice for bad weather. And finally, in an act of considerable courage – some say foolhardiness – Libby Riddles, a quiet, woman from Teller, a small village northwest of Nome, headed out of a checkpoint into the teeth of a howling gale only a couple hundred miles from the finish line. No other musher would risk traveling in the storm. But the few miles she made that night before being forced to make camp and sit out the storm gave Riddles the extra edge needed for victory, and she became the first woman to win in the 13-year history of the event.

Also in March is the Bering Sea Ice Golf Classic. Participants dress in wacky outfits for this game, played on artificial grass on top of the ice, next to the "Nome National Forest."

Today Nome is the transportation hub of western Alaska. It has a major airport with daily jet service to and from Anchorage and provides commuter plane service to every village in the region. Almost everyone touring western Alaska must at least pass through Nome.

Superb fishing: An hour by air southeast of Nome on the eastern edge of Norton Sound is **Unalakleet,** a pleasant Native village with good schools, churches and probably the best-kept secret in Alaska. The Unalakleet River, which runs through town, supports a large run of king salmon in late June, and the angling is superb. And, unlike most king salmon sport fisheries, bag limits are generous. Six fish per person per day has been the rule in recent years. Most other major fisheries only allow anglers a single king salmon daily.

Travel agents in Anchorage can set up a stay at a full-service fishing lodge on the Unalakleet River for those who wish to battle the giant salmon. Such a tour is

not cheap: $300 to $500 a day or more per person. But a couple of days fishing in the Unalakleet River when the kings are in is probably the experience of a lifetime for most fishermen.

North of Nome lies **Kotzebue**, a large, predominantly Eskimo community. Kotzebue is also served by daily jet service out of Anchorage.

Kotzebue is the headquarters for NANA, one of the regional Native corporations which was established in 1971 with the passage of the Alaska Native Claims Settlement Act. That act granted Alaskan Natives nearly $1 billion in cash and title to some 44 million acres (18 million hectares) of land: the money and the ground were divided up by 13 Native corporations formed to manage the sudden wealth. NANA's share was significant and it is believed to be one of the more successful of the 13 corporations.

NANA is actively involved in the reindeer industry, which is restricted by law to Alaska Natives. Several other business ventures of a more contemporary nature round out NANA's holdings. The company is providing jobs to its shareholders and is a significant economic force in western Alaska.

The big economic activity in western Alaska is the development of a world-class zinc mine just a short distance northeast of Kotzebue. Cominco, a Canadian-based mining concern, is developing the roads and other infrastructure necessary to support the venture. The state of Alaska guaranteed a $150 million loan in the spring of 1985 for the road system.

The Red Dog Mine project has provided more than 400 full-time jobs in the region, a tremendous economic impact for such a sparsely populated area. Zinc deposits are expected to last 20 years or more and recoverable quantities of silver, lead and other minerals have been detected in the same area of ground.

At the same time, however, Kotzebue is traditional. Fishermen still tend nets in Kotzebue Sound and nearby streams. Walrus, seal, whale and polar bear hunt-

Nome welcomes Iditarod winners.

ers still brave the elements in pursuit of their quarries. Kotzebue is a unique combination of the old and the new, and one of the few places where traditional and contemporary lifestyles are blending together in reasonable harmony.

Wilderness adventures: Kotzebue is also the jumping-off point for those seeking wilderness adventure in the **Noatak National Preserve** and **Kobuk Valley National Park**. Also accessible from Kotzebue are **Cape Krusenstern National Monument** and the **Bering Land Bridge National Preserve**. These lands were all set aside as part of the 1980 Alaska National Interest Lands Conservation Act, known to most Alaskans as simply "d-2."

There is no easy way to get to these remote parks and preserves. There are no roads. Charter airplanes from Kotzebue, starting at about $200 an hour, are about the only means of access. Before chartering to any of these areas, however, check carefully with the National Park Service office in Kotzebue. Various activities, such as reindeer herding,

are allowed to take place on portions of these lands. Those planning a wilderness adventure to seek solitude would probably be disappointed to land in the middle of a commercial reindeer drive.

One Kotzebue attraction that shouldn't be missed is the **NANA Museum of the Arctic**. Tours include a one-and-a-half-hour program that is unequalled anywhere in Alaska. The program includes story telling, traditional Inupiaq dancing and an award-winning slide show. In addition the museum's exhibits include display cases filled with artifacts and traditional art and examples of all of the animals indigenous to the region. It is a splendid introduction to the land and its traditional Native culture. Programs are offered twice daily from mid-May through early-September.

The biggest summer celebration in Kotzebue is again the 4th of July. But here it's a little different. Instead of the routine games found at most such festivities, Kotzebue awards prizes for traditional Native games, a *muktuk*-eating contest and seal-hook throwing

The waterfront at Kotzebue.

events. Visitors to Kotzebue can learn even more about the region's Native populations through an organization called Tour Alaska, which offers one- and two-day tours that include a city tour, the museum program, a visit to the National Park Service office to learn about the wildlife and wilderness areas, and a culture camp demonstration which explains Native culture from the spiritual to the practical.

Guides take visitors on a walk in the tundra to point out permafrost as well as plants and their traditional uses. Native Youth Olympic skills are demonstrated, as are traditional food preparations.

Another western Alaska destination that should rate high with history buffs is **Saint Michael** on the south shore of Norton Sound. Saint Michael was the major trans-shipment point for freight going to the Klondike gold fields at the turn of the century.

Almost everybody who has read of the Klondike Gold Rush (often called the Alaska Gold Rush although the Klondike was in Canada) knows about the struggles of the miners to hike the Chilkoot Pass out of the Yukon River. Lesser documentation tells the stories of the thousands of miners who reached the same destination by traveling in relative comfort aboard sternwheelers plying the Yukon River.

Saint Michael, near the mouth of the Yukon River delta, was originally the base for the river steamers loaded with supplies. Ocean steamers transferred cargoes bound for Dawson and other upriver points to the river boats at Saint Michael. Bits and pieces of old river steamers can still be found along the waterfront. Other than the gear miners carried on their backs over the Chilkoot Trail, most of the heavy equipment, food and freight that eventually reached the Klondike gold fields came through Saint Michael on Alaska's remote western coast.

Islands off the western coast of Alaska include the **Pribilofs**, the nesting grounds for hundreds of thousands of sea birds of 191 different species, and the breeding grounds and summer home of the Pacific fur seals. There's a small hotel in **Saint Paul** (population about 600) and two small restaurants. Scheduled air service is available from Anchorage to Saint Paul.

Today, the fishing industry is being developed as Saint Paul's main economic support. Past revenues were generated by the annual fur seal harvest and various government doles. With the discontinuation of the fur seal harvest, the community was forced to find other means of support. Saint Paul's newly completed harbor is a boon to local fishermen, who have had no safe haven for their boats, and is expected to attract industry to the island.

For the adventuresome traveler, a trip to Alaska's West Coast can be as thrilling as finding gold on the beach, or as daring as competing in the grueling Iditarod sled-dog race. The region's residents are fun-loving and hospitable – and sometimes rather unconventional. With a colorful past and a resource-rich future, Alaska's West Coast offers a look at the traditional way of life in the language of today.

Below, eskimo in ivory. Right, boys at Kotzebue.

CAPE KRUSENSTERN

It's hard to imagine a less likely place for buried treasure. There's nothing particularly conspicuous about **Cape Krusenstern**, no towering mountains, magnificent waterfalls, verdant forests. Only a low, ridged spit with deep furrows, dotted with countless ponds, and bordered by a relentless sea on one side, and a large lagoon on the other. Resembling a giant scythe clipping the waves of the Chukchi Sea, Cape Krusenstern stretches into polar waters in northwestern Alaska. Hidden beneath beach ridges on the cape are archeological treasures reaching back at least 4,000 years. This earthbound chronicle of early man in Alaska brought about the establishment of the 560,000-acre (226,600-hectare) **Cape Krusenstern National Monument** in 1980.

Charter planes and boats headquartered in **Kotzebue** take visitors to the monument, 10 miles (16 km) northwest across Kotzebue Sound at its southern border. The small village of **Kivalina** stretches out along the Chukchi shore north of the monument and to the east of Krusenstern, across the Mulgrave Hills, lies the village of **Noatak**. Kivalina and Noatak have airstrips although most visitors arrive via Kotzebue, which has a jet service from both Anchorage and Fairbanks.

Cape Krusenstern is a bring-your-own-shelter monument, and that goes for stove, food and water also. Highlands beyond the beaches have fresh water streams, but it's still best to carry water along. The National Park Service has built no public shelters, and there are no campgrounds. The Krusenstern tableau is waiting, but visitors should come prepared to be self-sustaining.

Planes can land on some beaches of the monument, and floatplanes put down on nearby lagoons. Many beach areas are privately owned; visitors should check with monument headquarters staff in Kotzebue for specific locations of private property. No signs mark private areas. Travelers are free to explore archeological zones, but no digging for artifacts or other disturbance is allowed.

Winds sweep almost constantly across the lowlands of Cape Krusenstern. In winter they bring instant freezing to an already-cold land. In summer, fog blankets coastal areas, although temperatures are from 40–65°F (4–18°C). Inland, the skies are often clear in June and July, but visitors should always carry rain gear and be alert for hypothermia, the severe lowering of the body's core temperature.

Formation of the cape: The cape at Krusenstern didn't always exist. In fact, as recently as about 10,000 years ago, the coastline angled straight southeast from Point Hope, skirted a small mountain, and turned east. Kotzebue Sound was mostly a giant sandy lowland and not the busy waterway it is today. During the Pleistocene era, about 2 million to 10,000 to 15,000 years ago, great ice sheets covered much of the northern hemisphere. These ice masses absorbed water, causing the sea level to recede.

Preceding pages, migrating sandhill cranes. **Below**, an archeologica dig.

As the sea shrank away from the shore, it exposed a land bridge connecting North America and Asia. At the end of the Pleistocene era, when the ice sheets melted, the sea level rose once again and covered the land bridge.

Sweeping down the newly aligned coastline, prevailing winds from the northwest propelled waves, which carried bits of gravel in their churning surf, down the beach. When the waves hit the turn where the coastline swung east, they dropped the gravel offshore. Every so often, usually in the spring, the winds shifted to the southwest. Great chunks of ice were driven onshore, but not before the ice scooped up gravel from shallow offshore beds and deposited it on the beach beyond the surf. Ridge after ridge built up on the outer shore of the cape.

Slowly the cape pushed seaward. Hardy beach plants colonized the ridges, their root systems helping to stabilize the gravels. Year after year the birth and death of beach plants built up a thin layer of soil, creating suitable habitat for other plants. Throughout the centuries, a carpet of green followed the shoreline, advancing seaward, until 114 ridges lined an approximately three-mile-wide (5-km) spit. Lt. Otto von Kotzebue, sailing for the Imperial Russian Navy, gave geographical recognition to the cape by naming it Krusenstern after the first Russian admiral to circumnavigate the globe in 1803–04.

Arctic archeology: Not until the late 1950s was the significance of the beach ridges correlated with the history of early man in Alaska. Professor J. Louis Giddings, anthropologist and archeologist, unlocked the treasure chest buried in the frozen beach gravels and began a new chapter in arctic archeology.

Giddings had sought signs of ancient man at several sites in northwestern Alaska prior to coming to Krusenstern in 1958. In 1948 he had uncovered artifacts from the Denbigh Flint people at Cape Denbigh in Norton Sound to the south. These ancient Alaskans left their calling cards – tiny chipped flints – in the soils of prehistoric Alaska about

4,000 years ago. (The discoverer placed the date at about 5,000 years ago, but more recent studies lead scientists to think 4,000 years is closer to the mark.) Archeologists view these discoveries as the first from the Arctic Small Tool tradition which eventually spanned the top of the continent from the Bering Sea to Greenland.

At Krusenstern, Giddings probed the ridges back from the shore to discover artifacts related to the succession of early man in northwestern Alaska and probably the entire northern portion of the continent. Laid out in order of their occurrence along the series of beach ridges were the remains of houses or hunting camps for every ancient man culture known to northwestern Alaska. Excavations over several years opened the prehistoric record, ridge by ridge, of the ancestors of modern Eskimos and those cultures which preceded them across the land bridge from Asia to arctic North America.

From the ninth to the 19th ridges, Giddings and his assistants unearthed bits of pottery, ivory and whalebone harpoon heads, snow goggles and other tools of a coastal dwelling lifestyle. Carvings and other decorations on these items pointed to the Thule culture which spread along the northwestern arctic coast about AD 800. Scientists have concluded that the Thule people are the first of the early cultures which can definitely be linked with modern Inupiat Eskimos of northern Alaska.

Giddings continued poking among the beach ridges, and at a large ridge extending much of the length of the cape he came upon artifacts of the Ipiutak people, a highly artistic prehistoric culture dating to about 2,000 years ago. First discovered when archeologists uncovered remnants of a huge village near Point Hope, 100 miles (160 km) to the northwest, the Ipiutaks carved elaborate designs on bone and ivory and fashioned fanciful items whose practical use has remained a mystery.

Moving inland once again, Giddings came upon a more moist habitat. Here pottery decorated with waffle-like **Cleaning salmon for drying racks**

rectangles provided the clue to the early residents of the next series of beaches. Unknown to the Ipiutaks, pottery of the Norton culture, which is unlike pottery of more recent peoples, lay scattered over nine ridges that guarded six centuries of this prehistoric culture.

Earlier in the archeological parade came the Choris people, first discovered on the Choris Peninsula of southern Kotzebue Sound. Identified by their large oval house depressions, the Choris people left no signs of permanent houses at Krusenstern. But tiny flakes lying exposed on early beach ridges led scientists to the hearths of temporary hunting camps which were set up by Choris people about 1,000 BC. At one prized find, the scientists chanced upon a bounty of flints, flaked diagonally, and including a single blade nearly seven inches (18 cm) long.

The Old Whalers: Every once in a while the continuity of the archeological record was broken when scientists unearthed artifacts from a culture that did not fit in to the spectrum of early man in north-

western Alaska. One such find was the record of Old Whalers on the beach ridge inland from the Choris remains. These prehistoric people who lived for a brief time at the cape year-round sometime between 1,800 and 1,500 BC relied almost exclusively on the sea for sustenance. Their record indicates a greater use of whales than either preceding or subsequent cultures.

The cape still had more to offer. On the innermost ridges beyond the Old Whalers and adjacent to the lagoon, Giddings came full circle, back to the prehistoric people he first encountered a decade earlier at Cape Denbigh. Beaches a mile and a half from the current Chukchi coast yielded hearths with bits of charcoal, burnt stones and tiny chips – remains of the earliest inhabitants of the beach ridge system, the Denbigh Flint people.

The archeological treasure chest buried in the beach ridges had now been opened, but there remained one final chapter to write in the story of ancient man at Krusenstern. **Ingitkalik Moun-**

trips of ried salmon fill winter tores.

tain, whose prehistoric ancestor guarded the Pleistocene coast before the beach ridges formed, rises across the lagoon at the beginning of the benchlands above Cape Krusenstern. At several elevations on the mountain's slopes Giddings found signs of ancient man's presence even older than those of the beach ridges below. Not until excavation of the vertical stratigraphy at the **Onion Portage** site in the Kobuk Valley, east of Kotzebue, were scientists able to confirm that the Palisades findings of the benchlands above Krusenstern were indeed older than any of the artifacts found buried in the beach ridges.

Giddings and others had now exposed the archeological treasures of Krusenstern and added to our knowledge of ancient man in Alaska. Man had subsisted at Krusenstern for thousands of years, and still does.

The Cape today: Each spring, the rivers and streams of Kotzebue basin cleanse themselves when snow melt fills the channels which dump their load into Kotzebue Sound. Whitefish join this migration, leaving their inland wintering grounds and moving into summer feeding areas in coastal estuaries. This annual flooding acts as a catalyst for one of the region's major subsistence hauls.

As the flood waters fan out into Kotzebue Sound, several species of whitefish swarm into sloughs along the Krusenstern coast, fattening throughout the summer in the brackish waters. Local residents congregate at the sloughs each fall when ground swells from the Chukchi Sea push gravel and sand across the channels by which the whitefish exit the saltwater areas on their return migration. Residents harvest the fish, now trapped in the sloughs, to add to their winter staples.

Subsistence controls the lifestyle of Krusenstern residents today as in ancient times. Travelers should take extra care not to disturb fishing nets, boats or other gear on which local residents rely.

Also crucial is the 6-mile (10-km) flatland at the monument's southern tip – **Sheshalik**, "Place of White Whales." Several families maintain year-round

Musk-ox hide in Tunanak.

236

homes at Sheshalik, a traditional gathering place for hunters of beluga, a small, light-colored, toothed whale.

Life at Sheshalik revolves around stockpiling the meat, fish, berries and greens that see these families through nine months of winter.

When snow and cold blanket the region, families keep busy ice fishing and trapping for small furbearers. In spring, marine mammal hunters take to the ice in search of seals. When leads open in the sea ice, belugas become the quarry. For centuries, hunters have gathered at **Sealing Point** on the narrow isthmus separating the Chukchi from the inner lagoons. Returning, their boats loaded with sea mammal carcasses, the hunters portage the isthmus and continue their southerly journey over calm lagoon waters rather than fighting the waves of the open sea.

In May waterfowl return from their winter sojourn and head for Krusenstern where snow melt has weakened the ice and open water spreads early throughout the lagoons. Several species of geese and ducks nest on the ponds, joined by their cousins on stilts, the sandhill cranes.

Later in the summer residents harvest salmonberries, cranberries and blueberries. Women pick greens, preserving some in seal oil for later use. Fish – grayling, arctic char, whitefish – hang to dry on wooden racks. Chum salmon are taken for subsistence as well as for the commercial fishery in Kotzebue Sound.

After waterfowl leave in the fall, hunters turn to caribou, ptarmigan and sometimes walrus or – rarely nowadays – bear. Black bear and brown bear have been found on the Cape; polar bear roam offshore ice in winter and spring. Agile arctic fox follow behind these northern barons, ready to inspect any tidbit left by the bears. Onshore, elusive furbearers – wolves, wolverines, red fox, lynx, mink, short-tailed weasels, snowshoe and tundra hare, and arctic ground squirrels – patrol the tundra. Hunters take moose in low-lying areas or Dall sheep in the Igichuk Hills. A small group of musk ox, descendants of the shaggy mammals which once roamed all arctic North America but were wiped out by hunters in Alaska in the mid-1800s, thunder across the tundra of the Mulgrave Hills.

Other species, generally not part of the subsistence catch, share Krusenstern's bounty. Lesser golden-plovers, western and semipalmated sandpipers, whimbrels, Lapland longspurs and Savannah sparrows add their beauty and song. Arctic and Aleutian terns float gracefully above the tundra, ready to defend their nests from the purposeful forays of glaucous gulls and jaegers. An Asian migrant, the handsome yellow wagtail, builds its nest in tiny cavities in the beach ridges. Overhead, rough-legged hawks soar from their nests in the highlands to hover over the tundra, piercing eyes searching for voles and lemmings.

The ambience at Krusenstern is understated, but for the curious and the thorough, the history of early man in the north and its modern translation in the subsistence world of local residents are only a step away.

arctic tern
vers over
pe
usenstern.

THE NORTH SLOPE

Bush pilots on Alaska's north coast have little use for aerial charts. There are few usable landmarks that can be depicted on a map to aid a pilot in this world of myriad tiny lakes and meandering rivers. Pilots plot their positions by counting the number of rivers crossed from a known starting point.

Rivers flow from south to north on the North Slope, a vaguely defined but huge chunk of territory that includes everything north of the summit of the Brooks Range. Once a pilot locates a particular river by flying east or west, he turns inland toward terrain with more features, the treeless northern side of the mountains about 100 miles (160 km) to the south.

Most people fly bush planes or helicopters in these latitudes. There are no roads and few means of overland travel except dogsleds and snow machines in the winter.

Hidden riches: There are, however, exceptional map readers who can chart a course across Alaska's northern fringe. Union Oil Company geologist Norm Kent – not a flier but riding in the co-pilot's seat – can read a map better than most people can read a book. When his company is paying $500 an hour and up to rent a helicopter for oil exploration, he knows where he is every second of every flight.

Kent flies out of the coastal oil production zone into the Brooks Range, seeking clues that might lead to oil. His clues are the rocks and fossils laid down in a bygone age and thrust upwards when the Brooks Range was born. The same rock strata that underlie the mountains also underlie the North Slope oil-fields; the varied terrain in the mountains, however, allows that strata to be seen and evaluated. The next rock Kent cracks with his hammer, seemingly in the middle of nowhere and maybe during a lunch break, could eventually lead to an oil strike worth millions, even billions of dollars.

Map-reading problems aside, a con-stant fog is the next biggest problem facing pilots navigating visually along the coast. A 1,500-foot (458-meter) thick cloud of mist blankets the north coast of Alaska most days of the year. It usually stretches inland about 20 miles (32 km); most of the airports are hidden in the fog. Helicopter pilots, who rarely fly on instruments, roar along at 120 mph (200 kph) through the perpetual mist. Just inches above the ground, they can usually only see objects within a quarter-mile of their cockpits. They joke that the only navigational hazard on this flat landscape is a caribou that suddenly stands up. A haunted look in their eyes after such a flight dampens laughter the remark might otherwise elicit.

When ferrying a geologist such as Kent, the pilot flies south, out of the fog, then lets the passenger do the navigating. Usually geologists are heading for the foothills of the Brooks Range, a different world but still considered part of the North Slope.

Stark, trackless beauty and the undisturbed miracles of nature surround the fragile helicopter. The country is so remote that Alaskan law requires firearms be carried aboard aircraft for use in possible survival situations. Aircrews forced down in the northern Brooks Range may have to survive for weeks on only their wits and the gear they have aboard the aircraft. A gun is handy for killing food animals or defending against marauding bears.

But there are lighter moments. A sack lunch on a 6,000-foot (1,830-meter) ridge overlooking a glacier is one. Discovering a bushel-basket full of 300-million-year-old fossils under the helicopter might be another. These moments are there, and more.

Almost every stone or fossil is a clue to the varying layers of rock underlying the flat coastal plain, a clue that can lead to the eventual discovery of oil. And every clue is zealously guarded by the company that finds it, for finding and developing oil is the name of the game on the North Slope. Initial explorations by geologists are just the first move by the players.

Alaska's economy floats on an ocean

of black gold, most of it pumped from beneath the tundra on the North Slope. Oil generates 85 percent of the state's income and a large transient population of oil-industry workers who live on the Arctic coast.

Prudhoe Bay is a working person's world. Several thousand people live and work at the Prudhoe Bay industrial facility – there are no schools, no public roads and few entertainment facilities. The workday is 12 hours long, seven days a week. The pace, though, is temporary. After two or three weeks on the job, workers fly to Anchorage, Fairbanks or even Dallas, Texas, for a week or sometimes two of vacation. It's not uncommon for a worker on the slope to make $75,000 a year for only 26 actual weeks on the job.

The larger oil companies house and feed their personnel, at no expense to employees. Meals are more than just sustenance. A common Friday night entree is steak, all you can eat. Icecream, sweet rolls, pies, cakes, cookies and a host of other snacks are available at all hours. Living quarters usually include a library, gymnasium with an indoor track, weights room, game rooms and satellite television, but they tend to be quiet places where the workers settle into a routine – and there is little time for more than working, sleeping and eating.

Many Slope transient workers see nothing more than the inside of the housing building, work station and air terminal. For them, Prudhoe Bay is the latest example of US technology transplanted into a frozen wilderness. Little outside their doors interests them; it's only frozen tundra and fog. Frozen it may be for most of every year, but people have called Alaska's Arctic coast "home" for centuries, and for some workers on the slope their few hours of unscheduled time are a rare opportunity for photographing summer wildlife, such as migrating caribou or birds, or winter's northern lights.

North Slope native life: West of Prudhoe Bay and east of Barrow, **Nuiqsit** is geographically between big oil and tradition. Unlike most northern communi-

A drawing of the elusive Northern Lights.

ties, it is several miles inland from the coast, at the apex of the Colville River delta, about 60 miles (100 km) from Prudhoe. Eskimo men still hunt whales off the coast, as well as polar bears and seals. Although most still lead a traditional lifestyle of hunting and gathering, a few jobs are available, mostly in government. But for those who still venture onto the frozen sea in search of food and skins, their safety is less in the hands of chance these days. If they are late returning to their modern frame houses in the village, one quick telephone call launches a helicopter to search the coastline near the delta's mouth.

An early freeze caught five Nuiqsit hunters in the Beaufort Sea in September 1980, perhaps 40 miles (64 km) from the village. A helicopter dispatched from Prudhoe Bay later located the hunters gingerly crossing the sea ice on foot, their boat and most of their gear left behind on a barrier island, one of a broken ribbon of sand spits thrusting barely above sea level off the northern coast. The helicopter pilot carefully set his heavy machine on the soft new ice, cut the engine to idle, and exited the aircraft. The men of Nuiqsit politely asked the pilot if they could have a ride home, making no mention of their misfortune and offering no explanation for their dangerous trek over the uncertain ice. The pilot paused only long enough to ensure that these were the men he was hired to find, although it would have made little difference. The flier would have flown down to safety anyway.

Aboard the helicopter, the men consumed several gallons of hot soup and dozens of sandwiches; they had been without food for several days. In the village, only one hunter struggled to thank the pilot. The concept of expressing thanks is a white man's innovation; Eskimos traditionally return a favor or kindness with little or no comment.

On the Continent's edge: Located to the west and just south of Point Barrow, the northernmost tip of North America, **Barrow** is the largest Eskimo settlement in Alaska. It is the headquarters of the North Slope Regional Corporation,

ow chining ough the fog in the h arctic.

a Native corporation formed to manage the huge sums of money and vast tracts of land deeded to Alaska Native groups by the Alaska Native Claims Settlement Act of 1971. When that legislation was approved by the US Congress, Barrow and other key Native villages in Alaska instantly became corporate centers, modern enclaves of big business in a traditional land. Barrow today stands as the ultimate contrast between tradition and technology.

The corporation, further enriched by money gained from oil leases, boasts large new buildings with entire walls of glass, even though built in this cold and harsh environment. When your land rests atop billions of barrels of petroleum, you can afford costly heating bills.

Yet in the shade of these glass monoliths perch clapboard shacks and drafty shanties of every description. Most of the owners haul water to their dwellings as blocks of ice cut from a nearby lake. One of the earliest goals of the North Slope Regional Corporation, headed during the 1970s by the late Eben Hopson, was to provide flush toilets in every home. It's still a dream, although coming closer to reality with every passing year.

Skin whaling boats still dot the coastline, but most are being replaced by modern aluminium craft as they wear out – few Natives continue to make boats in the traditional way. Whaling captains teach their sons the secrets of harpooning and landing the bowhead whale, now more as a means of keeping the culture alive than as a necessary tool of survival.

The opportunity to see an ancient culture and its traditions, and a chance to stand momentarily on the continent's northern edge, lure visitors to Barrow – mostly as part of a package tour. Travel agencies offer overnight trips to Barrow from Anchorage and Fairbanks. A single fee covers a hotel room, a few local tours and the use of a parka.

Less timid souls venture into town on their own and perhaps discover **Pepe's North of the Border Restaurant**, which serves some of finest Mexican food in Alaska. Others may squeamishly try a bite of *muktuk* (whale blubber), or perhaps a piece of seal meat. These local delicacies are available sporadically and visitors may have to search for them.

For all too many visitors, though, the most vivid memory of their Barrow trip is the brief moment they stood on the sand at the tip of the continent. It's only a windswept stretch of dark-sand beach, often shrouded in fog, and usually littered with ice. But it is the edge of a continent.

Eskimo lore: It's unfortunate that most Barrow trips are so brief. Eskimo culture is varied and ancient, but for an outsider to gain a detailed knowledge of it is difficult and time-consuming. And, although English is spoken by most Eskimos (except for the very old), traditional behavior sometimes interferes with communication. For example, Eskimos are not being impolite when they fail to respond immediately to a question or statement. It is simply not their custom to do so. Outsiders who find this long pause uncomfortable often feel slighted, though there is no reason for such a feeling. Perhaps the best advice for tourists is to assume a slower-paced style of speaking and action, a pace more attuned to the traditional lifestyles of the region. Eskimos live not by the clock but by the change of seasons.

Prudhoe Bay's oilfields: In addition to Barrow, tour companies also offer flights to the Prudhoe Bay oilfields. Travelers more attuned to 20th-century civilization often find this a more comfortable experience; certainly, less chance for a clash of cultures exists.

Prudhoe Bay trips are managed just as the Barrow trips. A fixed fee provides a bed for the night, meals at a North Slope dining facility and roundtrip airfare. Bus tours of the oilfields round out the arrangement. Visitors are usually impressed by the neatness of the facility and how little the buildings seem to disturb the landscape. The silver slash of the Trans-Alaska oil pipeline originates here, then winds south toward the Brooks Range.

Here beats the heart that pumps black gold, the life blood of Alaska's contemporary economy.

Aerial view
the ice pac
off Barrow.

244

NATIONAL PARKS: DENALI

Alaskan Indians called it Denali, "The Great One." In later years, the mountain was officially designated **Mount McKinley** by the US Government but Denali is the name still used by Natives and locals.

Denali is the most spectacular mountain in North America. At 20,320 feet (6,195 meters), it is also the highest. In a sense, it could be called the highest in the world. The north face of Denali rises almost 18,000 feet (5,500 meters) above its base, an elevation gain which surpasses even Mount Everest.

The mountain is surrounded by one of the world's greatest wildlife sanctuaries – **Denali National Park**. A one-day trip through the park will almost certainly result in sightings of grizzly bears, caribou, Dall sheep, moose and perhaps a wolf. A visit to Denali Park is an adventure. It's like nothing you've ever seen. When you arrive, be prepared for the ultimate Alaskan experience.

Geology and history: Denali is part of the **Alaska Range**, a 600-mile (960-km) arc of mountains stretching across the southeast quarter of the state. The oldest parts of the Range consist of slate, shale, marble and other sedimentary deposits formed under an ancient ocean. Approximately 60 million years ago, the collision and subsequent overlapping of two tectonic plates produced such intense heat that portions of the earth's crust literally began to melt. A gigantic mass of molten rock was deposited beneath the current location of Denali. The molten material eventually solidified into granite.

Overlapping of the plates also caused the whole region to be uplifted. Granite and sedimentary rock were forced upward to form the ancestral Alaska Range. As this uplift gradually tapered off, the process of erosion slowly worked to wear down the Range. Since Denali is chiefly composed of erosion-resistant granite, it wore at a far slower rate than the surrounding sedimentary rock. A

more modern period of tectonic plate collision and uplift began 2 million years ago and continues to this day. This ongoing uplift is responsible for the towering height of Denali.

The first humans came into what is now Denali Park about 12,000 years ago, near the end of the last Ice Age. Use of the area appears to have been mainly limited to seasonal hunting trips. Ice Age hunters as well as the more recent Athabascans sought the region's big game species – but did not live here year round. Their permanent village sites were in lower, warmer and more sheltered locations. Almost all of the villages were built next to a lake or river which offered dependable fishing. The lack of significant numbers of fish in the Denali rivers probably limited Native use of the region.

The Athabascans of the Yukon and Tanana rivers gave Denali its name. They said the mountain was created during a great battle between two magical warriors. The raven war chief, Totson, was pursuing his enemy Yako down a river. Totson threw a magic spear at his adversary but Yako turned a gigantic wave to stone and deflected the weapon. The solidified wave became the mountain called Denali.

In another Indian story, Denali is called "the home of the sun." (During the longest days of summer, the sun makes almost a complete circle in the local sky and drops below the horizon for only a few hours. From certain angles, it appears that the sun rises *and* sets from behind Denali.) An Athabascan hunting party once camped on the south side of the Alaska Range. That evening they saw the sun disappear behind Denali. A few hours later, it reappeared on the other side of the mountain. They told their chief, "Surely we found the home of the sun, as we saw with our own eyes the sun go into the mountain, and saw it leave its home in the morning."

The first recorded sighting of Denali by a white man occurred in 1794. While sailing in Cook Inlet, English Captain George Vancouver sighted "distant stupendous mountains covered with snow." He was undoubtedly seeing the Alaska

Range. Other explorers, surveyors and adventurers saw the mountain in later decades. Many of them commented on its great height. Some correctly guessed that it was the highest peak on the American continent.

The naming process: Denali became known as Mount McKinley through a strange set of circumstances in 1896. That year, a man named William Dickey went on a gold-prospecting expedition in the area just south of Denali. While camped within sight of the mountain, he met other miners who argued at length with Dickey over whether gold or silver should back US currency. (They were against the gold standard while Dickey was for it.) When Dickey later returned to the Lower 48 states, he wrote an article about his Alaskan adventures. To spite the miners, he proposed that the highest mountain in the Alaskan Range be named after presidential candidate William McKinley, the champion of the gold standard. McKinley won the 1896 election and the name stuck. At least it stuck in the Lower 48.

The first white man to extensively explore the Denali region, Charles Sheldon, was also the first to suggest that it be set aside as a National Park. Sheldon made a six-week trek through the area in 1906 and returned for a much longer trip from 1907–1908. To Sheldon, the opportunity to see and study wildlife was the most impressive feature of the region. After leaving Denali, he used his influence as a member of the powerful Boone and Crockett Club to gather support for his proposed Denali National Park. Largely due to Sheldon's efforts, the Park became a reality in 1917. To Sheldon's disappointment, Congress chose to call it Mount McKinley National Park.

While Sheldon was campaigning for the park, others were endeavoring to make the first ascent of Denali. In late 1909, four miners, true Alaskan sourdoughs (old-timers) all, decided to climb the mountain. The four men (Billy Taylor, Pete Anderson, Charly McGonagall and Tom Lloyd) were quickly dubbed the Sourdough Expedition. They

Park shuttle bus is dwarfed by Mount McKinley.

were not intimidated by the fact that they had never climbed a mountain before. They figured if they had survived the Alaskan winters they could do anything. The Sourdough Expedition left Fairbanks with complete confidence to conquer the mountain.

On the morning of April 6, 1910, Taylor and Anderson set out for the summit from their camp at 12,000 feet (3,700 meters). By mid-afternoon they were standing on Denali's North Peak, the peak visible from Fairbanks and their mining claims. They had achieved their goal despite their total lack of experience.

Unfortunately for them, the North Peak is 850 feet (260 meters) lower than the South Peak, Denali's true summit. Taylor and Anderson were never credited for being first on the top. For several years, no one even believed that these two miners had really climbed the North Peak, so Taylor and Anderson insisted their story was true and claimed they had left a spruce pole in the snow on the top. A later climbing party was able to validate their claim when they saw the pole on the North Peak.

Hudson Stuck and a party of three climbers (Harry Karstens, Robert Tatum and Walter Harper) mounted the first successful Denali expedition in 1913. Using maps and route descriptions made by earlier parties, they ascended the Muldrow Glacier which flows down the east side of Denali. After a long and difficult climb, they reached Denali Pass, the saddle between the North and South Peaks, only 2,100 vertical feet (640 meters) below the summit. The high elevation, low oxygen and extreme cold made those last few hundred feet the hardest part of their climb. Harper, a young Athabascan native employed by Stuck and the strongest member of the team, was the first to stand on the summit of Mt Denali.

Recent changes: From 1917 to the early 1970s, visitation was relatively low in Mount McKinley National Park. The park's remoteness and lack of direct access by vehicle combined to limit tourism. In the five years prior to 1972, the average annual visitation was only about 15,000. In 1972, the Anchorage-Fairbanks Highway was completed and it suddenly became much easier for both tourists and Alaskan residents to travel to the Park. In a short time, the numbers jumped to more than 140,000 a year, almost a ten-fold increase over the previous figures.

This dramatic rise in use was foreseen by the National Park Service. Rangers were concerned about the effect it would have on the park and the quality of visitors' experiences. One major problem was that the single dirt road which bisects the park was too narrow to handle the increased traffic. Another concern was the park's wildlife, which in the past had always been readily visible from the road. The extra traffic and noise created by a tenfold increase in numbers would likely drive the animals out of sight. In addition, huge influxes of people could result in more encounters with the park's dangerous animals, grizzly bears and moose.

The creative solution to these problems was the initiation of a shuttle bus

Ranger shows young hiker Denali's sights.

system for travel in the park. Private vehicles are parked at the park entrance and visitors board buses which run thoughout the day. Because people are concentrated into the buses rather than a large number of private vehicles, wildlife experiences little disturbance.

In the late 1970s, Congress considered a number of proposals to establish new National Parks in Alaska. Most of the proposals also called for an expansion of Mount McKinley National Park to include scenic areas and critical wildlife habitat which had been left out of the original boundaries. The Alaska National Interest Lands Conservation Act was finally passed in 1980. One section of the act partially resolved an old controversy. Recognizing the longstanding Alaskan use of the name Denali, Congress renamed the area Denali National Park but although the park is now called Denali, the mountain is still officially McKinley.

Arriving in the park: The entrance to Denali Park is on Alaska Highway 3, 240 miles (385 km) north of Anchorage and 120 miles (193 km) south of Fairbanks. Access to the park is also provided by the Alaska Railroad which has daily service from both Anchorage and Fairbanks. The train depot, Information Center, Park Hotel, Riley Creek Campground, general store and Youth Hostel are all within easy walking distance of each other.

Denali National Park Hotel, McKinley Chalet Resort and McKinley Village (907-276-7234), the only room accommodations inside the park, offer an array of services. Visitors can book private wildlife bus tours, river rafting and flight-seeing excursions. Complete packages are available including transportation to the park. Accommodations are available from late-May to mid- or late- September. The park road is closed beyond Mile 3 in winter, but a campground loop is plowed for campers.

Campground and backcountry camping registration also takes place at the Information Center. Denali Park has six public campgrounds containing a total of 215 sites. A limited number of ad-

Moving pictures.

vance reservations are accepted for these campgrounds – and the rest are available on a first-come, first-served policy. During the peak summer season (late-June to mid-August, all sites are often occupied by mid-morning. (Private campgrounds located just outside the boundary normally have space, even when the park campgrounds are filled.)

While in the park entrance area be sure to visit the sled dog kennel, located behind the park headquarters building at Mile 3 of the park road. The kennel is the home of 30 of the hardest working government employees you'll ever meet. Since the 1920s, park rangers have used sled dog trips as a means of patroling the park. Dog sledding is still the most practical means of getting around Denali in the winter months. The dogs have become so popular with visitors that rangers put on four dog sledding demonstrations every day during the summer season.

The adventure begins: The adventure of experiencing Denali National Park really begins when you step on a shuttle bus for an all-day trip into the park. The 52-passenger buses start their routes at Riley Creek Information Center. The rangers can give you a bus schedule, explain how the system works and get you a reservation on the next available bus. Most shuttle buses turn around at Eielson Visitor Center, 65 miles (105 km) from the park entrance. This round-trip usually takes seven to eight hours. Some buses make a 10-hour round-trip to Wonder Lake, 85 miles (136 km) from the entrance.

Your chances of seeing wildlife as well as Denali itself are increased by taking as early a bus as possible. The first few depart at 6am. During the rest of the morning they leave every half hour. The early buses are often in high demand. No food or drinks are available along the bus route so be sure to take with you what you'll need for the day. Always be prepared for cool temperatures and rain regardless of what the early morning weather might be.

The first leg of the bus route is the 14-mile (22-km) stretch between the en-

trance and the **Savage River**. The first views of Denali occur in this area. If Denali is visible, your driver will stop the bus, point it out and allow time for photographs. This section of the park road goes through prime moose habitat. Any time a moose or other animal is spotted the bus will stop to allow the passengers to watch and photograph it. Wildlife-spotting on shuttle buses is a group effort. With 52 pairs of eyes looking for wildlife, your chances of seeing animals is far greater.

Moose are the biggest animals in the Park – mature bulls can weigh as much as 1,500 lbs (680 kg). During the spring, watch for calves in this area. Cow moose usually have one or two calves each year. At birth, a calf weighs about 30 lbs (14 kg). Moose calves are one of the fastest growing animals in the world. By their first birthday, they often weigh over 600 lbs (270 kg).

Each September and October this portion of Denali Park becomes the rutting grounds for moose. The huge bulls challenge each other over harems of cows. The bulls are deadly serious when it comes to these fights. A bull can kill his opponent with his sharp antler points. Rutting bulls and cow moose with calves should always be considered extremely dangerous and avoided. If they are approached too closely, both cows and bulls will charge a human.

As your bus continues beyond the Savage River, you will pass a mountain to the north known as **Primrose Ridge**. Dall sheep are often seen on the higher slopes of Primrose. The sheep have pure white fur, perfect winter camouflage, but in summer, they readily stand out against the green tundra or dark rock formations.

Like all wild sheep, the Dall sheep are almost always found on or near steep cliffs. The cliffs are their security. No predator can match their climbing speed or agility. Enemies such as wolves or grizzlies can only catch weak or injured sheep, or those that have wandered too far from the crags.

The Dall ewes utilize the steepest cliffs in this area as lambing grounds.

Wonder Lake, Denali National Park.

With luck, you may be able to spot young lambs on the higher slopes. Within a few days of birth, the lambs can easily match their mother's climbing ability. The lambs spend hours each day playing games of tag, king of the mountain and head-butting. All of this play helps them develop their strength, agility and co-ordination. When their lambs are young, the ewes are provided with free day care service. The mothers drop off their lambs with a designated babysitter. She will watch over up to a dozen lambs while the mothers go off to feed and rest. After a few hours the lambs get hungry and call out for their mothers who then return to nurse their young.

Bands of rams may also be seen in the Primrose Ridge region. Rams are very concerned with the issue of dominance. A band will establish a pecking order going from the top ram down to the lowest. In almost all bands, the top ram will be the one with the largest set of horns. To a ram, horns are his most important status symbol. The older rams have horns of such large size that they can easily intimidate the smaller rams.

Head-butting contests which occur between big rams are fights to determine which animal will be dominant. The two rams back off and charge each other at speeds of 30 mph (48 kph). They bash each other over and over until one gives up and backs off. The reward of dominance comes during the fall rutting season. The top rams are the ones who get to do most of the breeding.

By the time **Sable Pass** is reached at Mile 39 you are surrounded by tundra. Tundra is any area of plant growth above tree line. Sable Pass has an elevation of 3,900 feet (1,188 meters), well above the average local treeline of 2,400 feet (730 meters). The cool summertime temperatures and strong winds at these altitudes are too severe for trees. The low growing tundra vegetation survives by taking advantage of the slightly warmer and less windy micro-environment at ground level.

Sable Pass is grizzly country. So many bears use this area that the Park Service has prohibited all off-road hiking here.

e Alaska
inge from
onder
ke.

Denali Park's grizzly population is estimated at 200–300 bears. Grizzlies are omnivores; like humans, they eat both meat and vegetation. They would prefer killing and eating large animals such as moose, caribou and Dall sheep but the bears are not often successful as hunters. For this reason, tundra plants make up at least 90 percent of the diet of most grizzlies. The tundra vegetation in places like Sable Pass offers a dependable, easily obtainable source of nutrition.

Grizzly cubs are born in January or February in the mother's hibernation den. The sow gives birth to one to four cubs weighing about 1 lb. (½ kg) each. By the time the family leaves the den in April, each cub has gained 5–10 lbs. (2–4.5 kg) from their mother's milk. Sable Pass is one of the best places in the world for viewing grizzly families. If a family is visible, you may see the cubs racing across the tundra, playfighting with each other or nursing from their mother. The sow usually drives her young off when they are two and a half years old. At that point they may weigh 100–150 lbs. (45–67 kg). She then breeds again and gives birth to another set of cubs the following winter.

Without a doubt, the grizzly is the most dangerous animal in North America. Its behavior and reaction toward humans is very difficult to predict. Whenever you are in grizzly country, you have the responsibility of doing everything you can to avoid provoking a bear. Most of the local bears seem willing to avoid humans if given the opportunity. The few attacks by bears on people in Denali have almost always been provoked attacks – many made by mother bears on people who had deliberately approached their cubs. Park rangers can give you detailed information on ways to avoid problems with grizzlies.

Your shuttle bus will stop for a rest break at **Polychrome Pass** at Mile 45. The brightly colored Polychrome cliffs are volcanic rocks formed 50 million years ago. The spectacular view to the south includes part of the Alaska Range as well as a vast area of tundra.

Wolf observation: Polychrome Pass is a good place to watch for wolves. A local pack uses these flats as its hunting grounds, especially in the spring when the caribou are in migration. Use binoculars to scan the tundra below the Pass. The Denali wolves range from white to black but most are gray. They may be traveling singly or in small groups. If a pack is sighted, look for a wolf with its tail in the air. This will be the alpha wolf, the leader of the pack. He may not be the first wolf in line, and may well bring up the rear. The alpha male often delegates the lead position to the beta wolf, his second in command.

In a wolf pack, the only members who breed are the alpha male and the alpha female. Their litter is born in the spring and all other members of the pack help to raise the young pups. The other wolves are almost always related to the alpha pair as brothers, sisters or previous offspring. The pack is really a large extended family. Feeding a litter of five to ten pups is a difficult job, even for the entire pack. If all of the pack members tried to breed, the park's territory could not support the resulting large number

Denali grizz' finds a venu for back-scratching.

of offspring. The pack is better served by limiting breeding to the dominant pair, the wolves who have proven themselves to be the fittest animals.

Much of what is now known about wolves was discovered by Adolph Murie. Murie was a biologist who was assigned to the park in the 1930s to study wolves and their relationship with their prey. He was the first scientist who extensively studied wolf behavior in the field. For years, Murie would drive out on the park road and spend hours watching wolves. Much of his observation took place in the Polychrome area. In 1944, Murie published the results of his studies in his book, *The Wolves of Mt. McKinley*, one of the great classics of animal behavior. The book documented that wolves were primarily preying on the sick and weak Dall sheep, caribou and moose. He concluded that wolves were a necessary part of the Denali ecosystem because they ultimately helped to keep their prey species in a healthy and strong state.

Caribou country: Caribou are commonly seen in the Highway Pass area at Mile 58. Caribou are the most social of the large Denali animals. In the spring, herds of several hundred caribou pass through this area as they head toward their calving grounds to the east. Later in the season, they migrate back through the area as they move toward their wintering grounds in the western and northern portions of the park.

The herds are constantly on the move. Even as they feed, they rarely browse for more than a few moments at any one stop. This style of light browsing is perfectly suited to the type of slow growing plants which live on the tundra. If the caribou herds spent too much time feeding in one area, they would likely kill off the fragile tundra vegetation.

Caribou, like moose, have antlers rather than horns. Antlers are formed of bone and are shed every year. Sheep horns consist of keratin, the same materials as our fingernails, and are never shed. The caribou bulls' antlers are fully developed by September and are used to fight for harems. These matches usually

ose are
mmon
hts along
Denali
rk Road.

occur between Highway Pass and Wonder Lake. After their rutting season is over, the antlers drop off. The weight of the massive antlers would be a major hindrance during the winter. Shedding the antlers enables the caribou to have a better chance of surviving the winter, the most stressful time of the year.

As your bus approaches **Stony Hill Overlook**, Mile 61, be prepared for a spectacular view of Denali. From the overlook, it is 37 miles (60 km) to the summit. On a cloudless day, the crystal clear Alaskan air makes the mountain appear far closer.

After a stop at Stony Hill, your bus will continue 4 miles (6 km) to **Eielson Visitor Center**, where the view of Denali is equally as awesome. The park rangers at Eielson can answer any questions you might have and can suggest good hiking routes in the local area. Restrooms, drinking water, maps and books are available at Eielson.

Some shuttle buses continue on to **Wonder Lake**, an additional 20 miles (32 km) beyond Eielson. The round-trip from Eielson to Wonder Lake adds about two hours to your day. If the weather is clear, the extra distance is definitely worth the time. Denali remains in full view along the entire route. On the way, dozens of tundra ponds, home to many species of waterfowl, are passed. In the evening hours, beavers can be seen swimming across these small ponds.

Walks and hikes: The shuttle system has been set up to encourage people to get off the buses and personally explore the park. You may leave your bus, hike for a few hours and then return to the road to catch a later bus. If they have room, buses will stop to pick up passengers anywhere along the road.

Denali National Park is a true wilderness. There are few official trails and these are mainly in the entrance area. In the rest of the park, you are on your own. Despite the vast size of the Denali wilderness, route-making is not difficult. Since most of the park is open tundra, it is easy to choose a destination visually and hike straight to it. Good areas for day hikes include the Savage River, *Going with the flow.*

Primrose Ridge, Polychrome Pass, the Eielson area and Wonder Lake. Before you begin a day-hike, talk to a ranger at Riley Creek or Eielson about tips on safety. Maps of the area you'll be exploring are available at both centers. Permits are required for overnight hikes.

National Park rangers offer a wide variety of interpretive programs to help you better understand and appreciate your Denali experience. Schedules of activities are posted throughout the park. Slide shows and movies are presented in the auditorium behind the Park Hotel several times daily. Most campgrounds have nightly campfire talks. Nature walks and half-day hikes are given each day in different sections of the park.

Denali Park is a paradise for watching and photographing wildlife. A pair of binoculars and a telephoto lens will greatly assist you in these activities. This equipment will allow you to observe and photograph the animals from a safe distance and in a way that won't disturb or drive them away.

Remember that some wild animals are dangerous and will attack if provoked. Never approach a grizzly – view them from the protection of a bus or Visitor Center. Always stay well away from a bull moose and a cow with calf. Dall sheep and caribou bulls are fairly tolerant of people if you abide by their rules. Allow the sheep or caribou to spot you when you are still a long way from them. (It is critical that they have a chance to identify you as a person, rather than a predator.) Making sure that you are always in their field of view, approach them at a very slow walk with frequent pauses.

The standard viewpoints for photographs include Stony Hill, Eielson Visitor Center and Wonder Lake. Take shots from those angles but be sure to use your creativity to seek out less obvious photo points. A walk around some of the tundra ponds between Eielson and Wonder Lake will turn up many great Denali compositions. Lighting on the mountain is best in the early morning or late evening. Those are also the times Denali is most likely to be free of clouds.

NATIONAL PARKS: WRANGELL - ST. ELIAS

As late as the mid-1980s, **Wrangell-St. Elias National Park and Preserve** was an overlooked and under-valued mountain wilderness. Created in 1980, America's largest park – at 13.2 million acres (5.3 million hectares), the size of six Yellowstones – was also one of its least known, least visited.

But sometime in the late 1980s, Wrangell-St. Elias was "discovered." And Kit Mullen, a park staffer from 1981 to 1992, guesses this park abutting the Canadian border will become "the next Denali, in terms of visitor use. There's so much access, probably more than any other national park in Alaska; you've got two roads into the park and airstrips all over."

The northern entry is the unpaved, 45-mile-long (72-km) Nabesna Road, which connects the state's highway system with the tiny (population about 25) mining community of Nabesna. Only the first 30 miles (48 km) are currently suitable for two-wheel-drive vehicles, though there are long-range plans to improve the road; be sure to check for updated road conditions before making the drive.

Several metals – gold, silver, copper, iron and molybdenum – were discovered in the Nabesna area earlier this century, but a bigger attraction now is the wildlife. Caribou, moose and even grizzlies may be spotted in the open country bordering Nabesna Road and large populations of Dall sheep are found in the hills surrounding 9,358-foot (2,850-meter) Tanada Peak, about 15 miles (24 km) southwest of road's end. (Trophy hunting for sheep and other species is allowed in the preserve, which encompasses about 37 percent of the unit's total area.)

McCarthy and Kennicott: The principal avenue into Wrangell-St. Elias is McCarthy Road; 60 miles (96 km) long and also unpaved, it stretches from Chitina, at the park's western boundary (where it connects with the Edgerton

Highway) to the "gateway" community of **McCarthy**, located deep within one of America's most spectacular wildlands. At its doorstep are rugged peaks that rise above raging rivers, fed by massive glaciers. The number of people funneled down McCarthy Road has grown dramatically in recent years, from about 5,000 in 1988 to more than 20,000 in 1993. Overall park visitation has approached 50,000 – less than one-tenth of Denali's total, but a three-fold jump from the early 1980s.

Only a small percentage of those who drive the McCarthy Road actually visit the park's awesome backcountry. Most are content to hang out in McCarthy, take half- or full-day hikes to the nearby **Kennicott Glacier** and **Root Glacier**, or travel 4½ miles (7.2 km) to the historic and now abandoned **Kennicott** copper-mining camp. (To reach McCarthy-Kennicott, visitors must leave their vehicles behind and cross the Kennicott River on hand-pulled trams, although plans are in the works to replace the trams with foot bridges. Local residents remain adamantly opposed to any sort of vehicular bridge, which might open their community to large-scale "industrial" tourism.)

The short version of the Kennicott-McCarthy story goes something like this: At the turn of the century, a couple of prospectors named Jack Smith and Clarence Warner spotted a large green spot on the ridge between the Kennicott Glacier and McCarthy Creek. Initially thought to be sheep pasture, the patch instead proved to be mineral staining from a fantastically rich copper deposit.

Mining engineer Stephen Birch bought the copper claims and won the backing of financial heavyweights such as the Guggenheimer brothers and J.P. Morgan. Known collectively as the "Alaska Syndicate," the investors formed the Kennecott Mines Co. – in the process misspelling Kennicott – later to become Kennecott Copper Corp.

The copper discovery sparked construction of the 200-mile-long (320-km) Copper River Northwestern Railroad, connecting the mining camp to the coastal town of Cordova. When the mine

receding
ages: Skolai
reek valley.
eft, glacial
ick,
rangell-St.
lias.

closed in 1938, after three decades of operation, it had produced more than 4.5 million tons (4 million metric tons) of ore, worth a reported $200 million.

At its peak, 600 people lived at Kennicott. The main settlement included all the operations needed to mill the ore as well as houses, offices, stores and a school, hospital, post office, dairy and recreation hall. Just down the road, a second community, eventually named McCarthy, sprang up around 1908.

In a perfect complement to staid, regimented Kennicott, McCarthy played the role of sin city. Among its most successful businesses were several saloons, pool halls, gambling rooms and back-alley brothels. In its heyday, 100 to 150 people lived in McCarthy. But after the mine shut down, only a few people stayed on.

For decades after the mine's closure, McCarthy-Kennicott served as the quintessential haven for Alaska recluses. But more recently the region has become a major tourist draw, complete with two lodges, a hotel, a bed-and-breakfast inn,

a pizza parlor, two air-taxi operators, two shuttle-bus services, two or three wilderness guide operations, and even an espresso bar – impressive for a community whose "hard core" population numbers 20 to 30 people.

Treasures beyond the road: But the park's real treasures lie beyond such road-side attractions, in a wild and magnificent alpine world that wilderness guides call "North America's mountain kingdom." It's a kingdom that includes four major mountain ranges – the St. Elias, Chugach, Alaska and Wrangells – and six of the continent's 10 highest peaks, including 18,008-foot (5,490-meter) Mount St. Elias.

Here too is North America's largest subpolar icefield, the Bagley, which feeds a system of gigantic glaciers; one of those, the Malaspina Glacier, covers an area of more than 1,500 sq. miles (4,075 sq. km) – larger than Rhode Island. Hubbard Glacier, which flows out of the St. Elias Mountains into Disenchantment Bay, is one of the continent's most active glaciers; in 1986,

Kennicott Mine today.

Hubbard was nicknamed the "Galloping Glacier" when it surged more than a mile and sealed off Russell Fjord. The ice dam later broke, but scientists speculate that Hubbard will eventually close off the fjord permanently.

The glaciers have carved dozens of canyons; some, like the Chitistone and Nizina, are bordered by rock walls thousands of feet high. Rugged, remote coastline is bounded by tidewater glaciers and jagged peaks. The park's alpine superlatives, along with those of neighboring Kluane National Park in Canada, have prompted their combined designation as a World Heritage Site.

There's a certain irony to the new-found interest in Wrangell-St. Elias: much of what's been "discovered" by modern-day explorers was known to local residents centuries ago. This is especially true of the **Skolai Creek-Chitistone River** area, the most popular of the park's backcountry destinations.

Those who hike the Chitistone "Goat Trail" – so named because it's a game trail that you have to be a goat to get across – are following in the footsteps of the Ahtnas, an Athabascan tribe that used the route for hunting and trading.

There's evidence that the Ahtnas traveled the Goat Trail to trade copper nuggets, used for jewelry, with the Eyak people on the coast, according to local naturalists. In return, they would get ocean things, like shells or whalebone.

Later, both the Chitistone and Skolai Pass routes were used by stampeders traveling from McCarthy to Chisana, the site of Alaska's last major gold rush. (Less than 20 people now live year-round in Chisana, located within the Wrangell-St. Elias' northeast corner).

Chisana's boom times lasted only a few years, from 1913 to 1915. But during that short period, as many as 10,000 people may have traveled through the mountains. The routes were heavily used, to get both bodies and equipment to the gold fields.

Modern explorers: Eighty years later, the footsteps of the Chisana stampeders are being retraced by a different sort of boomer, one attracted by wilderness

values rather than gold: the baby boomers. This newest rush into the Wrangell-St. Elias backcountry is, so far at least, much smaller and more benign. Most modern explorers lured into this vast mountain landscape bring a minimum-impact ethic and leave little or no trace of their visit. Still, there's no question that the 1990s "boomers" are having a cumulative effect.

In the first four years that he explored the Skolai-Chitistone area, wilderness guide Bob Jacobs saw only one set of footprints not made by his own parties. Now it's almost impossible to go more than a day or two without seeing signs of other backpackers, or at least hearing aircraft traffic. "It's a much more fragile environment than a lot of people realize and in places you can find evidence of degradation," says Jacobs.

It was only natural that the Skolai-Chitistone area became Wrangell-St. Elias' heaviest-used backcountry area. It is the premier wilderness spot in the park, ruggedly spectacular country in the heart of the mountains.

This is "big country" in the truest sense of the word. The scale of things is immense in this still largely pristine world. In every direction are stark, jagged, ice-carved peaks, most them unnamed and unclimbed. Here, too, there are massive, near-vertical rock faces thousands of feet high, hanging glaciers and waterfalls by the dozens; some are torrents, cascading hundreds of feet to the valley floor, while others are more delicate mists.

And among the glaciers' morainal deposits are "rock gardens" composed of huge boulders, many of them lorry-sized (or bigger) and covered with lichens, moss or grasses.

Wildlife in the park: Yet for all the rock and snow and ice, this is not a barren or alien world. In the valley bottoms are alder groves and tundra meadows brightened with legions of rainbow-hued flowers: blue forget-me-nots, lupine and Jacob's ladder, purple monkshood, yellow paint brush, white mountain avens, pink fireweed and wintergreen.

Ptarmigan hide in the alder, clucking **Glacier country.**

in the early morning like wilderness roosters. Bands of Dall sheep inhabit the high rocky places, while occasional moose, wolves and brown bears prowl valleys and hillsides. The valleys are also home to pikas, ground squirrels, shorebirds and robins. And overhead, eagles soar.

Despite its vast, primeval richness, the Skolai-Chitistone area is easily accessible by plane, located less than 30 miles (48 km) from McCarthy – a short hop by Alaska backcountry standards.

Use takes its toll: All of those variables have dramatically boosted recreational visits to Skolai and Chitistone valleys. The increased use has taken a toll; there's been some trampling of vegetation, littering, crowding, increased air traffic and a growing potential of so-called problem bears that have learned to associate humans with food.

Park officials' biggest concerns aren't the traditional wilderness traveler, but novice explorers. Visitor education is one solution. Another, perhaps, is to spread the use to other beautiful but neglected areas. For instance Tebay Lakes, which are similar to the high Sierras, with beautiful granite peaks, good fishing and excellent hiking. Other areas that haven't been used as heavily include Goat Creek, which offers excellent hiking and has sheep "everywhere" and the wide-open and wildlife-rich upper Chitina Valley.

There's also the remote and stark coastline of the park's southeastern edge, where sea-kayakers can paddle among seals, sea lions, sea otters and orca whales in Icy, Yakutat and Disenchantment bays, or roam among icebergs loosed from tidewater glaciers.

Facilities: Most of Wrangell-St. Elias' natural wonders are inaccessible to those who remain along the road system. Air-taxi services provide transportation into the park and several guide outfits offer river-rafting, climbing and trekking opportunities. Increasingly popular are "flightseeing tours," out of McCarthy or communities that neighbor Wrangell-St. Elias. Overnight lodging is available at both McCarthy and Kennicott and a "wilderness lodge" is located in the backcountry, but park facilities are intentionally minimal. A list of commercial facilities and services is available from park headquarters in **Glennallen** (200 miles/320 km east of Anchorage).

Like much of Alaska, the park's summer weather is typically cool and cloudy, though July – the warmest month – may bring hot, sunny days. The weather can change with little warning and storm systems may delay drop-offs or pick-ups by several days, so extra provisions are recommended.

Other musts are rain gear and cold-weather clothing; in the mountains, sub-freezing weather is possible even in mid-summer. Many streams are glacially fed, making river crossings a special challenge in the Wrangell-St. Elias backcountry. Because assistance may be miles or days away, backcountry travelers must be self-sufficient and schooled in wilderness survival skills.

For more information, call (907) 822-5235 or write to the superintendent, Wrangell-St. Elias National Park, P.O. Box 29, Glennallen, AK 99588.

iew from
e Goat
rail.

NATIONAL PARKS: MISTY FJORDS

There are only two ways to get to **Misty Fjords National Monument**, near Ketchikan: by water or by air. Some travelers opt for a combination cruise/ fly tour – going in by water and out by air, or vice versa. Each summer, hundreds of visitors to the 49th State learn about the beauty of an area that is magnificent, mind-boggling and many an additional adjective as well.

Untouched backcountry: The area, Misty Fjords, is a national wilderness as well as a National Monument, and within the 3,570 miles (9,246 sq. km) of its largely untouched coast and backcountry lie three major rivers, hundreds of small streams and creeks, icefields, glaciers, snowcapped mountains and mountaintop lakes.

It is the southernmost of Alaska's 18 national monuments and visitors to this 2.2-million-acre (890,000-hectare) wilderness experience every major ecosystem of Southeast Alaska, from the ocean swells on the outer coast to the alpine lakes. There are forest groves so thick you can barely see daylight through them, tiny coves and great bays. Misty Fjords wildlife includes brown and black bears, Sitka black-tailed deer, wolves, mountain goats, beavers, mink, marten, foxes and river otters.

There are few marks of human activity inside Misty Fjords. The area's first human inhabitants – Native Tlingits and Haidas – may have settled here as much as 10,000 years ago, but visitors to the monument may stay for days and see no evidence of their passing.

But no roads lead to Misty Fjords. Some cruiseships visit the monument as part of an Inside Passage experience. You can fly there with any of several Ketchikan air charter companies; you can cruise there by charter boat; or (probably most convenient) you can sign on with an outfit called Alaska Cruises, Inc., and take one of the yacht tours the

Unmistakeably Misty Fjords.

company schedules four days a week in the summertime. These latter excursions, aboard the 50-foot M/V *Misty Fjord* or one of the company's other two vessels can be round-trip or one-way with either the coming or going portion by air.

Touring Misty Fjords: Here's what happens on a typical cruise/fly tour. Departure from near downtown Ketchikan is at about 8.30am, but coffee is on the galley stove and donuts are on the serving table for passengers who arrive on the ship early. It's a wide, beamy, comfortable cruiser with plenty of walking-around room, big view windows, and table seating for 32. When the weather is nice about half that number can be seated, if they want to, on an open-air deck above the cabin.

The sightseeing begins as soon as the boat's lines are cast off and the vessel begins its southeasterly path toward the lower end of Revillagigedo (the locals say "Revilla") Island, on which Ketchikan is located. Passing dockside fish processors, supply houses and the town's main business district, the *Misty Fjord* soon cruises past the entrance to Ketchikan Creek. Late in the summer, thousands of salmon assemble here before ascending the creek – and formidable waterfalls – to spawn in the upstream shallows and then die.

Shortly after Creek Street (Ketchikan's former red light district), the *Misty Fjord* cruises past **Saxman**, a Native village containing one of the largest collections of totems in the state.

Shortly thereafter, the *Misty Fjord* passes **Bold Island** and passengers line the port (left) rails and windows of the vessel to glass a huge bald eagle perched in the spruce tree on the island. Shortly, the yacht will pass another of the proud birds, this one sitting on top of a navigational marker out in the middle of the channel.

For southeast Alaskans, such sightings are commonplace, though they never become dull. For visitors, the frequent sight of America's national bird is a highlight of the trip.

At one point or another in the morn-

The coast along Misty Fjords.

ing's cruise, almost every passenger will crowd into the yacht's little wheelhouse and talk to Dale Pihlman, sometimes skipper and all times owner of the *Misty Fjord* and the Alaska Cruises excursion firm. Dale welcomes the intrusion. He's never reluctant to talk about the monument.

Glacial scenery: Eons ago, he explains, great glaciers thousands of feet deep filled what are now Southeast Alaska bays and valleys. Slowly but relentlessly they ground their way seaward from mountaintop heights. In the process they carved and scoured great steepwalled cliffs that now plunge from mountain summits to considerable depths below sea level. The effect of this carving and scouring has never been more beautifully evident than it is in Misty Fjords.

"But Misty Fjords," he says, "is not only a place of scenery on a grand scale, though it certainly is that. It also has tremendous commercial value. Some of Alaska's most productive fish rearing streams are located there."

Dale Pihlman should know. He is a former commercial fisherman and was, in fact, one of Alaska's fisher-folk who traveled back to Washington D.C. in the late 1970s to lobby for the bill that created Misty Fjords National Monument in the first place.

The provisions of the bill, incidentally, do protect most of the monument today from destructive exploitation. Conservationists are fearful that if the giant molybdenum mine within the monument is ever put into full production, the results for fish and wildlife values could be catastrophic.

Porpoise companions: As the boat cruises toward the fjords, the *Misty Fjord* guide and naturalist announces there are porpoises both fore and aft of the vessel. Everyone scrambles, half in each direction, for a view of the small marine mammals. The porpoises swimming behind the yacht are too far away for a close look. They are visible only as leaping, playing creatures 100 yards or more astern. But the ones in front are only a few feet away, clearly visible,

tives took vantage of e rich sources of e fjords.

and just as clearly having a wonderful time pacing the boat. For brief moments their dorsal fins break the surface of the water; at other times they dive. It's obvious they could outdistance the 16-knot vessel easily. They prefer to stay and play, and they do so for a quarter hour or so.

By noon the vessel is in the monument and Dale guides the *Misty Fjord* through a narrow channel into an exquisite little tree-shrouded cove on **Rudyerd Island**. The naturalist points out the steep granite rock formations on the shore and the occasional jet black vertical streaks, a few inches to a couple of feet or more wide, that appear among the brown granite walls.

These were formed 60 million years ago when earthquakes in the region cracked the granite, and hot molten magma came up from below the earth's surface to fill the cracks. The black streaks that you see are magma.

Shapely rock: A little later, **New Eddystone Rock** comes into view. Depending upon the time of day you see it and the angle from which you approach it, it can resemble a man-made building, a ship under sail, or it can look like what it is – a high-rising volcano "plug" from millennia past. It was named by the explorer Captain George Vancouver who thought it looked very much like Eddystone lighthouse off the shore of his native Plymouth, England.

Overnight campers and kayakers who want to go into the fjords often travel along with the day visitors on Alaska Cruises vessels. If there are any aboard the *Misty Fjord*, this is the time they leave the ship in their smaller craft to paddle the waters off Winstanley Island. There's a US Forest Service cabin there, one of relatively few located on saltwater sites in Southeast Alaska.

The comfortable, weathertight shelter is popular with campers who paddle around **Rudyerd Bay** during the day. The cruiser enters the bay – and a welcoming committee of at least 20 seals lie basking on the rocks of an island to port.

Minutes later, within the bay, the *Misty*

Touring Misty Fjords waterfalls by floatplane.

Fjord approaches the towering massive vertical walls of **Punchbowl Cove**. And it is here that the magical mystical effect of the place really comes upon you.

Mists and mystique: It can be truly eerie hereabouts, especially when there are – as the monument's name suggests – mists or clouds or fog in the air. Steep, stark granite walls descend from heights hidden in clouds. Waterfalls which range from torrents to trickles plunge from unseen sources just as high. Trees both large and small hang tenaciously to many of the cliffsides, seemingly on surfaces that don't have enough ground cover to support a house plant.

Waters around and beneath the boat are cold, slate gray, and they descend to depths of 750 feet (230 meters) or more. There has been no sea monster reported in these waters – but it's just the right kind of place for such.

Enough of musings and mystique. On board, it is time for a luncheon of seafood chowder, rolls and tossed green salad. After lunch, the *Misty Fjord* leaves Punchbowl Cove and cruises toward the head of Rudyerd Bay. Several of the passengers glass the shoreline that now replaces the steep cliffs, looking for bears, wolves or other wild creatures.

Creeks and waterfalls: The boat stops again an hour later, this time at **Nooya Creek** where, in season, 1,000 or more pink salmon descend to saltwater each year from Nooya Lake in the high country. Here a trail leads to the uplands – much less steeply, Pihlman says, than one which also takes off, and up, from the Punchbowl Cove area visited earlier. The camping and trout-fishing opportunities at the ends of the trails are, he says, outstanding.

Then it's time for another memorable experience. Dale edges his boat right up to a large plummeting waterfall, where passengers are given paper cups to fill with the icy water.

Promptly at 2.30pm, it is time for those who fly back to Ketchikan to leave the *Misty Fjord* and board the floatplane which taxis gently to the boarding platform.

From the air: Fifteen minutes later, goodbyes are yelled to those remaining and the pilot drifts his plane away from the vessel. He then gives the aircraft full throttle, and within a minute the aircraft is airborne. Within three or four minutes more the passengers may well be spotting white, furry mountain goats, usually nannies and youngsters, negotiating impossible cliff faces to the right of the plane. It is a dramatic flight back through the fjords and the wildlife is only part of the excitement as the dark granite walls seem to be just inches away from the plane's wingtips.

Shortly thereafter the aircraft exits the monument, flying low over New Eddystone Rock and heading back to Ketchikan. The trip takes in hydro projects, logging shows, and no small quantity of land and water and mountain scenery in the process.

By the time you're back at the floatplane dock in downtown Ketchikan, your mind's eye will be full of images and your camera bag full of exposed film, and it is hard not to reflect that visiting Misty Fjord is, indeed, one of Alaska's premier experiences.

the verdant astal rain rest.

NATIONAL PARKS: GATES OF THE ARCTIC

In 1929, Robert Marshall suggested that all of Alaska north of the Brooks Range should be preserved as wilderness. His vision never came to pass, but the place most dear to Marshall, the central Brooks Range, is preserved in **Gates of the Arctic National Park and Preserve**.

In the heart of northern Alaska, the park is 200 miles (320 km) northwest of Fairbanks, and 200 miles south of Barrow, Alaska's largest Eskimo community. No maintained roads or trails exist within the park – no phones, TVs, radios, gas stations, restaurants, stores or hotels. No emergency services are available: no hospitals, first aid stations, ambulances, police or fire stations. There is one permanent ranger station at Anaktuvak Pass, a small community in the middle of the park. Other park staff operate out of Bettles.

Such wilderness offers a real opportunity to experience freedom from civilization and its attendant trappings. A person, liable to meet a bear, in 8 million acres (3.2 million hectares) of wilderness is on his or her own. Unless visitors arrange for someone to rescue them, no one will. People still freeze and starve to death in remote cabins in the Brooks Range wilderness; months may pass before their bodies are found. This unique experience is called self-reliance – or suicide.

A rewarding risk: Yet inherent in the risks are opportunities for wilderness recreation on a grand scale. In the summer, the park provides opportunities for mountaineering, hiking and camping. The lakes, rivers and streams allow for motorboating, rafting, canoeing, kayaking and fishing. Photography is the most popular recreational activity. Also popular are birding, flight-seeing and wildlife viewing. The arctic summer provides 24-hour sunlight – no flashlight needed.

Fall activities include blueberry and cranberry picking, as well as hunting for bear, caribou, moose, ducks, geese, rabbits and ptarmigan. In winter, the park is quiet. The sun drops below the horizon in November and doesn't surface again until February. The temperature can drop to -70°F (-57°C).

As the sunlight comes alive between February and April, the park comes alive with cross-country skiing, dog sledding and snowshoeing.

The Gates of the Arctic area is personalized by the Athabascan Indians and several Eskimo cultures. The lifestyles of trappers, homesteaders and others who live in isolated cabins add color and character. Visitors, flogging past a Native fish camp, may see orange-red salmon strips drying on birch poles or a fish net bobbing with the flow of the river. They may even encounter a trapper's secluded log home with snowmachine outside, traps and a bearskin hanging from the cabin walls. But people are rare. The area population is less than one person per 5,000 acres (2,000 hectares).

Gates of the Arctic National Park and Preserve is remote, pristine wilderness. The meaning of "remote" becomes im-

eceding ges, ooks Range sta. Left, d cabin with owshoes. low, ditional otwear.

A CHILCAT MAN.

From a Drawing by Mrs. Willard.

The buckskin suit is trimmed with fur and quills. The narrow snow-shoe is used in hunting and running, and the broad one in packing.

mediately evident when trying to reach the Gates. Visitors must fly there in their own plane or charter one. Those who don't fly must instead have the time and the physical stamina to backpack miles to the park, after driving along the Dalton Highway.

The Dalton Highway winds through wilderness as wild and beautiful as the Gates and nears the Gates' vicinity at **Coldfoot**, approximately 250 miles (400 km) north of Fairbanks. In early September, when the birch leaves are golden in the hills and the weather is sunny and dry, the drive alone is worth the trip. Coldfoot was named when Klondike gold miners traveled that far north and got "cold feet." Coldfoot was then, and still is, history in the making. Here, the last frontier lives in truckers snaking up the haul road, in mountains and lakes with no names, and in people who tell bear stories from experience. The latter eye with disbelief visitors wanting to sleep in tents and travel unarmed through prime bear habitat.

A stop at the **Coldfoot Services Truckstop** is a must for any visitor. A touch of the modern-day trucking frontier is evident in the racks of personalized coffee cups of the truckers. In the lodge-style dining hall restaurant, meals are eaten on oilcloth-covered tables with wooden benches, mining camp-style. Motel rooms are also available. A summer visitor center at Coldfoot is operated jointly by the National Park Service and other federal agencies.

The most easily accessed trail into the park is in **Wiseman**, 15 miles (24 km) north of Coldfoot. Wiseman is a turn-of-the-century mining community. Its weathered buildings are still home to a small group of miners. The road from Dalton Highway to Wiseman extends on to several trails that enter the Park. The **Nolan-Wiseman Creek Trail** goes through the historic mining area of the park to the Glacier River. Another popular trail follows the Hammond River north from Wiseman.

Gateway to Gates: For those who fly into the National Park, the town of **Bettles** is the gateway to Gates. Another

friendly outpost, Bettles provides visitors to Gates with potential outfitters, guides, air taxi service and a lodge. From Bettles, any number of trips are possible into the park.

The most popular Gates of the Arctic trip is to the north fork of the Koyukuk River, where the peaks, **Frigid Craigs** and **Boreal Mountain**, stand guard. They are the climax of a backpacking trip that starts at **Summit Lake** and ends at **Chimney Lake**; a trip that averages 10 days. Another favored excursion involves flying down the river to the Eskimo village of **Noatak**, past exquisite mountain scenery. Moose and Dall sheep are often spotted, and fishing for grayling, pike and char is excellent.

Float trips – and combination backpack/float trips – can be arranged throughout Gates. Or seek fish-filled **Walker Lake**, a blue jewel nestled in the deep forested hills in the southern part of the park. A few private cabins are the only places where a visitor can sleep indoors in the park. Winter cross-country ski trips, dogsled rides and ice fishing are also available at Walker Lake.

Anyone who wants to visit the Gates needs to do considerable research: terrain and customs can be likened to those of a third-world country. Topographical maps are a must, and problems must be anticipated and planned for. When you are hundreds of miles from the nearest tree it is *not* the time to inquire about how to start a fire without wood!

For maps, information and supplies, Fairbanks is a recommended stop before going to Gates. The National Park Service office in Fairbanks, which has jurisdiction over Gates, has a complete list of air services, commercial services, information books, maps and pictures. Information is also available from the Alaska Department of Fish and Game, the Department of Transportation, the Alaska State Troopers, the State Department of Tourism and the Fairbanks offices of the Bureau of Land Management.

Fairbanks is generally the last stop to shop for supplies. Since all fuel must be flown in, many communities have er-

beaver
ılls an alder
ranch back
his dam.

ratic or nonexistent fuel supplies; camp stove fuel is not allowed on regularly scheduled airlines. Villages are often not equipped with facilities for visitors, so travelers should have adequate food supplies and arrange return air transportation well in advance.

Also check in at Fairbanks for road conditions on the Dalton Highway. (Call the Alaska Department of Transportation, road maintenance, tel: (970) 451-2294.) The road is rough gravel, very narrow and dominated by commercial trucks. Most local people refuse to take cars over the road, preferring vehicles with stronger suspension systems. Only two places sell gas (or anything else) on the road: the truckstop at the Yukon River Bridge and the truck stop at Coldfoot. Beyond Disaster Creek, the Dalton Highway is closed to the public.

The world of air service opens the Gates to visitors. The average flight into the park lasts from half an hour to 1½ hours and can cost from $150 to $300 per hour for flight time. Passengers pay for the pilot's return trip, plus fees for baggage in excess of 40 lbs (18 kg).

Those desiring to cut costs are encouraged to travel in a group. A trip for six from Bettles can cost $364 a person, less than half the cost of the same trip for two. An average two-week trip for two can add up to $2,000 per person. Compare services to prices and ask for references. Reputable guides will have names of people to contact who have taken their trips. The steep price of visiting Gates of the Arctic National Park can be an advantage. In 1993, only 2,245 people made their way in. Just an elite few, endowed with finances, physique and time, vacation here.

Visitors whose goal is the solitude and isolation that this huge wilderness offers may be better off avoiding favored places, such as the north fork of the Koyukuk and the Gates of the Arctic peaks area, where they might meet other park visitors. Customized trips to unnamed valleys are available for those who want to vacation alone.

Sport-hunting is only allowed in the preserve portion of Gates of the Arctic

Cache keeps intruders away from backcountry supplies.

and non-Alaskans must have a guide to hunt for certain big game animals. Given the remoteness and unique problems associated with hunting in the arctic wilderness, a guide who is familiar with local conditions is recommended even if not required. Some game can be taken only by permit or drawing. Contact the Alaska Department of Fish and Game for specifics.

Along with the bears – yes, guns are allowed for protection – Gates is also home to hordes of mosquitoes. During certain times of the year, wilderness travelers survive the ever-present swarm of bugs by keeping their entire body, including their hands, completely covered. Carry a good mosquito repellent and a finely screened tent.

Another wilderness creature that inhabits Gates is *giardia lamblia*, a microscopic water organism that causes "beaver fever," an unpleasant intestinal disorder. The best prevention is to boil all drinking water or use chemical disinfectants such as iodine or chlorine.

June and July are the wettest months in Gates; thunderstorms are frequent occurrences. Rain has been known to start in mid-August and not quit until it turns to snow in September. Temperatures can range from -70°F (-57°C) to 92°F (32°C). Snow may fall in any month of the year. The average summer temperature ranges from freezing to 85°F (29°C), prime hypothermia (body-chilling) conditions. Wool clothing allows for both warmth and dryness, and hiking boots are needed to survive in wet, rocky and soggy conditions.

As a final word, avoid the tragic wilderness experiences. People have drowned sleeping on sandbars and others have suffered delays in their travel plans because a gentle stream became a raging white-water river in a matter of hours in a downpour. Three to 10 days' leeway should be allowed for water level changes if any river or creek crossings are involved. Gates of the Arctic is no place to live by the clock and, although offering a unique encounter with nature, the park requires some careful vacation planning.

he basic
esign has
ot changed.

NATIONAL PARKS: GLACIER BAY

Glacier Bay National Park and Preserve encompasses 3.3 million acres (1.3 million hectares). Located in Alaska's southeastern panhandle, the park's center lies approximately 90 miles (145 km) northwest of Juneau and 600 miles (965 km) southeast of Anchorage.

In a land comprised of three climatic zones – marine to arctic – seven different ecosystems support a wide variety of plant and animal life. From the endangered humpback whale and threatened arctic peregrine falcon to the common harbor seal, black and brown bears, mountain goat, marmot, eagle and ptarmigan, Glacier Bay provides a rich overview of Alaska's wildlife.

One can navigate the narrow inlets by large cruiseship, small tour boat or kayak, or fly low over crevassed glaciers and rocky ledges in chartered aircraft. Gaze at towering walls of blue ice and watch the antics of lazy harbor seals sunbathing on floating bergs. Snap pictures of mountain goats perched precariously on steep slopes and take home tales of adventure and beauty.

Glaciers are rivers of ice, snow, rock, sediment, water and organic debris originating on land and moving downslope under the forces of weight and gravity. Alaska is one of the best places in the world to observe the impressive splendor of this natural phenomenon.

Glacier Bay's physical environment is as diverse as any found in Alaska. Sixteen massive tidewater glaciers flowing from the snow-capped mountain peaks of the **Fairweather Range** literally plunge into the icy waters of the fjords. Besides the jagged icebergs, ice-scoured walls of rock lining the waterways, salt-water beaches and protected coves, numerous freshwater lakes and thick forests of western hemlock and Sitka spruce are also found here.

Prehistory and exploration: Evidence of man's habitation in the Glacier Bay region dates back approximately 10,000 years. The absence of archeological remains over long time periods, however, prompts questions of early cultural success, as settlers struggled to survive postglacial eras. Researchers outline seasonal patterns of hunting, fishing and gathering from semi-permanent winter villages. Native Tlingit folklore includes tales of village destruction periodically from shock waves and other natural forces.

European exploration of Glacier Bay began as early as July 1741, when Russian ships of the Bering Expedition sailed the region's outer coast. French explorer Jean François La Perouse arrived 45 years later. His detailed observations and map of Lituya Bay, published in 1797, with its five surrounding glaciers, provide scientists with valuable data, from which glacial changes over time are computed. Other explorers such as Captain George Vancouver followed. But it was the widespread publicity soon after well-known naturalist John Muir's first reconnaissance of the area in 1879 that stimulated scientific investigations and early tourism.

Visitors to Glacier Bay today are treated to views much different from those which were observed in the 1880s. At that time, the network of fjords had not yet been established; a huge glacier extended into the area which is now open water.

Early steamship excursions into Glacier Bay during the 1880s carried up to 230 passengers. People came from around the world to ride the ships sailing close to the mighty icewalls. The flock of curious scientists and tourists halted abruptly, however, when on September 10, 1899, a violent earthquake struck the area, causing tremendous amounts of ice from the Muir Glacier to calve, falling into the sea. An unbroken jam of floating ice choked the waterway and extended more than 10 miles (16 km) from the glacier's terminus.

When tour ships could no longer sail closer than 5 or 7 miles (8–11 km) to the very popular Muir Glacier, excursions to Glacier Bay ceased. Touring slowly developed again after 1925, when the Glacier Bay National Monument was originally established.

286

Glaciers and icebergs: The glaciers of Glacier Bay National Park and Preserve have, over time, retreated and advanced due to severe climatic fluctuations. La Perouse and Vancouver both observed glacier ice at the mouth of the bay in 1786 and 1794. During Muir's trip to Glacier Bay in 1879, however, the ice had retreated 32 miles (51 km) to a point near what is now the mouth of Muir Inlet. Another 90 years later, the Muir Glacier had receded another 24 miles (39 km).

Visitors to Glacier Bay traveling via water or air routes can often watch entire sections of glacier ice calve from 150-foot (46-meter) walls. From the water, the cracking ice produces a thundering roar. Huge bergs are set adrift. Waves sweep across sandbars outward from the glacier's tidewater base. Kayakers are warned to maintain a safe distance from the glacier faces.

From the air, the sound emitted from the crashing ice cannot be heard over the drone of an aircraft engine, but the aerial perspective of shimmering ice flowing from mountaintop to sea will convince even the most ardent disbeliever that the forces of nature in Glacier Bay are alive and very active.

Those on the water, close to ice chunks slowly melting in the salty bay, may hear a crackling sound similar to breakfast cereal, seltzer water or champagne. The sizzling actually comes from the release of thousands of air bubbles which became entrapped in the glacier ice from high pressure during its formation.

Plant and animal life: Two hundred years ago, when a glacier entirely filled what is now a network of inlets in Glacier Bay, only a small number of plant and animal species inhabited the region. Since the rapid retreat of the ice, life in the water and on the surrounding land has flourished. Today, the nutrient rich waters of the fjords are important feeding grounds for large marine mammals. Even the wind-swept and insect-free upper slopes of the glaciers provide welcome refuge for mountain goats and other animals.

The four land and three marine eco-

systems in Glacier Bay support lifeforms adapted to the environment. Near **Gustavus**, a wet tundra ecosystem is home to shrubby willow, lodgepole pine and Sitka alder. Sandhill cranes rest in the open marshes here during migration, while river otter, wolf, bear, coyote and moose roam.

Bartlett Cove, the park's only area of major development, lies within a region dominated by coastal western hemlock and Sitka spruce. Watch for bald eagles flying overhead.

Those who spend time in the magnificent backcountry of Glacier Bay National Park and Preserve may climb to elevations of 2,500 feet (762 meters). Here, in the alpine tundra ecosystem, the thick vegetation of lower elevations is replaced by shrubby plants – alpine grasses and dwarf blueberry. The terrain is rocky, and snow patches remain in early summer. Delicate flowering plants and lichens should be treated with respect, for regeneration in this environment is extremely slow.

Although few visitors venture onto the higher snowfields and glaciers, life in this seemingly barren, mountainous environment does indeed exist. The legendary "ice worm," which is the only earthworm known to live on snow and ice, feeds on a red-pigmented green algae and organic debris swept onto the frozen surface. Only three-quarters to an inch (2–2.5 cm) long, these tiny black creatures hatch their eggs in subfreezing temperatures and remain extremely sensitive to heat.

The Glacier-flea – a vegetarian insect – also lives above the treeline, as do many species of lichens – algae and fungus in a symbiotic relationship. Glacial history can actually be computed by studying lichen growth, a slow process which occurs at a steady rate.

Possibly the most controversial species found within Glacier National Park is the endangered humpback whale. A migratory marine mammal that winters near Hawaii or Mexico, humpbacks feed in the icy waters of southeastern Alaska and Glacier Bay in the summer. Killer and minke whales are sometimes spotted in the bay as well. Besides small intertidal creatures, Glacier Bay is also home to many fish and shorebirds. Sea lion and otter, harbor seal and porpoise are frequently sighted.

There are no improved roads leading to Glacier Bay National Park and Preserve, and the area is not serviced by Alaska Marine Highway ferries. Most visitors arrive by large cruiseships or package tours, but travelers on their own can reach the small community of Gustavus by either scheduled flights or small air and boat charters from Juneau.

Overnight accommodations within the park are limited to **Glacier Bay Lodge** – 55 rooms with baths, a dining room, cocktail lounge, lodge and gift shop. A 10-mile (16-km) road links the park headquarters in Bartlett Cove to Gustavus, where lodges and cabins are open May through September.

Park facilities and attractions: A small walk-in campground located in Bartlett Cove usually fills to capacity only two or three times a season. **Sandy Cove**, approximately 20 miles (32 km) north, offers a good anchorage for those traveling by boat.

Although clear, warm days in the park are marvelous, providing unlimited views of the higher peaks and glacier walls, Southeast Alaska is famous for its rain and fog. Summer temperatures in upper Glacier Bay can differ 20 degrees F (7°C) from those in Bartlett Cove (10 to 16°C). Don't forget a warm sweater, hat and raincoat.

The main attraction in this beautiful national park is, of course, the spectacular scenery and abundant wildlife. The National Parks Service provides interpretive programs and activities to make visits even more exciting. Guided nature and walking tours on two well-maintained trails start from Bartlett Cove, and slide-lecture shows are given in the lodge and on concessionaire vessels.

Backcountry travel in Glacier Bay is becoming increasingly popular. Kayakers often spend a week or more in the area, and July is usually the busiest month. A floating ranger station in **Blue Mouse Cove** is opened up during the summer months.

The mystery of an ice cave.

288

NATIONAL PARKS: KATMAI

Nature is, simply put, "awesome" in **Katmai National Park and Preserve**. Here in this isolated location the scenery is breathtaking, the weather is unstable, the winds can be life-threatening, and the past is reckoned in terms of pre and post-volcanic eruption.

Located 290 air miles from Anchorage on the Alaska Peninsula, the park is a haven for lovers of the unspoiled wilderness. No highway system touches this area; the usual access is by small plane. Within Katmai National Park and Preserve backcountry routes may be suggested to summer explorers, but the only trails they will find to follow are made by animals.

On **Naknek Lake** is **Brooks Lodge**, recipient of around 20,000 visitors, sightseers and flightseers, fishermen, hikers, climbers and canoeists each year. Park Service campgrounds and lodges at **Kulik** and **Grosvenor Camp** are available for serious fishing enthusiasts.

For those who prefer to enjoy the wilderness from a distance, air taxi services can be chartered for sightseeing and package tours are available, with guides, food and lodging provided. At Brooks Camp, tourists can enjoy several easy walks, bears can be viewed summer-long from a place of safety as they feed on spawning salmon, and a tour bus provides transportation to the scene of volcanic devastation in the **Valley of Ten Thousand Smokes**.

Three-quarters of a century after the eruption that justified this National Park, the valley remains awe-inspiring. Ash, pumice and rocks from the 1912 eruption produced over 40 sq. miles (100 sq. km) of lunar landscape, sculpted by wind and water. The once-verdant valley floor, covered with shifting pumice, still resists vegetation and quickly erases the imprint of a hiker's boot.

Historic Katmai: Before the great eruption, a portion of the historic Katmai Trail would have passed through this valley. Today the trail is no longer visible and its ancient route a path of obstacles. Blowing ash, rugged terrain, dense undergrowth, quicksand, narrow canyons and braided streams challenge the most seasoned hiker.

During severe weather, travelers are warned against the old route at Katmai Pass at the head of the Valley of Ten Thousand Smokes. The interchange of air between the Gulf of Alaska and the Bering Sea streams through this pass and can cause winds over 100 miles per hour (160 kph) – strong enough to blow a hiker off his feet.

Archeologists believe that two separate cultures once existed on either side of the Alaskan Peninsula. Some time after 1900 BC, however, trade began across Katmai Pass between the Pacific Coast and Bristol Bay, and the dissimilar cultures began to merge.

As Russians infiltrated coastal regions in their quest for furs, the Katmai Trail was traveled by traders and missionaries. After Alaska's purchase by the United States, traders still used this route, although less frequently.

The trail became popular again in 1898 when a flood of gold seekers found it a shortcut to Nome: prospectors used it to avoid a stormy sea passage around the Alaska Peninsula. Mail carriers also found this route convenient, but by 1912 the gold rush had subsided and the Katmai Trail was seldom traveled.

Earth tremors and eruptions: When the great eruption occurred in 1912, news was slow to reach the outside world because the area was so isolated. The closest account was furnished by a Native named American Pete, who was on the Katmai Trail only 18 miles (29 km) northeast of Mount Katmai when the violent explosions began.

Earth tremors that preceded the eruption were so severe that the residents of Katmai and Savonoski, small Native villages on the Alaska Peninsula, gathered their possessions and fled to Naknek, on Bristol Bay.

Later research gave credit for the devastation not to Mount Katmai, but to **Novarupta Volcano**, a volcano formed by the eruption itself. The explosion was heard 750 miles (1,200 km) away in

Juneau, 650 miles (1,050 km) away in Dawson, and 500 miles (800 km) away in Fairbanks. Most heavily impacted were the Native villages of Katmai and Savonoski, later abandoned because of heavy ashfall, and the town of Kodiak on Kodiak Island, across Shelikof Strait to the Southwest.

One hundred miles (160 km) from the eruption, Kodiak residents noticed a peculiar fan-shaped cloud in the sky. As the cloud grew steadily higher, darker and closer, they grew more and more uneasy. Especially alarming were flashes of lightning within the cloud, an oddity in an area where electric storms do not occur.

Terror increased as the sky became dark – in June in Kodiak there is almost continuous daylight – and earthquake shocks grew frequent. As ash began to fall, accompanied by nauseating gases, people believed they would suffer the fate of Pompeii and be buried alive.

Kodiak's ordeal: Ash sifted through cracks around windows and doors, clogged nostrils and scoured eyes, fill-ing rooms with such an impenetrable haze that people could not see each other. A 20-room log building burned, yet residents who stood only a few hundred yards away saw no flame and felt no heat: falling ash was so heavy it insulated the air.

When the ash fall grew heavier the people of Kodiak tied dampened layers of cloth over their faces. Groping along fences and ditches they followed the sound of a foghorn to the harbor, where they boarded the revenue cutter *Manning* or the barge *St. James*. Five hundred people huddled on the decks of the *Manning*, so cramped they could not sit down. Lack of visibility made it difficult to leave the harbor, but eventually the vessel was anchored two miles away where an escape to sea would be possible if conditions worsened. But after two days and nights of terror, the cloud dispersed and the Kodiak people returned to their village. There they found ash 18 inches (45 cm) deep, landslides, collapsed roofs, choked water mains, pumice-laden rivers and streams over-

flowing their banks. Lakes normally five feet deep had been filled in, and wildlife was decimated.

Ash fall from the great eruption covered more than 3,000 sq. miles (7,800 sq. km). As far away as Vancouver, British Columbia, acid fumes weakened the threads in clothing hung out to dry. (Until the reason was known housewives accused merchants of selling inferior goods). In addition, particles from the ash cloud affected the upper atmosphere so much that the average annual temperature in the Northern Hemisphere was reduced by 1.8° F (1°C).

Valley of Ten Thousand Smokes: In the following years several expeditions were sent to the eruption site by the National Geographic Society to satisfy worldwide interest and do scientific research. Scientists were initially prevented from reaching the source of the eruption by seas of mud, ash slides as deep as 1,500 feet (450 meters), and evidence of one of the most powerful water surges ever.

In 1916 the crater of Mount Katmai was reached and a smoking valley discovered at Katmai Pass. The valley, named the Valley of Ten Thousand Smokes by explorer R.F. Griggs, covered up to 40 sq. miles (100 sq. km) and held thousands of steaming fumaroles. Some of these emitted periodic columns of steam that reached 1,000 feet (300 meters) in the air. Here, explorers found that by moving their tents in relation to a fumarole, they could regulate floor temperature. Steam from the fumaroles, they found, could not only fry bacon, but would hold the fry pan aloft.

In 1918 the Valley of Ten Thousand Smokes was made a national monument in order to preserve an area important to the study of volcanism. Later additions for a wildlife sanctuary brought the Katmai National Park and Preserve to its total of 4,268 acres (1,700 hectares).

When the Katmai monument was first created it was believed that the Valley of Ten Thousand Smokes would become a geyser-filled attraction to rival that of Yellowstone National Park in Wyoming. Scientists then believed that the geyser field at Yellowstone was dying. Since that time, however, the reverse has come about. The Yellowstone geysers are still active, but the fumaroles at the Valley of Ten Thousand Smokes have subsided, and now number fewer than 10.

A rugged wilderness: Katmai National Park and Preserve makes available to visitors not only an area of amazing volcanic involvement but a representative and undisturbed portion of the Alaskan Peninsula. Great varieties of terrain in Katmai include the rugged coastal habitat of Shelikof Strait on one side of the Alaskan range and the rivers and lakes of the Naknek River watershed on the other. Mixed spruce-birch forests, dense willow-alder thickets and moist tundra are found at lower elevations, and alpine tundra on the higher slopes.

A series of small lakes and rivers provide opportunities for canoeing, kayaking and fishing. Rainbow trout, lake trout, char, pike and grayling are popular sport fish here, as well as sockeye, coho, king, pink and chum salmon. Nearly one million salmon return each year to the Naknek River.

Brown or grizzly bears are common in Katmai and can be safely viewed all summer at the Park Service viewing area as they feed on spawning salmon. Other wildlife that may be encountered are moose, caribou, land otter, wolverine, marten, weasel, mink, lynx, fox, wolf, muskrat, beaver and hare. Off coastal waters, seals, sea lions, sea otters and beluga and gray whales can be seen. Birdwatching is also a popular pastime at Katmai.

Weather in Katmai National Park is variable, and heavy rain is characteristic of most areas during the summer months. The most comfortable weather occurs on the northwestern slope of the Aleutian range, where at Brooks Camp average daytime temperature is 60°F (15°C). Here, skies are only expected to be clear or partially cloudy 20 percent of the time. Warm clothing, rain gear and boots are recommended.

Katmai can be reached by an hour's jet flight from Anchorage to King Salmon, and a 20-minute trip by floatplane or amphibian chartered from King Salmon to Brooks Camp.

Bears enjoy the annual salmon run.